Just boys doing business?

One of the most significant facts about crime is that it is almost always committed by men. Despite this, academic consideration of crime tends to overlook this most obvious feature. If gender is discussed at all, the focus is usually on women. *Just Boys Doing Business?* is the first collection to challenge mainstream criminology by taking the social construction of 'masculinity' as its focus.

The book brings together a broad range of criminologists with established international reputations. It comes at a time when there is increasing concern about levels of crime – especially among young men. The contributors come from three continents and illustrate the international significance of a focus on masculinity when looking at crime. The editors are both established criminologists and have published widely within and outside the discipline.

Just Boys Doing Business? will be of particular appeal to teachers and students of criminology, sociology and gender studies, as well as to criminal justice practitioners.

Tim Newburn is Head of Crime, Justice and Youth Studies at the Policy Studies Institute, London. **Elizabeth A. Stanko** is Reader in Law, Brunel University.

Contributors: John Braithwaite; Kathleen Daly; Nigel Fielding; Jewelle Taylor Gibbs; Alberto Godenzi; Dick Hobbs; Tony Jefferson; Michael Levi; Joseph R. Merighi; James W. Messerschmidt; Kenneth Polk; Rogan Taylor; Joe Sim; John Williams.

Just boys doing business?

Men, masculinities and crime

Edited by
**Tim Newburn and
Elizabeth A. Stanko**

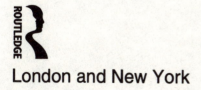

London and New York

First published 1994
by Routledge
11 New Fetter Lane, London EC4P 4EE

First published in paperback 1995

Simultaneously published in the USA and Canada
by Routledge
29 West 35th Street, New York, NY 10001

Typeset in Baskerville by LaserScript, Mitcham, Surrey
Printed and bound in Great Britain by
Mackays of Chatham PLC, Chatham, Kent

British Library Cataloguing in Publication Data
A catalogue record for this book is available from the British Library

Library of Congress Cataloging in Publication Data
A catalogue record for this book has been requested

ISBN 0–415–09321–X (hbk)
     0–415–09320–1 (pbk)

Contents

Figures

Contributors

John Braithwaite is a Professor in the Research School of Social Sciences, Australian National University. He received his Ph.D. from the University of Queensland in 1977. He is author of numerous articles and books, most notable of which is *Crime, Shame and Reintegration* (Cambridge University Press 1989). Co-authored with Brent Fisse, his next book is *Corporations, Crime and Accountability* (Cambridge University Press).

Kathleen Daly is Visiting Associate Professor of Sociology at the University of Michigan. She received her Ph.D. from the University of Massachusetts in 1983, taught at the State University of New York at Albany, and was a member of the faculty at Yale University from 1983 to 1992. She is interested in applying feminist, sociological and legal theories to problems of crime and justice. Her book *Gender, Crime and Punishment* (1994) is published by Yale University Press.

Nigel Fielding is a Reader in the Department of Sociology at the University of Surrey and editor of the *Howard Journal of Criminal Justice*. He is currently completing a book about community policing. Among his previous books are *Joining Forces* (Routledge 1988), a study of police training, *The Police and Social Conflict* (Athlone 1991), and *Negotiating Nothing* (co-author with Kemp and Norris, Avebury 1992), a study of police decision-making in disputes.

Alberto Godenzi is currently Assistant Professor in Sociology at the University of New Hampshire, Durham. He has been a development expert in Ecuador, a research associate in social psychology

at the University of Zurich, a senior lecturer at the Universities of
Zurich, Fribourg, and Berne, and director of GOAL Research and
Consulting. He is a pioneer of studies on masculinity, inter-
personal violence and crime, and the author of numerous articles
and books (most published in German), including: *Rape in
Marriage* (Social Research Institute Press 1987); *Sexual Violence*
(Union Publishing 1989); *Family Violence and Woman Abuse*
(Helbing and Lichtenhahn 1993).

Dick Hobbs is a Lecturer in the Department of Sociology and Social
Policy at the University of Durham, UK. He is author of *Doing the
Business* (Oxford University Press 1988), which won the Philip
Abrams Prize in 1989, and editor (with Tim May) of *Interpreting the
Field* (Oxford University Press 1993); *Policing Matters, Policing
Changes* (Bellew Publishing/Howard League 1993), and
Professional Crime (Dartmouth Publishing 1994). He is currently
working on a study of professional and organised crime to be
published by Oxford University Press. He has published chapters
and articles on a range of issues concerned with enterprise culture,
criminal justice, research methods, and the sociology of deviant
cultures.

Tony Jefferson is a Reader in Criminology at the University of
Sheffield where he recently completed some research on race and
the criminal justice system. He has written widely on questions
relating to policing, race, crime, the media and youth culture
including *The Case Against Paramilitary Policing* and several
co-authored books; *Introducing Policework* (with M. Brodgen and
S. Walklate); *Interpreting Policework* and *Controlling the Constable*
(with R. Grimshaw); *Policing the Crisis* (with S. Hall *et al.*) and
Resistance through Rituals (co-edited with S. Hall). He is a member
of the editorial group responsible for *Achilles Heel* and is currently
working on a book about Mike Tyson and masculinity.

Michael Levi is Professor of Criminology at the University of Wales
at Cardiff. He is the author of *The Phantom Capitalists* (Gower,
1981); *Regulating Fraud* (Routledge 1988); *Customer Confidentiality,
Money-Laundering, and Police–Bank Relationships* (Police Foundation
1991); and *The Investigation, Prosecution, and Trial of Serious Fraud*
(Royal Commission on Criminal Justice Research Study No. 14,
HMSO 1993). In addition to many articles on fraud and general

policing issues, he has written a major review of explanations of violent crime for *The Oxford Handbook of Criminology* (Oxford University Press 1994). Recent research includes an interview-based study of credit card fraudsters and a review of what happens to reports by financial institutions of suspected money-laundering.

Joseph R. Merighi received his MA in clinical psychology from Connecticut College and his MSW from the University of California at Berkeley where he is currently a doctoral student in social welfare. He has co-authored articles on differences in French–American love styles, interracial dating, mother–child interactions, and personality and motivational factors as they pertain to developmentally disabled children. Currently, Mr Merighi is interested in investigating issues of sexuality among adolescents, cross-cultural issues in mental health, and psychosocial aspects of AIDS in gay male and drug using populations.

James W. Messerschmidt is Associate Professor of Sociology and Criminology at the University of Southern Maine. He received his Ph.D. from the University of Stockholm in sociology, specialising in criminology. His research interests focus on the interrelation of class, gender, race and crime, and he has authored *The Trial of Leonard Peltier* (South End Press 1983), *Capitalism, Patriarchy, and Crime: Toward a Socialist Feminist Criminology* (Rowman and Littlefield 1986), and *Criminology* (with P. Bierne, Harcourt Brace Jovanovich 1991), and *Masculinities and Crime* (Rowman and Littlefield 1993).

Tim Newburn received his Ph.D. in the sociology of law from the University of Leicester, where he first began work as a researcher. More recently he has worked at the Home Office Research and Planning Unit and the National Institute for Social Work. He is currently Senior Research Fellow at the Policy Studies Institute in London. He is author of *Permission and Regulation: Law and Morals in Post-war Britain* (Routledge 1991), *Disaster and After: Social Work in the Aftermath of Disaster* (Jessica Kingsley 1993), *Persistent Young Offenders* (with A. Hagell, PSI 1994) and editor of *Working with Disaster: Social Welfare Interventions Before and After Tragedy* (Longman, 1993).

Kenneth Polk received his post-graduate education at North-western University and the University of California, Los Angeles. He was Professor of Sociology at the University of Oregon for many years before moving to Melbourne University in Australia in 1984, where he is now Reader in Criminology. Much of his previous work concerned juvenile delinquency, as is reflected in his book *Schools and Delinquency* (co-authored with Walter Schafer) published by Prentice-Hall. His most recent work deals with issues of homicide and negligent work death and is funded by the criminology Research Council and the Australian Research Council, which has resulted in several published papers on these topics.

Joe Sim is Professor of Sociology, Institute of Crime, Justice and Welfare Studies, School of Social Science, Liverpool John Moores University. He is the author of *Medical Power in Prisons* (Open University Press 1990) and co-author of *British Prisons* (with M. Fitzgerald, Blackwell 1982) and *Prisons Under Protest* (with P. Scraton and P. Skidmore, Open University Press 1991).

Elizabeth A. Stanko is Reader in the Department of Law, Brunel University, UK, and has been a pioneer of feminist criminology on both sides of the Atlantic. She received her Ph.D. in Sociology from the City University of New York, Graduate School in 1977. She is the author of *Everyday Violence* (Pandora 1990), *Intimate Intrusions* (Routledge 1985), editor of texts on gender and crime, and has published widely on issues of prosecutorial discretion, violence against women, victimisation and gender, crime prevention, and policing.

Rogan Taylor first came to public prominence in 1985 as a founder member of the Football Supporters Association. Since 1990 he has been a researcher at the Sir Norman Chester Centre at Leicester University. His book *Football and its Fans* was published by Leicester University Press in 1992. He is co-author of *Three Sides of the Mersey* (with A. Ward and J. Williams, Robson Books, 1993).

Jewelle Taylor Gibbs, MS.W. and Ph.D., joined the faculty of the University of California at Berkeley in 1979 and now holds an endowed Chair as Zellerbach Family Fund Professor of Social Policy. Her areas of research include adolescent psychosocial adjustment, minority mental health and brief treatment methods.

She has authored a number of articles and book chapters and is a frequent lecturer and consultant on these topics. She is the editor of *Young, Black and Male in America: An Endangered Species* (Auburn House, 1988) and the co-author of *Children of Color: Psychological Interventions with Minority Youth* (Jossey-Bass Publications 1989).

John Williams is the Football Trust Research Lecturer at the Sir Norman Chester Centre for Football Research, Leicester University. He has written widely on football and football spectator culture and his most recent book in this area is *British Football and Social Change* (with S. Wagg, 1991). He is currently writing a book (with J. Woodhouse) on women and football.

Introduction
Men, masculinity and crime

Tim Newburn and Elizabeth A. Stanko

The most significant fact about crime is that it is almost always committed by men. In 1991, for example, of the offenders found guilty or cautioned for indictable offences in England and Wales, only 18 per cent were females. In general terms – and this holds true both across countries and across time – women commit fewer crimes of all types and proportionately fewer serious and violent crimes than men. Although one in three men in the UK will have a conviction for a serious offence by the age of 31, this is only the case for approximately one in thirteen women (Home Office 1993). Despite this very strong contrast, academic consideration of crime tends to gloss over what is perhaps this most obvious feature of offenders and offending. Indeed, when gender is discussed at all, women are most usually the subject.

The purpose of this book is to begin the process of charting the territory of masculinity/ies and crime. The concept of masculinity, underdeveloped as it is,[1] opens up the possibility of a critical illumination of troubling public issues. Thus, if ramraiding, hot-rodding, joy-riding and rioting (Jefferson 1992) are unimaginable in the absence of men, the same is true of almost all crimes. It is not that sociologists and criminologists have ignored the role of men in crime – indeed, they have not – it is that the dominant theoretical models have rarely gone beyond the simple association of masculinity with, say, 'machismo'.

From the work of W.B. Miller in the late 1950s onwards (Miller 1958, see also Parsons 1954), theorists studying the structural cultural context of crime stressed the importance of 'toughness', 'excitement', and an emphasis on male sexual prowess to the core values of those communities most usually associated with high crime rates. Later, subcultural theorists located similar insights within a predominantly Marxist analysis of post-war social conditions (see, for example, Cohen 1976 and Corrigan 1979). The key problem confronting these commentators, however, was, as Downes and Rock (1982) expressed it, 'that many are called but few are chosen or self-elected'. The subcultural activists are generally outnumbered by the conforming majority despite their common exposure to similar pressures.

Similar problems remain with the theorisation of masculinity that is at the centre of more recent and generally more sophisticated attempts to explain (working-class) crime. While there is much to be learnt from writers such as Paul Willis (1990), a number of significant questions remain: how many competing versions of masculinity are visible within, say, the working class? How is it that some people exhibit one form rather than another, and why do some young men – and by implication why do not *all* young men – exhibit the aggressiveness that so many writers over the past thirty years have identified and associated with 'delinquency'?

The subtitle of this book makes clear that we believe that referring to masculini*ties* is more helpful than referring simply to masculinity. There are a number of reasons for this, but the dangers of reification and essentialism are key. On the one hand the use of the singular term can imply an all-pervasive reified ideal-type, or on the other hand a form of crude reductionism where the existence of one 'masculinity' is, in its explanatory power, little different from the efforts of those who would reduce everything to the level of biology. It is crucial therefore to think about the power and variety of masculine values, the processes by which they become internalised, the processes of identification, the ways in which certain core values become associated with specific social groups, together with an historical analysis of masculinities and masculine practices. As one example of such variation in values and practices, Tolson (1977) describes some of the family cultures and associated masculinities found in different social classes:

> The lower middle-class image of patriarchal authority – based on moral dignity and 'respectability' – remains socially influential; but within the working class family it constitutes a distant reference, an imposition, rather than a coherent family

mythology. Working class families maintain collective memories of poverty, and physical insecurity, rather than a nostalgia for Victorian provincial life. And working class masculinity is characterised more by an immediate, aggressive style of behaviour, than a vision of personal achievement.

Such practices and values are mediated not only by class but also, of course, by race. For as Jefferson (1992) has recently argued:

> The fact that the next heavyweight champion of the world, like the last and the one before that *ad nauseam*, will almost certainly be black (if he survives the lottery of the ghetto and escapes the prison house) has nothing to do with chromosomes and natural aptitude – but it has everything to do with the way racial and class disadvantages combine not only to reduce opportunities but also to heighten the salience of certain forms of manliness.

Of all the current theorisations of masculinity/ies, it is that by Bob Connell that is most influential – and indeed this is illustrated by the number of references to his work throughout the chapters in this book. The key distinction that he has introduced is that between 'hegemonic' and 'subordinated' masculinities (Connell 1987). The former is that which is socially dominant, though not necessarily the most widespread. Hegemonic masculinity is 'a question of how particular groups of men inhabit positions of power and wealth, and how they legitimate and reproduce the social relationships that generate their dominance' (Carrigan *et al.* 1985: 592). 'Subordinated' masculinities by contrast 'are discredited or oppressed (such as homosexual masculinity in our culture)' (Connell 1991: 186). Such a dichotomisation should not, however, be taken to imply differentiation only by power relations, but also in relation to a division of labour and patterns of emotional attachment, psychological differentiation and also institutional differentiation as part of collective practices (Carrigan *et al.* 1985).

Such a conceptualisation is important for the study of crime for a variety of reasons. First, it allows one of the important lessons of feminism – that the aggressive and often violent behaviour of men should be viewed as *normal* rather than unusual or abnormal – to take on a more pivotal role in criminological theorising. Second, relatedly, and again largely as a result of the impact of feminist theory, it locates the behaviour of men (and therefore the criminal behaviour of men) within a context of unequal power relations with women. Thus 'crime' or 'criminal behaviour' is not a series of relatively unproblematic givens but, rather, a wide range of activities which all need to be understood within the context of gender relations, and indeed a conceptualisation of gender relations which allows for a broad and differentiated understanding of what it means to be *a man*.

In addition, by emphasising identity, in this case masculine identity, as something that needs to be accomplished – indeed always temporarily accomplished – it focuses attention on 'practice': that masculinity (and femininity) is not an essence, but simply a way of living one type of relationship. It provides a tool with which to begin the task of unpicking why it is that certain boys/men become involved with one sort of activity rather than another, and how, if it is considered important to do so, they might be persuaded to stop. The task then is to use the developing understanding of masculine identities to make sense of male over-involvement and female under-involvement in criminal activities. We are not talking about a tendency that is either universal or inevitable, but it remains clear that crime is in the main a male behaviour. Both the behaviour itself and the discourses that define it need to be understood for, as was argued above, masculine ideology is constantly (re)-produced – 'men are not simply the passive embodiments of the masculine ideology' (Brittan 1989: 68). Not all men become involved in a succession of criminal activities, many eschew violence, and yet it is clear that in modern western patriarchal culture the dominant or hegemonic masculine form is aggressive and misogynist. Furthermore, the fallout from hegemonic masculinity affects men as well as women (Newburn and Stanko, this volume) and it is only by challenging the taken-for-grantedness of much of what it is supposed to mean to 'be a man' that the appalling consequences of the strait-jackets in which we live can be mitigated.

The purpose of this collection of essays is to place masculinity/ies into the foreground of our theoretical work and understanding. For too long now, the discipline of criminology has ignored the power of gendered analysis. While feminist criminologists have illustrated how this oversight has affected women, gender, as a significant contributor to explanations of social control, criminality, or victimisation, remains on the margins. Excluding women allowed many criminologists to attempt theoretical generalisations without having to grapple with the difficult realities of women's victimisation, and of their under-involvement in criminal activities. Criminology's major concern, as a discipline, has been the control of marginal and working-class men. Even now, all the evidence suggests that when the greatest threat to internal financial security and public safety is at the hands of corporations and insider-dealers, criminology focuses largely on the random violence of young men.

The aim of this collection then is not to provide the answers, but to ask some awkward questions and to encourage the development of a more humane, as well as realistic approach to crime, victimisation and criminal justice, not only by academic criminologists but by professionals. Clearly, as Heidensohn (1992) has observed, women are not in control of criminal justice decision-making. It comes as no surprise that men continue to dominate, in criminal justice, and, to their own detriment, in crime.

THE COLLECTION

What can we learn about criminology, crime, victimisation and its control from a study focused upon men and masculinity? The following chapters offer innovative directions. Tony Jefferson courageously offers us some ways to conceptualise men's psychic and social complexities. Jefferson suggests that it is men's psychic vulnerability coupled with their social positioning which weave the complexities of each individual man. Here we find both the potential for emergent new masculinities and the pull towards destructive forms of masculinities. He challenges us to account for how men come to adopt particular masculine positions, for without this sensitivity the difficulties of uniting social and psychic process which often pull men in different directions makes theorising, and the practice of preventing crime, impossible.

Jefferson warns of settling for the simplicity of binary categories, a point Betsy Stanko makes in her chapter. Stanko suggests that much theorising about men's individual violence obscures criminology's vision about violence itself, with devastating consequences for women as well as for men. By typifying violent men as evil, biologically driven, or as reacting to provocation, criminological theorising is missing what so many men do to each other, and to many women they know and share intimacies with. Alberto Godenzi, in his reflection on his study of non-detected rapists in Switzerland, suggests that non-detection has consequences for how men conceptualise themselves as ordinary and normal. While the criminal justice process may not evoke remorse from the rapists it incarcerates (Grubin and Gunn, unpublished), men who have not been so labelled report feeling vindicated. At the same time, Godenzi's study raises questions about the standard methodological approach to the study of incarcerated rapists. Such studies are more likely, he argues, to capture the motivations and rationalisations of men who did not know their victims, or only knew them slightly. Inspired by feminist critiques of sexual violence, Godenzi calls for further research on offenders, and in particular those men who have not come into contact with the criminal justice system.

These chapters raise questions about criminology which notes, but fails to make notable, men's significant contribution to criminality and its control. Nigel Fielding's analysis of the dilemmas facing contemporary policing in Britain suggests that the intrusion of women has had an effect. Fielding examines the variety of occupational cultures visible within the police, and attempts to account for the current move towards community-style policing, proposing that the masculine precepts of 'crime-fighting' policing are the subject of challenge from within and outside the police force. In particular, it is the very fact of women's current and increasing visibility within the police that opens up many of the internal contradictions of the police service today.

Sumner (1990) has been critical of the failure of criminology to respond to the critique of hegemonic masculinity, and this failure is perhaps clearest within the sub-discipline of victimology. The failure to *see* men, as, for instance, victims, has allowed criminology to maintain a largely stereotyped gendered analysis in this area. Thinking seriously about men as victims of crime, Tim Newburn and Betsy Stanko argue, challenges the notions of victimisation as some form of weakness. Moreover, men respond to crime in very different ways, but they do so as *men*. While research is beginning to address the link between victimisation and offending, we continue to have little real sense of what this might mean. There is clearly no simple connection between victimisation and offending, for if that were the case, there would certainly be many more women offenders than there currently appears to be. The incorporation of the notion of 'masculinity' within victimology contests the simple separation of offenders/offending and victims/victimisation.

What is perhaps even more surprising is that the link between masculinity and offending has been largely overlooked in the study of men as prisoners, a population which represents almost 95 per cent of inmates. In a powerful essay, Joe Sim questions the institutionalised thinking of prisoners as 'hard men'. Prison regimes are not strangers to gender, as the work on women in prison has demonstrated (Dobash, Dobash and Gutteridge 1986; Carlen 1985; Eaton 1993), but Sim demands that such a theoretical understanding extended to men is essential if the 'orthodox study of penal power' is to be reconstructed.

The link between the imagery of prisoner and the marginality of some men is the core of the chapter by Jewelle Taylor Gibbs and Joseph Merighi. In the US, they demonstrate, young black men, as a cohort, have been equated with crime: one in four black males between the ages of 20 and 29 are involved in the criminal justice system either in prison, on probation, or on parole. Homicide tops the list as the cause of death for young black men. Marginality, segregation, poverty, lack of education and employment blight these men's lives. It is impossible to analyse the position of young black men without the mixture of race, class and gender. Masculinity and 'manhood' are central features of the lives of young men who are structurally excluded from possible mobility rendered to white society.

A detailed exploration of homicide in the Australian context in the chapter by Kenneth Polk underscores the work of Gibbs and Merighi. He argues that it is impossible to understand the fact that men kill each other, in competition and over honour, without the aid of gender. Supporting the earlier work of Daly and Wilson (1988), Polk provides detailed accounts of homicide encounters, showing the complexities of arguments, disputes and disagreements which have lethal consequences. The failure to explore so male a phenomenon lies in the generally marginal position of the men killing each other in these everyday encounters.

Social structure and masculine identity also combine to mould the pattern of involvement of young white men in youth crime. James Messerschmidt suggests that institutions such as schools play an important part in the configurations of deviancy, as does the social class context within which schooling supports or discourages youth crime choices. The school, which is a place where young boys can find encouragement despite external pressures, may consequently act as a structural barrier against masculine values and practices which result in destructive consequences. One avenue, some commentators argue, which offers positive alternatives for boys, is involvement in sport.

John Williams and Rogan Taylor offer a detailed analysis of the connections, both in myth and in practice, between masculinity and football in England. Though football in England is a national pastime, for women and men, its image of rowdyism and hooliganism, at home and abroad, reflect one traditional model of British masculinity. And while the prevailing stereotype of fan as 'hooligan' has been disrupted in recent years, both the game and the climate in which it is watched remain doggedly resistant to alternative masculine forms. Additionally, commentators have speculated recently that the watching of football has become the cover for other criminal activity, such as that explored by Dick Hobbs. In his chapter on father and son low-level criminal entrepreneurs, Hobbs provides a rich account of how the skills of illegal enterprise are passed down as family legacies, most often through the men in the family. His ethnographic data becomes a text about work, and about finding and learning innovative ways to make a living. Danny and Chris, the two featured characters, give voice to how 'doing business' makes market sense, within, of course, a world that privileges the men's access to 'business'.

Michael Levi features another aspect of business, that of the so-called legitimate fraudster or insider-trader. Levi examines aspects of the lucrative white collar entrepreneur. Whether for greed or to feed other habits (gambling, women or drugs), white collar criminals often separate themselves from 'real' criminals – in a manner that is not dissimilar to that utilised by non-detected rapists. Business competition is mostly inter-male, as Levi points out, and this form of ecomonic competition appears to be the acceptable face of the sometimes lethal violence which characterises masculine competitiveness at the lower end of the social scale. White collar criminals are clearly not subjected to the same forms of policing as other law-breakers, and there is little evidence that confinement of such offenders does anything more than delay future law violation.

All of the areas of offending considered in this volume present a challenge in thinking about the processing of law-breakers. Using the case of men who are violent to women, John Braithwaite and Kathleen Daly suggest some alternative ways of using the criminal justice system to condemn such behaviour, in a way which both shames and reintegrates the individual (Braithwaite 1989). They describe community conference strategies, as currently operating in New Zealand. These community conferences, where both offender and victim are supported and given voice, offer an integrative alternative to incarceration. This, together with Sim's chapter, is a salutary reminder that confinement, reflecting the most destructive aspects of hegemonic masculinity, is no way to transform the lives of men, and ultimately (and hopefully) women.

NOTE

1   A large literature in the general area of men's studies/masculinities has, however, developed in recent years. Readers looking for a broad but sympathetic introduction to some of the key issues in this literature should probably consult David Morgan's recent text, *Discovering Men* (Routledge 1992).

Chapter 1

Theorising masculine subjectivity

Tony Jefferson

INTRODUCTION: EXEMPLIFYING THE PROBLEM

LOOKING BACK ON IT (AGAIN)

AT NINETEEN I was a brave old hunchback,
Climbing to tremendous heights,
Preparing to swing down on my golden rope
And rescue Accused Innocence.

But on my swooping, downward path one day
Innocence ducked,
And I amazed at such an act
Crashed into a wall she had been building.

Twenty-one years later,
Sitting stunned beside that same brick wall
I see others climbing their golden ropes
And hear innocence sniggering.

I say nothing much,
But sit with bandages and the hope
That maybe after all
Some sweet fool might in time
Swing right through that wall.

(Patten 1988: 62)

Like all poems, Patten's poem has many meanings. But one I take from it concerns the chastening effect of experience on the unrealistic desire to live up to the ambitious ideals ('tremendous heights') of masculinity. Yet, despite the inevitable failure, the hope lives on that 'some sweet fool' might one day achieve the unachievable and 'swing right through that wall'. Its surreal humour, self-deprecating honesty, and wry optimism make it a lovely poem; but what makes it special for me is its ability to connect concretely with my own experience. My aim in what follows is to trace a critical path through 'theorising masculine sujectivity' that remains similarly connected to the level of experience, albeit in a rather less immediately recognisable way. Without this, I fear, critiques of masculinity, however well-intended, will fall on deaf ears.

The poem's notion of 'climbing to tremendous heights' is not dissimilar to the quest for 'transcendence' – the desire to achieve immortality through some extraordinary act ('rescue Accused Innocence') – that has been identified as masculinity's ultimate value. Robin Morgan (1989), for example, identifies it as central to the heroic 'death or glory' appeal of terrorism to young men; while Cameron and Frazer (1987) cite transcendence as the 'common denominator' for understanding why sexual murderers are overwhelmingly men, and the sadism behind their 'lust to kill'. Important though these accounts are, the truth is that most men's transcendent strivings get thwarted *en route* as the poem graphically recounts ('crashed into a wall'), or, thankfully, find less obviously harmful outlets than either terrorism or sexual murder. Put another way, the gap between the ideal of transcendence ('preparing to swing down on my golden rope') and mundane reality ('sitting stunned . . . with bandages') may be too great to bridge, or, perhaps consequently, undesirable even to attempt.

Bell hooks' moving account of the difference between her strict, fearsome, provider-father and her 'easygoing . . . affectionate, full of good humor, loving . . . brother' would find echoes in many families, as would her brother's lack of interest 'in becoming a patriarchal boy' (1992: 87). She also remembers being 'fascinated and charmed' by a whole gallery of other black men 'who were not obsessed with being patriarchs: by Felix, a hobo who jumped trains [and] never worked a regular job; by Kid, who lived out in the country and hunted . . . rabbits and coons . . . by Daddy Gus, who spoke in hushed tones' (ibid.: 88), and by countless others. Like her brother, these men were clearly dancing to a very different tune than that of the 'patriarchal masculine ideal' (ibid.) which inspired her father. It is not clear whether this is because they felt they did not match up to the ideal, did not desire it, or were resisting it; but it certainly suggests that the notion of a single masculinity that all men aspire to must be given up. Rather, we need to be thinking about a range of masculinities, though undoubtedly some, like the patriarchal ideal embodied by bell hooks' father, are more dominant than others. Connell's notion of a '"hegemonic masculinity" [which] is always constructed in relation to various subordinated masculinities as well as in relation to women' (1987: 183) best captures both notions: the variety of masculinities and their hierarchical ordering.[1]

It is this hierarchical ordering, of course, that largely accounts for the pressure exerted by the 'ideal'. As bell hooks sadly relates, her brother eventually succumbed, in early adult life, to the pressure 'to become a man's man – phallocentric, patriarchal and masculine' (1987: 87). Moreover, once the 'pressure' has become internalised, a part of one's sense of self, then failure to live up to the ideal can have painful, even catastrophic, consequences. Bell hooks' brother was 'forever haunted by the idea of patriarchal masculinity' (bell hooks 1992: 87). So too was Peter Sutcliffe, as Joan Smith (1989) convincingly argues; yet he never felt it achievable because of his strong identification with his beloved, oppressed mother. This internal conflict in Sutcliffe, between an unachievable ideal of masculinity embodied in his bullying father, and an all too real identification with a femininity embodied in his weak, downtrodden mother, eventually manifested itself as an obsessional search for a way to eradicate 'this weakness within himself. And he found it only when he began ripping, stabbing, mutilating and *destroying* women's bodies' (Smith 1989: 148).

This sense of insecurity or fear of failure usually takes more benign, though still damaging, forms; the feeling of vulnerability precipitated for men on entering an emotionally significant relationship, for example. Here the need for and dependence on another is posed most starkly, in direct contradiction to the notions of self-sufficiency and independence central to hegemonic masculinity. It is almost as if to succeed in love one has to fail as a man. This is so even for (especially for?) men who are considered socially powerful. Martin was one such; but it was a power secured at some psychic cost, as the following quotation reveals:

> just by showing that you're *soft* on somebody . . . you put yourself in an *incredibly* insecure state . . . as soon as you've shown that

there is this terrible *hole* in you – that you want somebody else –
then you're in an absolute state of insecurity.

(Hollway 1983: 127; emphasis in original)

This widespread feeling of insecurity amongst men problematises
those accounts of masculinity that see only its highly visible social
power and miss its often hidden connection with psychic vulnerability. It also renders untenable the still dominant explanation of
how notions of masculinity are internalised, namely, through
constant exposure to the masculine sex-role model in the home,
the school, the media, etc.(cf. Staples 1989: 75).[2] Such an
explanation removes any notion of the difficulties actual men
experience in relating to these 'models', and any sense of the
variety of models on offer. Moreover, its overdeterministic, overly
sociological thrust renders the notion of change impossible to
conceptualise; how, for example, are we to understand the
emergence of new masculinities – critical gay culture or the 'cool
pose' of some young black men (Majors 1989: 84–5) – if not as in
some ways a response, or resistance, to existing masculinities,
rather than their simple reproduction?[3]

Let me summarise. So far, I have argued that the idea of
masculinity as an ideal that all men aspire to and which is
unproblematically internalised by successive generations of male
children being exposed to a range of socialising agencies is simply
contradicted too often at the level of experience to take us very far.
It ignores the obvious difficulties that boys and men often have in
either accepting or achieving the ideal, or both. This all but
universal experience of failure can lead to an active rejection of
the ideal on offer and a positive identification with an alternative,
albeit subordinate, masculinity; painful, sometimes frenzied,
attempts to drag an unwilling psyche into line with the unwanted
social expectations; living a life of quiet desperation; or, perhaps
most commonly, a lot of faking it. All this means we are going to
have to think about masculine subjectivity in a way which does
proper justice to the complexities of both the external and the
internal world (the task of the sections 2 and 3) and then to the
very difficult question of the relation between them (the task of
section 4). As we shall see, this involves approaching the specific
question of masculine subjectivity through the more general
literature on subjectivity.

2   A MULTIPLY DIVIDED SOCIETY

Phil Cohen's use of the phrase 'multiply divided subjects in a multiply divided society'(Cohen 1986: 52) neatly sums up the complexity of both the internal and external world on which the last section ended. But how can we 'think' this complexity? Let's start with a multiply divided society. The primary question is: do we live in a world that is structured according to some set of principles, or are we 'post-structure'?

Connell, practice, and a multiply structured gender order

Connell (1987) is the most sophisticated theorist of masculinity who operates with the notion of a structured world. 'Social structure' for him refers to 'the constraints that lie in a given form of social organisation' (1987: 92). However, to avoid the familiar problems with structuralism and thereby offer 'an opening towards history' (1987: 95), he needs to produce a notion of practice which is primary (yet structured). This he does in the following way:

> Practice is the transformation of . . . [a] situation in a particular direction. To describe structure is to specify what it is in the situation that constrains the play of practice. Since the consequence of practice is a transformed situation which is the object of new practice, 'structure' specifies the way practice (over time) constrains practice.
>
> (Connell 1987: 95)

Connell's object of enquiry is the field of gender relations, which for him consists of three structures, namely, labour, power and cathexis, though this is neither a necessary, nor, necesssarily, an exhaustive list (ibid.: 96). These are interrelated, but there is no 'ultimate determinant' (ibid.: 116). There is, however, 'an orderliness, which needs to be understood' (ibid.), but this is not 'the unity of a *system*. . . . It is a unity – always imperfect and under construction – of historical composition . . . the real historical process of interaction and group formation' (ibid.). The product of this process at any given moment is the 'gender order', a term Connell borrows from Jill Matthews, which he defines as 'a historically constructed pattern of power relations between men and women and definitions of femininity and masculinity' (Connell, 1987: 98–9).

All this is impressive: the notion of structure enables the obvious hierarchical ordering of the field of gender relations to be addressed, whilst the notion of multiple, interacting but irreducible, structures allows for considerable complexity; and placing constrained practice in command ensures a central place to questions of history and change. But questions still remain. How, for example, are we to conceptualise relations *among men*, especially when class and ethnic and generational relations are included? Is the relationship between hegemonic and the various subordinated masculinities structured? If so, how many structures are needed to think this series of relationships? Finally, if structure is simply the outcome of prior practice, albeit constrained practice, how does practice produce, and continually reproduce, something as systematic as the gender order? It is the difficulties posed by some of these questions which have led many to abandon the notion that explanations are usefully to be sought in underlying structures in favour of one of the many variants of poststructuralism. Of these, the Foucauldian version with its focus on 'historically specific discursive relations and social practices' (Weedon 1987: 22) is undoubtedly the most important for us.

Poststructuralism, Foucault and discourse

Essentially, Foucault argues that meaning is not to be sought, *pace* structuralism, in underlying structures, nor in the intentions of speaking subjects. Rather, we must turn to the historically specific discursive relations within which particular practices (social and institutional) with their specific modalities of power and accompanying knowledges are necessarily located, and particular subjectivities constructed.

Giving primacy to discourse has created many confusions. These hinge on the precise meaning of discourse – is it confined to words and texts or can it include non-linguistic phenomena? – and on its relationship to objects and events outside discourse – is there a non-discursive realm, a world beyond discourse, or is everything discourse? I think the confusion disappears once the centrality of meaning is understood. Although the importance of language to meaning-production necessarily makes linguistic phenomena central to the notion of discourse, it is also the case that social meanings are carried by non-verbal phenomena as well. Thus there seems to me no difficulty in accepting Macdonell's paraphrasing of Laclau that 'any institutional practice and any technique "in and through which social production of meaning takes place" [Laclau 1980: 87] may be considered part of discourse' (1986: 4)'. The focus on meaning also eliminates problems of the relationship between the discursive and the extra-discursive. Michele Barrett summarises her understanding of Foucault's *The Archaeology of Knowledge* (1990) on this point in a wonderfully brief phrase, namely, 'the production of "things" by "words"'(1991: 130). In other words, though 'things' have a pre-discursive existence, they only lose their object status and thereby acquire a social and historical meaning, in discourses ('words'). More simply still: the world cannot be 'thought' other than in discursive categories.[4] Discourses are set off from each other by the 'regularities' discoverable in what would appear to be a heterogeneity of statements ('dispersions of statements'); though the results of Foucault's brilliant historical researches into various 'dispersions of statements' – of madness, punishment, sexuality and so on – are more illuminating than the method advocated for discovering their discursive regularities (cf. Barrett 1991: 126–9). This certainly poses problems for those attempting to identify particular discourses. However, I think that within this approach, Connell's hegemonic and subordinate masculinities become so many competing discourses.

If everything that produces social meaning is part of discourse, and the world cannot be thought except through discourses, then discourses become ubiquitous. This, of course, dissolves the problem of 'how many structures' which besets structural approaches; but in the process, it also makes a systematic understanding of the social whole all but impossible. Given this, it is somewhat ironic that, as Dews points out, the effect of this plethora of discourses and practices has been fairly singular, in practice: 'Power in modern societies is portrayed as essentially oriented towards the production of regimented, isolated and self-policing subjects' (1984: 77).

If the notion of discourse threatens to undermine the notion of a gender order, it also, as with poststructuralism generally, obliterates the subject. By reducing subjects to the effects of discourses, either to a sum of discursive positionings or to a product of the interplay of discourses, it effectively erases them; in so doing, poststructuralism echoes structuralism's corresponding reduction of subjects to the effects of structures. As Dews neatly puts it, Foucault's 'peremptory equation of subjectification and subjection erases the distinction between the enforcement of compliance with a determinate system of norms, and the formation of a reflexive consciousness which may subsequently be directed against the existing system of norms' (Dews 1984: 95).[5]

At this point it is time to consider the question of the subject more directly.

3   MULTIPLY DIVIDED SUBJECTS

Freud, the unconscious and repression

Traditional Freudianism exhibits many problems. Perhaps most often cited are: the universality, and hence incipient ahistoricism of the psycho-sexual order (the Oedipal complex), that founds the unconscious and 'normal' gendered identity; the incipient biologism in talking of motives founded on instincts or drives; and the patriarchal assumptions behind the focus on relations with the father and the notion of penis envy (cf. Barrett 1991: 112–19; Weedon 1987: 45–51). In addition, there is the common belief that its apparent focus on the individual necessarily renders it an asocial theory. Whilst the former criticisms are largely justified, the latter, as we shall see, is mistaken. But the reason why psycho-analytic theorising is enjoying the resurgence it is, particularly amongst feminist writers, has to do with the undeniable relevance of Freud's core notion of the dynamic unconscious. This totally undermines the simplistic notion of the unitary, rational subject. Since the material of the unconscious is composed largely of that which is socially unacceptable to the conscious mind, the two parts of the mind are in conflict. This is why things get repressed, constantly to obtrude in transformed ways, in slips of the tongue, jokes, dreams, etc. (cf. Hollway 1989: 29). If reason rules the conscious mind, desire drives the unconscious. The implications of this for socialisation have been well put by Jacqueline Rose:

> What distinguishes psychoanalysis from sociological accounts of gender . . . is that whereas for the latter, the internalization of norms is assumed roughly to work, the basic premise . . . of psychoanalysis is that it does not. The unconscious constantly reveals the 'failure' of identity. Because there is no continuity of

psychic life, so there is no stability of sexual identity, no position for women (or for men) which is ever simply achieved.

(Rose 1987: 184)

The introduction of notions of desire and the unconscious somewhat at odds with our reasonable, conscious selves is surely necessary in any attempt to think through some of the difficulties in achieving and sustaining a sense of masculine identity that I pointed to earlier. As for the accusations of asociality, Freud's argument in *Civilization and its Discontents* (1963) that 'civilization is built on the renunciation of instinct' is a classic statement relating the psychic and the social realms (cf. Connell 1987: 197). This laid the basis for other such attempts, which I return to in section 3. But it was Lacan's revisions of traditional Freudian theory which were to provide the critical breakthrough in this enterprise. So, we need to consider these first.

Lacan, the deconstructed subject, language and desire

Lacan's revisions of Freud, focused through the importance of language and a revised concept of desire, have produced a notion of the self which is radically non-unitary since inherently split. Moreover, Lacan's notion that entry into language founds the unconscious and self-identity provides a decisive route into a social understanding of the psyche. This is not just because 'language is by definition a social system' (Henriques, *et al.* 1984: 213), but more profoundly because Lacan operates with a post-Saussurean model of language in which 'meaning is constituted within language and is not guaranteed by the subject which speaks it' (Weedon 1987: 22). Subjects are thus the products of language, and hence of the social world – Lacan's 'Symbolic order', which is similarly 'structured by language' (ibid.: 52).

Within this conception of language, words ('signifiers') do not possess fixed meanings by being linked with particular concepts (or 'signifieds'), but acquire meaning only through their difference from other signifiers, and then only temporarily since meaning is always context-specific. However, what rescues Lacan's account of signification from the relativistic extremes of Derrida's *differance* in which there is never any final fixing of meaning, is his controversial notion that 'meaning and the symbolic order as a whole, is fixed in relation to a primary, transcendental signifier . . .

the *phallus*, the signifier of sexual difference, which guarantees the patriarchal structure of the symbolic order' (Weedon 1987: 53). Here Lacan's fidelity to Freud is very evident; the biological differences underpinning the resolution of the Freudian Oedipal complex and the institutionalisation of gendered subjectivity have simply been transmuted in the light of modern structural linguistics. The penis becomes the phallus, but both uphold the Law of the Father, a fact which makes Lacan as troubling for feminists as Freud.

What rescues the Lacanian subject from being merely a product of language (in Foucauldian terms, an effect of discourse) is the introduction of desire, which 'Lacanian theory assumes . . . to be the motivating principle of human life' (Weedon 1987: 53). What distinguishes Lacan's notion is the idea of 'lack': the inevitable 'disjunction between desire and the prospects of fulfilment' (Frosh 1987: 132) resulting from the unattainability of the wholeness that is desire's constant objective. The infant's early experience of fragmentation, during which time s/he 'has no sense of the self as the central point of existence' (ibid.) nor any sense of desire since 'there is no sense of difference, no boundary between desire and gratification' (ibid.), is only ever overcome (and human subjecthood achieved) by successive illusions of wholeness. This fictive sense of wholeness is experienced first during the moment of entry into the Imaginary order, the first step in becoming a human subject inaugurated by the 'mirror phase' when

> the child's perception of her/himself in the mirror (that is in the gaze or responses of the other with whom the child interacts) leads to a joyful but mistaken perception of bodily unity as the site of a unified self.
>
> (ibid.)

This sense of wholeness thus originates, simultaneously, the possibility of desire (through producing the desiring subject) and its object (the experience of integration), as well as the impossibility of its satisfaction (because the experience of integration is based on something – mirror/mother/Other – outside itself and is, thus, only ever imaginary). Desire's point of origin is thus its constant point of return, as it endlessly seeks to remedy the lack which is the condition of its existence.

The second moment which encodes an illusion of integrity is

that of entry into the Symbolic order. At this point it is the acquisition of language and the accompanying identification with the self that speaks, as if the speaking self – the 'I' of language – were the author of meaning, that is the source of the illusion. As Lacan neatly puts it, 'I identify myself in language, but only by losing myself in it like an object' (1953: 86). This moment of entry into language is also the moment of the formation of a properly human subject, as opposed to the narcissistic subject of the mirror phase; and, since meaning in the Symbolic order is ultimately guaranteed by the transcendental signifier, the phallus, entry into the Symbolic realm necessarily coincides with the installation of everything associated with the Law of the Father, i.e. 'the discovery of sexual difference and the repression of desire in the Oedipus/castration complex' (Frosh 1987: 135).

Though based on fictions, the desire for wholeness is real enough since it is the sense of ego-wholeness, inaugurated by the mirror phase, that first enables the infant 'to experience separation from the mother in a new way' (Henriques, *et al.* 1984: 276). Through experiencing the self as object, the infant 'is now in a position to . . . want the mother' (ibid.) and to control her by being what she wants, the object of her desire; and since, 'following Freud, the mother is . . . the primary source of satisfaction in Lacan's account' (ibid.), controlling the mother is the indirect route to guaranteeing satisfaction. So, the desire for (an illusory) integrity becomes played out in the form of a ceaseless and unrealisable desire for the Other, a desire originating in the mirror phase, 'constantly replayed in human language' (ibid.: 278), but 'ultimately rooted in desire for the mother' (ibid.: 277).[6]

Though Lacan's notion of a self desiring what can never be had, locked within a patriarchal social order which can never be changed, takes psychoanalytic theorising to a new low of pessimistic conservatism, it does so, ironically, using concepts with truly radical implications, namely, a decentred self, the role of signification in the construction of subjectivity, and desire for the mother/Other. I shall, therefore, return to these in the next section.

4 BRINGING IT ALL TOGETHER: SOCIAL SUBJECTIVITIES

The social Freudians and 'embedding'

Freud's imaginative attempts to think through the relationship between psychic structures and the social order foundered on the rock of his universalistic assumptions. His idea of a conflict between instincts and reality which results in the repression of the former and their subsequent reappearance, in sublimated forms, to found civilisation was never properly historicised, despite implicit hints of its possibility (cf. Connell 1987: 197–8). The result generally has been to saddle psychoanalysis with the charge of pessimistic conservatism: because repression is the general characteristic of human relations which also founds civilisation, 'normal' unhappiness is inevitable and progressive social change impossible. But once the notion of repression is rendered historical, i.e. is shown to vary according to historical context, then it becomes possible to use psychoanalysis as a tool of social criticism directed towards progressive outcomes. This was the route that various radical social Freudians, such as Reich, Fromm, Adorno, and Marcuse, were later to take.[7]

Broadly speaking, these theorists were attempting to weld psychoanalytic and Marxist concepts in their efforts to explain 'the psychological underpinnings of capitalism' (Connell 1987: 200). In other words, they were interested in looking at the particular character of repression in a particular historical period. Marcuse, for example, argued in *Eros and Civilization* (1955) that capitalism was a system based socially in class exploitation and psychologically in 'surplus repression' – the latter made necessary by the requirement of a 'willing' workforce, and possible by narrowing down the arena of spontaneous eroticism to a depleted genital sexuality. His later *One Dimensional Man* (1964) changed tack somewhat in introducing the famous notion of 'repressive desublimation' – the idea that advanced capitalism now required less repression ('desublimation') in order to encourage consumption (for example in the use of sex to sell everything from cars to aftershave), but that this was still socially repressive (i.e. narrowly genitally based) since geared to stabilising the system, not to the uncontrolled flowering of an expanded eroticism.

But whatever the particularities of these arguments, they are all examples of what Connell usefully calls 'a theory of embedding': 'Their purpose is to explain how a social movement like fascism or a social system like capitalism can establish links with unconscious mental processes and thus gain mass support regardless of its irrationality and destructiveness' (1987: 201). The basic problem with such approaches is that they are ultimately socially determinist. That is to say, the requirements of the social system are embedded easily in a too pliant unconscious. Moreover, the question of differences between groups, such as gender-based ones, tends not to be a central focus. More recently, however, some feminist theorists interested in a psychoanalytically informed theory of gender have begun to remedy this aspect, though without breaking with the more fundamental problem of embedding theories.

Chodorow, mothering and the pre-Oedipal phase: a feminist variant of 'embedding'.

Chodorow's concern is to explain how the social system of patriarchy gets embedded psychologically. Focusing on the pre-Oedipal stage and relations with the mother, as opposed to the more traditional Freudian focus on the Oedipal complex and relations with the father, she argues that 'the selves of women and men tend to be constructed differently – women's self more in relation and involved with boundary negotiations, separation and connection, men's self more distanced and based on defensively firm boundaries and denials of self–other connection' (Chodorow 1989: 2). The result, as Chodorow spells out in her most famous book *The Reproduction of Mothering* (1978), is that girls grow up both wanting to mother and psychologically equipped to do so, whilst boys, with their more clear-cut ego boundaries, are better equipped emotionally to succeed in the public realm, albeit that much male activity is a defensive reaction to insecurity.

The fact that Chodorow managed, simultaneously, to explain the facts of male dominance and widespread female acquiescence in their subordinate mothering role, and to present an empirically recognisable psychological portrait of many men, has made her work very popular, especially amongst men interested in the construction of masculinity (cf. Brod 1987: 13; Seidler 1989: 170; Kidd 1987: 257; Edwards 1990: 119; Richards 1990: 163). But for all that, it remains, as Connell suggests (1987: 201–2), a theory of embedding.[8] Chodorow herself now admits as much in confessing that now she 'would not, as I believe I do in *Reproduction* give determinist primacy to social relations that generate certain psychological patterns or processes' (Chodorow 1989: 7). But it is not clear how she proposes to correct this particular error. This failure to address the difficulty of internalising the social – what

Rose calls 'the fundamental impasse of . . . Chodorow's work' (1987: 184) – also enables her to work with undifferentiated categories of 'men' and 'women'. However, in stressing the importance of early *object* relations (mother/carer–child), she does move decisively away from the residual biologism associated with traditional Freudianism. As we shall see later, in conjunction with Lacan's revisions, this will prove an important break.

Sartre and existential psychoanalysis

The existential project of Sartre, with its commitment to notions of choice and responsibility, still poses the most significant challenge to all forms of psychoanalysis:

> The problem with 'empirical psychoanalysis', as Sartre called Freudian thought, is that it takes as a necessary structure of the person what should be regarded as the product of choice. For one's psychic life to be determined by libido is certainly a possible form of existence, but it is not the only one. It is a way of being that a person may take up, may choose. What is human is precisely the process of constructing oneself by choices that transcend given circumstances.
>
> (Connell 1987: 211)

As Connell goes on to point out, this position is neither voluntaristic, since present choices are always constrained by the consequences of past ones, nor predicated on the equation of consciousness with self-knowledge, since Sartre famously distinguishes the unreflective, 'bad faith' consciousness of 'being-for-itself' from the knowledge-based 'good faith' consciousness of 'being-for-others'. Within this approach, then, the Freudian 'unconscious' becomes the alienated part of the conscious self: the self in retreat from itself, refusing responsibility for past actions. If classical psychoanalysis seeks to uncover the particular pattern of repressions motivating a person's present behaviour, existential psychoanalysis seeks to decode a life in terms of original, constitutive choices.

Effectively, such a choice-based focus produces a theory of gender oppression which is

> almost exactly the reverse of 'embedding' in psychoanalytic sociology. The power relations of the society become a

constitutive principle of personality dynamics through being
adopted as personal [*sic*] project, whether acknowledged or
not. At the social level, what this produces is . . . a *collective project
of oppression.*

(Connell 1987: 215)

Unsurprisingly, therefore, the core problem with this theory is also
the reverse of that found with embedding theories. With the latter
the difficulty was the too *easy* internalisation of social relations;
with the Sartrean project the central difficulty is how *hard* it is to
conceptualise a collective project of oppression, and its
institutionalisation, built solely out of millions of individual
choices. That being said, it is impossible to duck the questions of
choice and responsibility in talking about the maintenance of
systems of oppression. Sartre's efforts here need to be properly
acknowledged, even though I think, in line with psychoanalytic
reasoning generally, that people's choices are often impossible to
comprehend without acknowledging their unconscious, driven
dimension. Imaginatively combining some features of the work of
Foucault, Lacan and Klein, the authors of *Changing the Subject*
(Henriques *et al.* 1984) demonstrate this point decisively, in
illustrating the possibility of thinking about the social production
of subjectivity. It is, thus, to their work I now turn.

Changing the subject

In *Changing the Subject*, published in 1984, Henriques and
colleagues produced a series of linked essays committed to
retheorising subjectivity in a thoroughly social fashion, but without
obliterating the subject. Subsequently, Wendy Hollway, one of the
authors, was to develop some of these ideas further in her
Subjectivity and Method in Psychology (1989). Jointly, this work
represents the best attempt yet to weave together the strands of
discourse-based and psychoanalytic theory that I have variously
touched on above. In what follows, I outline its main contours.

Their starting point is the Foucauldian one of discursive
relations viewed in their historical specificity. It is a thoroughly
social starting point, but one which avoids the universalism of the
Lacanian Symbolic order. Moreover, in order to distance their
approach from simply linguistically based usages of discourse
analysis, they stress the connection with practice: 'the analysis

which we propose regards every discourse as the result of a practice of production which is at once material, discursive and complex, always inscribed in relation to other practices of production of discourses' (Henriques *et al.* 1984: 106). The notion of 'discursive practices' endlessly vying with each other forefronts Foucault's 'power/knowledge' point, namely, that discursive relations are always also relations of power.

The social order, therefore, is comprised of a multiplicity of discursive practices and the different power relations these inscribe. These produce a corresponding multiplicity of subject positions, all differentially accessed to power. That is to say, at any historical moment any given discourse will display a particular patterning of power relations. Insofar as these implicate gender-based power relations, they will ensure that the taking up of particular subject positions is not equally available to men and women. Take, for example, the discourse of sexuality that Hollway calls 'the discourse of male sexual drive' (Hollway 1989: 54). Given that 'the central proposition of this discourse is that men are driven by the biological necessity to seek out (heterosexual) sex' (ibid.), there is literally no subject position for women to occupy; they can only be the (sexual) object of the discourse, by definition. Despite the so-called sexual revolution of the 1960s, and the production of a new 'permissive discourse' in which women 'became, in principle, equal subjects' (ibid.: 55–6), present gender-based power relations still continue to ensure that the only safe subject position for women to adopt in the realm of sexual relationships is that offered by the traditional 'have/hold discourse', namely, the idea 'that sex should take place within the framework of a lasting relationship' (ibid.: 55).

However, the production of subject positions is not sufficient for theorising subjectivity. The fact that an individual is located within a variety of discursive relations means 'the subject is composed of, or exists as, a set of multiple and contradictory positionings or subjectivities' (Henriques *et al.* 1984: 204). But the question still remains as to how the fragmented positionings are held together within individual subjects so as to produce both the subjective experience of identity and the predictability of people's actions (Henriques *et al.* 1984). In other words, the question of how potential subject positions become actual subjectivities also needs to be addressed; what motivates people to 'choose' to invest in or identify with one discursive position rather than another?

Here, the question of desire re-enters, and hence Henriques and colleagues' engagement with psychoanalysis.

It is the radical potential of Lacanian psychoanalysis – the deconstruction of the unitary subject, the emphasis on signification, and desire for the mother/Other – which provides the starting point for their proposed reworking of the psychoanalytic subject. We have already seen how they have replaced 'Lacan's emphasis on a universal and timeless Symbolic order with an emphasis on discursive relations, viewed in their historical specificity' (Henriques, *et al* 1984: 217); what remains is to see how they rework his notion of desire.

The basic modification, again, is to render Lacan's notion less abstract and universal, this time by linking it to concrete inter-subjective relations of power. Analytically, this involves drawing on the work of Melanie Klein, especially her focus on the pre-Oedipal, relational defence mechanisms. This is what enables them to make desire a phenomenon which is socially produced, but also uniquely linked to individual biographies. Klein's relational defence mechanisms include 'splitting' (the ego disowning part of itself or dividing an object into good and bad parts in order to stop the latter contaminating the former) and 'projection' (filling an object with the ego's unwanted, split feelings). For Klein these were linked with biological assumptions about the existence of the Life and Death Instincts and the consequent inevitability of anxiety. In other words, she saw anxiety, and the defences against it partly an inevitable consequence of the existence of the Death Instinct.

The shift towards a more social reading of Klein is achieved first by suggesting how anxiety can be conceptualised as a product of human relations, not nature, without losing its ubiquitous character; then by showing how the defence mechanisms of splitting and projection are constantly implicated in the inter-subjective management of anxiety; and finally by illustrating how 'the continuous attempt to manage anxiety, to protect oneself . . . provides a continuous, more or less driven, motive for the negotiation of power in relations' (Hollway 1989: 85). This continuous attempt to defend against a feeling of powerlessness within a person's actual relationships thus gives substance to what is 'unsatisfiable and contentless' (ibid.: 58) in Lacan's notion of desire, rescues Klein's notion of anxiety from its biological moorings, and links both with a Foucauldian-derived notion of power:

Over and over again in my material, I found that the positions people took up in gender-differentiated discourses made sense in terms of their interest in gaining them enough power in relation to the other to protect their vulnerable selves. . . . It led me to think that it was not so much desire but power which is the motor for positioning in discourses and the explanation of what is suppressed in signification. Certainly the relation of power and desire needs to be clarified.

(Hollway 1989: 60)

The resulting conception of subjectivity is not reducible to the intentions of consciously choosing subjects, nor to the effects of language/discourse, but is the complex outcome of 'two or more people's unique histories, the contradictions between meanings (suppressed and expressed), differentiated positions in available discourses, the flux of their continuously negotiated power relations and the effect of their defence mechanisms' (Hollway 1989: 84–5)

Thus, historically specific discourses, such as the male sexual drive discourse mentioned earlier, provide the normative, power-conferring public significations and subject positions; an individual's specific history of desire (or defending against feelings of anxiety) provide a set of meanings which are unique to that individual and, insofar as these are in conflict with available public significations, these may need to be defended against, by suppression, or splitting/projection. Given the power-conferring nature of taking up 'appropriate' positions in particular discourses (being heterosexual rather than homosexual, mother rather than childless, etc.), it is not hard to see why particular power/ knowledge configurations get routinely reproduced. But the pattern of anxieties of any particular individual will be unique and will be defended against, through choosing appropriate subject positions in discourses, and/or repressing them, and/or splitting them off and projecting them elsewhere. One way, for example, of understanding traditional masculinity is in terms of this splitting/projection; quite simply, heterosexual men often disown their feelings of vulnerability and dependency by saddling their partners with them.

Though such an account addresses both the social and the psychic dimensions in convincing and non-reductive ways, it still leaves unaddressed the systematicity of the whole: how to explain the systematic reproduction of discursive positions, and hence the 'single structural fact [of] the global dominance of men over women' (Connell 1987: 183), through the sum of the idiosyncratic personal histories of anxiety?

CONCLUDING REMARKS

This is as far as I am able to take the theoretical issues that I identified in the Introduction to this piece. But I hope that it provides a framework for theorising masculine subjectivity. Foucault's historically specific discursive relations, within which power is always implicated, offer a fruitful starting point for thinking about available discourses of masculinity, and their dynamic, changing inter-relationship, as is amply demonstrated by Hollway's analytical illustrations of various discourses of sexuality with their different subject positionings. They enable, for example, an entry-point for thinking about one dimension of the difference between bell hooks' patriarchal-provider father (who looks to have firmly taken up the male subject position in the 'have/hold' discourse) and her more labile brother (whose discursive positioning in the discourses of sexuality is far less clear). But the discursive field of sexuality is only one significant site of gendered oppression, probably corresponding to Connell's structure of cathexis. His structures of labour and power constitute the other two. Insofar as discourses are everywhere, and therefore present a chaotically unwieldy field for analytical work, it might prove useful to utilise Connell's three structures as principles for organising the sites of gendered oppression requiring discursive deconstruction. Such analyses could then be used to uncover the state of play inside particular institutions, like the family – what Connell calls its 'gender regime' (1987: 120), as well as at the level of the society as a whole – what Connell, following Jill Matthews (1985), calls the 'gender order' (1987: 134).

But how do particular men like bell hooks' father, or brother, come to adopt the particular masculine positionings they do, if only provisionally, as in her brother's case, and with much psychic cost? Without addressing this issue, the notion of practice is meaningless. So, the individual subject had to be theorised. The location of individuals within an array of discursive positionings broke with the traditional asocial subject of psychology; the break with the unitary, rational subject, via the notion of a dynamic unconscious with hidden desires, prised open the possibility of making sense of the contradictions and difficulties that particular men experience in becoming masculine. Without this sensitivity to the difficulties of uniting social and psychic processes – often pulling in different directions – it is not possible to theorise masculinity in a way that men will recognise.

Discourses and structures point towards societal and institutional levels of analysis; desiring subjects point towards the importance of life-history research. Both levels are necessary; both are implicated in the other; yet they remain different. As Connell succinctly puts it:

> Personality has to be seen as social practice and not as an entity distinct from 'society'. Personality is what people do, just as social relations are what people do, and the doings are the same. Yet there is a difference which makes personality a coherent object of study. Personality is practice seen from a particular angle, which I will call the perspective of the life-history.
>
> (Connell 1987: 220)

Later, to ensure that the point about the interpenetration of personality and structure is not lost, Connell re-emphasises the structural bases of life-histories:

> However much detail is known about a given life, personal life becomes unintelligible if the structural bases of practice are not kept in view. . . . In the context of a theory of practice, personality appears as one of the major sites of history and politics. It is connected with other sites like institutions, but has its own configurations.
>
> (ibid.: 221)

Society, structures and discourses/the subject, personality and life-histories; the question of conceptualising their interpenetration in a non-dualistic, non-deterministic fashion remains. In addressing the crucial question of motivation, I have followed *Changing the Subject* in suggesting the importance of defences against anxiety and the constant negotiation of relations of power. Herein lies an important conceptual knot encompassing power, anxiety and desire which needs further untangling. As Hollway acknowledges, 'the relation of power and desire needs to be clarified' (1989: 60). In the meantime, this nexus does provide a principle (like Connell's structures) with which to interrogate what may otherwise prove a bewildering variety of life-history events. So, the question of how anxiety gets expressed or suppressed by particular groups of men in particular settings could provide a handle for opening up life-histories. For those who think this too individualistic a handle, ponder for a moment the example I gave earlier of heterosexual men disowning their feelings of vulnerability by saddling their partners with them. With that in mind, think, finally, of the question of masculine subjectivity and crime, especially crimes where issues of gender are obviously central, such as wife-battering, child sexual abuse and rape. The worst motivational accounts in this area are tawdry variations on a theme of 'bad, mad or sad'; while even the best tend to get stuck on one side or other of the individualistic/socially deterministic divide. Finding a way of transcending that dichotomy, of producing accounts which are intellectually coherent and experientially recognisable, is one important way we can begin to take the question of 'men and crime' more seriously.

NOTES

1   Connell's use of hegemony here is a borrowing from Gramsci (1971) for whom it meant the achievement of a class-based ascendancy predominantly through consensually based authority rather than coercion.
2   For a comprehensive critique of sex-role theory, see Connell (1987: 47–54).
3   Though I find problems with Majors' account, his notion that 'cool pose' is an 'aggressive assertion of masculinity' which 'emphatically says "white man, this is my turf. You can't match me here"' (1989: 84) poses very strongly this notion of subordinate masculinities resisting the imposition of hegemonic masculinity.
4   For a useful discussion of Laclau and Mouffe on this point, see Barrett (1991: 76–7).
5   This is not to deny the enormous debt modern social theory owes to Foucault. For a useful, short and balanced introduction to his work, see Smart (1985).
6   The precise meaning of Lacan's notion that all desire is 'ultimately rooted in desire for the mother' remains unclear to me. This is because of some confusion over the sequence of stages the infant passes through on its journey from neonate to human subject. I have followed what appears to be a consensus amongst commentators of a two-stage model, namely, entry into first the Imaginary order and then the Symbolic order (cf. Weedon 1987: 51; Frosh 1987: 132–4 and 1991: 59; Flax 1990: 93; Henriques *et al.* 1984: 276–8; Hollway 1989: 82).

However, Frosh also conceptualises this process as if there is a stage prior to the mirror phase, namely, a moment characterised by separation from the mother. His exact words are:

> the subject is split during development through a complex process that separates it first from the sense of linkage with the primary object, the mother, and then from the illusory, narcissistic identification of the self as a perfect unity, until the subject's place in the symbolic world is found, and the unconscious produced.
>
> (Frosh 1987: 132)

Insofar as this suggests the importance of early 'object-relations' in the formation of desire, it moves in the direction that I explore further below. For the moment though, I merely signal that my use of Lacan's 'desire for the mother' collapses the moment of separation from the mother and the mirror phase, in line with what seems to me, in the absence of more work on the subject than the purposes of this paper can justify, to be the dominant reading of his work.

7 Though space does not permit any consideration of it here, the critical, suggestive but largely forgotten, early work of Adler on masculinity would appear to warrant a re-examination, as Connell (1987: 199) forcefully argues.

8 More recently we have witnessed a sociologist of Giddens' eminence grapple seriously with the relationship of 'self and society', even devoting two whole books to the topic (Giddens 1991, 1992). This is still an unusual project for a sociologist. But, despite its insightful and challenging argument, and the 'correction' in the later book of a certain gender-blindness in the former, it too remains a theory of embedding.

Chapter 2

Challenging the problem of men's individual violence

Elizabeth A. Stanko

Violent crimes continue to fascinate the public and are both attributable to and an attribute of the media. Despite their apparently infrequent occurrence, such incidents are good news in ratings and circulation wars (Chibnall 1977). Perhaps this is because life can be portrayed as precarious or exciting, the love affair of the media with violence thus sensationalises and distorts its typical form (Soothill and Walby 1990). The brutal attack by a stranger on a pensioner provides hot copy, as does the sex attack by an unknown, 'deranged' man. This idealised image of violence is not only accepted uncritically and enthusiastically by the media, but, I suggest, also rests upon unstated, and unquestioned commentaries about gender, and masculinity in particular: violent incidents represent allegories about the inevitability of some men's violence and the peculiarity of women's violence.

The current state of the art of collecting, analysing and building policy about the prevention of violent crime is based on traditional definitions of violence. These definitions are wedded both to theories constructed to explain unsafe streets as well as to methodologies which count separate, legally framed actions. Such approaches neglect many experiences that people have which are not officially counted as crime, but nonetheless contain valuable lessons about danger and safety (Stanko 1990; Anderson *et al.* 1990; Bowling 1993). The state of knowledge about victims and offenders of violence seems to be growing every day. Several journals are devoted to its study. But while we gather knowledge about the most significant factor of violence – men's involvement as offenders, victims (Newburn and Stanko, this volume) and commentators (see also Heidensohn 1985), our limited thinking about masculinities and crime remains.

INDIVIDUALISING VIOLENCE

In using the legal framework to define criminal violence, criminologists usually embrace the tacit assumption that the law's violence (the use of legitimate violence by the state) is not as problematical and subject to scrutiny as the use of violence by individuals. The law's treatment of violence, reflected in how we count violence, how it is prosecuted, and how we punish it denies its own use of violence in that aim (see Sarat 1993). What is missing from the dominant criminological discourse is a discussion of institutional violence and the state's sanctioned violence, as in the contested arena of policing public order, for example (see Green 1990; Scraton 1985); or as in contested accounts that have arisen in debates about the Bosnian War or in the 1991 Gulf War. The predominant theme in criminological work is the conceptualisation, explication or construction of policy which aims to prevent individualised acts of violence committed by individuals.

As such, criminologists' empirical evidence highlights only one perspective in defining violence: that which is within the parameters of criminal statutes. These specify that force or the threat of force are located within physical and sexual harm as *legally defined* elements. Furthermore, the offences must be committed by an identifiable if not identified individual, against victims (or witnesses) who are willing to report them to official authorities, such as the police or crime survey researchers, who might in turn treat such reports as criminal. Thus only the violence that fits the state's definition of crime makes official figures. However, surveys and studies of police recording practices also indicate that a significant proportion of violence never reaches the police. Nor do police treat every reported incident of violence as criminal by recording it as such. Violent crime is usually defined by grouping crimes together, such as those of robbery and wounding, which involve legal elements of threat and/or force, and/or injury. Common assault involving little or no injury is often recorded separately, thus excluding it from being counted as truly serious crime: 'real violence'. In Britain, crime survey researchers do not ask men whether they have experienced sexual assault, and even the data that is gathered on sexual assault of women is considered unreliable (Mayhew and Maung 1992). This highly particular ordering of serious violent crime is fed into the multi-national agenda generating information about victims and crime around the world (Van Dijk *et al.* 1990) which even publishes league tables of violent crime, with New Zealand, in the last survey, topping the list. What this says about New Zealand is not entirely clear.

As a consequence of accounting procedures, violent victimisation, as a criminal offence, appears to be an aberrant event, piercing the harmony of normality. The 1981 British Crime Survey, for example, suggested the following: 'a "statistically average" person aged 16 or over can expect: a robbery once every five centuries (not attempts); an assault resulting in injury (even if slight) once every century (Hough and Mayhew 1983: 15).

Violence, according to criminological information, is an intruder upon what is assumed to be a serene, problem-free, crime-free life. It is within this terrain, for instance, that the feminist analysis of violence against women has had its greatest opposition (Gilbert 1991). Women, suggest researchers such as Russell (1984), Stanko (1985, 1990) and Kelly (1988), live in *potential* danger from men's violence as an ordinary part of their daily lives: unsafety, not safety, is the foundation of women's understanding of personal and sexual integrity (Stanko 1990). But whatever impact the awareness of violence against women has had, it has little or no impact upon the hegemonic image that 'real' violence and crime is something that occurs on the street, in public, and is committed by strangers. Men, therefore, who are statistically least likely to fear personal violence and who spend more time in those public spaces that regularly feature in the demonology of personal violence (the pub, football ground and the picket line) not surprisingly appear at the top of official figures as victims (and perpetrators) of 'crime'. What this says about class and crime is sporadically explored by criminology. What this says about gender, never.

FOCUS ON STREET CRIME: PUBLIC VIOLENCE, PUBLIC MAN

Criminological myopia about violence stems from a nineteenth-century criminological discourse, one that is as much about the safety of the streets (Pearson 1983) as it is about visions of order (Ericson *et al.* 1991). The concern about the safety of public space is yet another illustration of the privileging of men's domains within criminology. Embedded within this historical development too are the intricacies of class conflict and attempts to control working-class men (Cohen 1971), the poor and the disenfranchised on the public streets. Despite the fact that criminology rarely considers elite deviance (for the exceptions, see, for example, Braithwaite 1984; Levi 1987; Clarke 1986), and that the criminal justice system is geared to the policing and prosecution of public street crimes and the maintenance of order (Reiner 1985; Sanders 1987), criminological evidence suggests that 'crimes of the powerful' (Pearce 1976) are much more physically, economically and environmentally threatening than what criminologists consider to be conventional crime (Box 1983).

While feminist work continues to make women visible (though still marginal) within criminology, men and masculinity are largely taken-for-granted backdrops in the counting games. Though aspects of masculinity remain invisible, or at least largely unconsidered, evidence from crime surveys and elsewhere (Shepherd 1990) suggests that men are more commonly the victims of serious interpersonal violence (Hough and Mayhew 1983, 1985; Mayhew *et al.* 1989), are least likely to report fear of crime (Maxfield 1984), and are even more commonly the perpetrators of violence, as well as the targets of institutionalised violence of the state at the hands of the police, prison system (see Sim, this volume) and the military (Morgan 1987; Connell 1987). Concerns about violence however focus on the actions of the individual, in public, between strangers. And while there has been an explosion of work exploring women's experience of non-stranger, often private, violence, this work has not affected the dominant discourse about danger in criminology. It is only the growing literature on masculinity which is attempting in a limited way to come to terms with the impact of violence throughout individual men's lives (Seidler 1991; Connell 1987; Morgan 1992; Segal 1990, see also Newburn and Stanko, this volume).

Criminology's tradition is to explore the personal motivations, justifications, or explanations for street crime. Because of the historical focus on the criminalised actions of working-class and marginalised men, the ideological and practical strength of the image of 'real' violence remains firmly fixed on the street. This focus on the street, and on faceless, lurking assailants, has serious consequences for treating what happens to (largely) men in public, and results in 'stranger danger' as the prime concern in the policy and practice of criminal justice. It also has consequences for the way we conceptualise harm to women (Stanko 1990). This can be seen in the way we think about policing and the nature of protection. We are told time and time again that the way to reduce violence, and all crime for that matter, is to put more police on the *street*. Confronting violence such as domestic violence, racial harassment, and in some ways, homophobic violence, has been approached by special police initiatives, and by appointing dedicated officers to handle such violence. Even police practice suggests that policing the streets will not reduce these forms of violence.

A second distortion arising from linking violence to unsafe streets is in our understanding of the concept of fear of crime. The classic, and universal question, serving as the core measurement of fear of crime is: how safe do you feel walking alone in this area after dark? Some researchers ask questions about how safe an individual feels at home, but this is usually linked to the possibility of intrusion from the outside. Overwhelmingly reported by women, fear of crime is characterised as a problem of not trusting strangers inside and outside the home. As I have forcefully argued elsewhere (Stanko 1990), women's fear of crime is not solely associated with their safety in public places. Women's fear, and understanding of the potential for violence, weaves their experiences of known men with those unknown. Assuaging fear, then, will take more than better outdoor lighting. But what about men's fear, particularly if men's violence against men holds such prominence in the official statistics (see Newburn and Stanko, this volume)? What about some men's fear of institutionalised violence, such as harassment of gay men or the stops and searches of black men at the hands of police (Smith and Gray 1985)? 'Fear' in criminological circles, it seems, only refers to that victimisation encountered at the hands of lone assailants, men who run amok (see also Daly and Wilson 1988).

The anxiety and harm caused by corporate actions such as manufacturing faulty goods or drugs, or failing to maintain adequate safety standards at work, which some have termed violence (see Box 1983), is also absent from conventional criminological thinking about fear of crime. The conceptual development of 'fear of crime' focuses entirely upon individuals' fear of personal violence, a form of violence which more than any other form of criminal behaviour is restricted to the actions of *individual* assailants. Indeed, the study of fear of crime has shored up the discipline's fixation on unsafe streets. Fear of crime, as a concept, is used as a barometer of the safety of the street. Any glance at a local newspaper when crime statistics are released shows how criminal statistics about violence serve to quell or magnify fears about personal safety (Grade 1989).

The third, and perhaps the most insidious distortion, is that found in crime prevention literature. In Britain, the Home Office's crime prevention campaigns feature women as a particular audience for advice. Yet, men's harm seems to come to the attention of the police *and* crime surveys more than women's (see, Stanko 1988). No crime prevention advice is available for young men, who according to the Home Office's own crime surveys, report the most personal violence. Though women are recognised as targets of violence, the literature barely acknowledges the greatest risk to women: known men. Instead, the crime prevention advice is devoted to advising individual, adult women on how to walk in the street, sit on public transport, park their cars, and lock their doors. What is even more extraordinary about the crime prevention literature, is that it is seemingly unaware of *all* empirical evidence which shows that women already take far more precautions for their safety than do men (see, for example, Gordon and Riger 1988).

Why is there little or no crime prevention advice for men? The British Crime Surveys suggest a strong association of some young men's lifestyle and their victimisation: being outside the home, drinking three times a week places young men at a higher risk of physical assault. Should we also assume that somehow men who wish to avoid violence know how to do so, that is, stay in rather than meet friends at a pub? Or is it because we assume that victim and offender are one and the same, thus tacitly accepting men's harm as somehow deserved or provoked? The work of Sampson and Lauritsen (1991) suggests that there is a strong association between male victims and male offenders, but why hasn't this association been explored further?

Virtually everything we know about encountering the threat and the reality of physical and sexual brutality, though, forces us to recognise that, for a sizeable proportion of the population – both women and men – encounters with violence are part of their daily lives (Stanko 1990). This is even more pervasive for those who occupy our institutions, such as mental health facilities, children's homes and prisons. Such violence is also integrally connected with

people's structural positions within a white-European, heterosexual, male-dominated, class society.

But when an individual acts violently, criminologists
immediately resort to isolating the behaviour of that individual, as
Murdock (1982) observes, as the product of two intersecting
forces: the influence of external stimuli, which lower inhibitions
on aggression, and the inability of individuals to withstand these
inducements owing to their personal inadequacies and/or the
breakdown of normal cultural controls (1982: 62).

Violence within the home, bullying at school or in the neighbourhood, courtship violence, gay-bashing, racial harassment and
crime, sexual harassment and intimidation, 'fair' fights between
adolescent men or women – little of which comes to the attention
of the police or any official agency– are commonplace and rarely
classified within the narrow confines of the criminal law. Even
when these activities are treated as criminal offences, the structural
context of the actions is especially relevant in understanding men,
masculinities and violence. One way forward is to explore how
thinking about masculinities informs our understanding of the
violence men commit, and often, participate in, sometimes by
choice.

MASCULINITY AND VIOLENCE OF INDIVIDUALS

Broadly speaking, violence involves the infliction of emotional,
psychological, sexual, physical and/or material damage. The harm
felt by the recipient varies, as does the long-term impact on
his/her everyday life. A recent experience of violence, or its threat,
may have significant effects, altering an individual's routines and
personal lifestyle or it may have little noticeable influence on daily
life. In order to explore more fully how explanations of men's
individual violence are saturated by thinking about masculinity, we
must unpick some of the approaches to explanations of men's
violence and violent men within contemporary criminological
thinking. Some of these are:

1   the nature versus nurture debate;
2   the use of violence debate: instrumental versus expressive;
3   negotiating masculinities: hegemonic masculinity and the
    structure of power.

Nature versus nurture

Media images of aberrant men with 'natural' aggression abound, especially when the violence is sexual (Soothill and Walby 1990). As Campbell (1976) suggests in an early essay on violence, 'press reports often sensationalize, chastise, moralize and blame.' (1976: 27). But the blame is often placed on the influence of hormones or deranged psyches. The contribution of biological or psychological aberration to men's violence and aggression lingers uncomfortably in portrayals of violent acts with regularity (Bland 1984). According to some theorists, the problem with street criminals (most of whom are male), is that they cannot control their biology. Thus, the popular characterisation of men who commit street crime is that their ability to control aggression, fuelled by testosterone, is limited. These limitations may be caused by race (see Gilroy 1987, for a critique of racism and crime), psychological impairments, head injuries, sexual addiction, and so forth.

Even when authors such as Wilson and Herrnstein (1985) write:

> Young men are everywhere more likely than females or older persons to commit common street crimes, because of the way nature and nurture combine to make male children more impulsive and aggressive and less concerned with the well-being of others than are females or adults.
>
> (1985: 508)

questions about the influence of nature and what kind of nurturing fosters violence remain. As scholars turn to descriptions of how young men learn violence, peers, family members, neighbourhoods, schools, institutions, subcultures, and cults are examined for their adverse influence on boys and young men. But explaining why some boys or men use violence, and others don't, is theoretically difficult. Sometimes, the nature card is played as the final explanation, though the thesis that all men are violent is one solution to the need to differentiate.

Radical feminists are often castigated for suggesting that all men are violent, by relying upon essentialist biologically based explanations for men's violent actions. Perhaps the statement quoted the most is that of Brownmiller (1975), who suggests that man's lust for power combined with his 'biological capacity to rape' explains sexual violence. Yet Brownmiller is most criticised

for stating that rape ideology is a 'conscious process of intimidation by which all men keep all women in a state of fear.' (1975:
14–15) I cannot help but think that many (see, in particular,
Elstain 1981) have missed the point of much radical feminist work
about women's experiences of violence and its implications for
thinking about men's violence. By raising the potential for danger
in women's encounters with *any* man, feminist explanations for
men's violence rest upon women's inability (and indeed anyone's
inability) to predict which individual man will be individually
violent to an individual woman. Social scientists, when noting
trends, observations, and aggregate findings, cannot specify which
men might be violent. But women, as individually responsible for
their own safety, are in effect forced to sort the safe from the
unsafe man. Taking my own work (Stanko 1985) as an example,
some (see, for example, Messerschmidt 1993) interpret the work
to suggest that all men are violent.[1] I (Stanko 1990), and others
(Kelly 1988; Gardener 1990) illustrate how many women's
everyday lives are organised in such a way as to minimise the
possibility of encountering a dangerous man, known or unknown.
Therefore, in practice, women may be accused of acting as if all
men, *by nature*, are violent. This is, of course, not the case. What is
crucial, however, is that the explanations of when and how men
are violent include commentaries about men's structural power
and the negotiation of this power with others. The socio-structural
context of violence, and how violence is used and interpreted, are
important commentaries which shed light upon the connections
between masculinity and violence, not its biological origins (or
otherwise).

Take, for instance, the groundbreaking work of Diana Scully
(1990), who unpicks rapists' explanations for their sexual
violence. As the men themselves suggest, sexual violence, whether
it be directed at women known or unknown, can be understood
within patriarchal, structured relations between women and men.
Sexual entitlement, the devaluing of women and their wishes, the
desire to harm women: such misogyny can only stem from a
climate within which such hatred can *structurally* fester, be
reinforced, and in many ways encouraged (see Radford and
Russell 1992). Scully (1990) terms rape as a low risk, high reward
crime. Men rape, because within such a cultural context, they can,
not because they are biologically driven, but because they are
driven by a combination of cultural and social hatred of women as

part of the very foundation of society. With all the criticism that has been directed at Brownmiller's work, it is worth remembering her most powerful chapter is on rape in war (see also Godenzi, this volume). Few commentators have suggested that the Bosnian rape camps are the product of a few, deranged men.

Yet the vestiges of biologically based thinking seep into standard explanations for man's use of violence in criminal acts. Such distinctions appear in a standard criminological dichotomic classification of violence: instrumental and expressive.

Use of violence: instrumental versus expressive acts

Categorising the use of violence into instrumental and expressive types overlooks the important contribution of the gendered context, knowledge, and the meaning of violence. Instrumental violence has been defined as violence for gain, or profit. Katz (1988) in his critique of 'sentimental materialism' suggests that instrumental violence, as a way of characterising violent theft, just doesn't make sense. Street robbery, he observes, makes little rational sense as a way of making money. The fact that street robbery is virtually an entirely male activity should not go unnoticed. He writes:

> Unless it is given sense as a way of elaborating, perhaps celebrating, distinctively male forms of action and ways of being, such as collective drinking and gambling on street corners, interpersonal physical challenges and moral tests, cocky posturing and arrogant claims to back up 'tough' fronts, stick up has almost no appeal at all
>
> (Katz 1988: 246–7).

Yet students of criminology are taught to separate instrumental from expressive violence, because, it is felt, it is understandable why most men who rob would resort to violence to acquire material goods. Moreover, there is an assumption that crime prevention may be able to impact on violence which is instrumental violence, that is for material gain, but not on violence that is the result of an impulsive explosion of temper.

Expressive violence, too, can be deconstructed through the lens of masculinity. Losing one's temper, losing control and blind rages are typical explanations given to men's battering of women in intimate relationships. It is somehow understandable for a man to have a fight with his wife, then go to attack another woman, as did a recently convicted man in France, given a sentence of fifteen years for manslaughter. Throughout feminist exposes of femicide (Radford and Russell 1992), such seemingly adequate explanations for men's outrage, forwarded as part of the cultural understanding of men's natural tempers, have been debunked. What the feminist critiques show is the wider context within which men's outrage can be understood: propriety over women and the 'right' to sexual and domestic services from women (Daly and Wilson 1988).

Daly and Wilson's (1988) careful examination of homicide reveals the use of men's violence to control their wives across industrial societies, aboriginal peoples, and ethnographies of many other social groups. It is therefore best understood as instrumental rather than expressive violence. While they argue that the killing of women is relatively rare, the widespread use of violence is not, and the predominant issues which inspire such violence are 'adultery, jealousy and male proprietariness'. So, while men's violence to women is usually characterised as 'losing control' or flying into a 'blind rage', all the evidence suggests that both battered women and the men who batter tell the same story: that men's behaviour is used as a means of control (see also Dobash and Dobash 1979).

Daly and Wilson (1988) raise challenging questions about men's violence. They illustrate throughout their treatise on homicide that: 'Intrasexual competition is far more violent among men than among women in every human society for which information exists' (1988: 161). These authors, moreover, demand that social scientists stop ignoring the powerful lessons, drawn from a multitude of sources, from the study of homicide. They suggest that patterns of homicide are better understood within the range of adaptive strategies of complex human development. Their paradigm, evolutionary psychology, is neither reductionist, nor does it eschew social conditions. It locates homicide within an understanding of how men relate to one another as competitors. And a major influence upon how men relate to one another is where they are located within the social structure. In this way, homicides among young men constitute the variable component in overall homicide rates (see, especially, pp. 279–91).

Examining lethal violence between men shows how men use violence within particular contexts. Polk's exploration of confrontational homicides in this volume, Stanko and Hobdell's (1993) study of assaulted men, and Katz's (1988) narrative on violence suggest that the complexities of how violence is used cannot be captured adequately in the all-too-simplistic dichotomisation of violence into the categories instrumental and expressive. Men say they use violence, whether they be its recipients or its perpetrators (or both) for a number of reasons: to save face, to resolve an argument, to defend personal territory, to cajole compliance, to enhance their status, to 'have fun', to attract the affections of women. Yet criminology's focus remains on those who use apparently random violence on the street. Quoting Katz again: 'Distinctive features of violence already noted – strategic calculation, militaristic delight, symbolic representation of enemies, and melodramatic self-absorption – indicate a pride in ruling the streets by terror' (1988: 112). But what Katz and others spotlight is the actions of young men who wish to control people and places within specific jurisdictions. But the spotlight upon young men's violence in gangs, or targeted towards certain local populations, neglects the vast amount of violence which is not involved in 'ruling the street'. The public face of violence, made visible because of the presence of a body, as in murder, or as in the mobilisation of police to quell concern about losing the control of the streets to unruly young men, obscures many of the experiences that women and men define as violent or threatening.

Equally important are the gendered dimensions and consequences of violence, and it is these gendered aspects which are most likely to be pushed out of the frame of understanding violence and its consequences. Women who have experienced violence cope with those experiences in the context of their understanding of what it means to be female, and by and large, women experience femaleness as *unsafety*. Whilst many women are abused by men known to them, they are acutely aware that some men they do not know may wish to violate them *because they are women*. Men's experiences of violence are all too often attributed to their experiences of normal masculinity. The way men cope with violence is multi-dimensional, yet has been almost entirely overlooked by criminologists (Stanko and Hobdell 1993; Newburn and Stanko, this volume). Women and men of colour feel potentially vulnerable to violence in a white-dominated society, and indeed, many have experiences of verbal and physical abuse because they are not white.

Using the frame of masculinity, let us explore what contribution this additional perspective might give to the study of individual men's use of violence.

The power of violence in negotiating masculinities

Jefferson (this volume) challenges the reader to find a way of transcending the individualistic/socially deterministic divide. One way to do so is to recognise how the individualisation of men's violence is moulded by criminological discourse, a discourse, I argue, which relies upon individually attributed explanations for men's individual behaviour.

On a general level, men's use of violence on an individual level by and large asserts control over individual women (Daly and Wilson 1988). Men use violence between each other as mechanism for negotiating the hierarchies of power. By all accounts, violence between men, as a solution to an argument or to save face or status, is most prevalent among working-class, poor, and disenfranchised young men. The intransigence of this fact, and its persistence and presence in virtually all societies today, should alert us to general observations about how men use violence: 'poor young men with dismal prospects for the future have *good reason* to escalate their tactics of social competition and become violent', say Daly and Wilson (1988: 287).

Men's use of violence has special implications for women and for men. As I have argued elsewhere (Stanko 1985, 1990), many women, in action and in anxiety, tacitly understand the potential danger in their encounters with men. Men's negotiations of danger and violence take place with other men and, in many ways, are illustrations of the way in which complex structures of men's lives, in racial, sexual or economic terms, are actually reproduced as features of mundane realities. Gibbs and Merighi (this volume) show the devastating impact this has had and continues to have on young black men in the United States. The growing awareness of racial and homophobic threats and violence is testimony to how ordinary passage in public is made problematic by those in dominant positions (see Gardener 1993).

But because we have fixated on the street in the way we characterise individual violence, we have limited our approaches to minimising the impact of violence on all our lives. It is not enough to uncover and make visible the hidden violence against women in order to expose features of women's lives. We must expose the way violence works in men's lives. The focus on street violence also deflects attention away from the realities of violence in men's lives, both as perpetrators and victims. But it should not be in a way that fuels the headlines about the growing violence in society (although we should always be monitoring how violence works and grows). It should be for the purpose of deconstructing men's power and privilege, which, as all the evidence suggests, is killing men more than it is killing women. Here, I challenge the foundation of criminological work, not just that devoted to the study of violent crime, but as a theoretical enterprise devoted to thinking about crime in general, for its failure to take the lessons about violence and its patterns revealed through the lens of gender.

NOTE

1   While I would not disagree with the statement, 'all men are capable of violence', I would suggest that how violence is invoked or provoked will differ widely among men.

Chapter 3

Cop canteen culture

Nigel Fielding[1]

> At the end of (Home Secretary) Kenneth Clarke's address to
> the Police Federation, the chairman presented him with a fluffy
> toy dog . . . in response to Mr Clarke's claim that he was more
> of a 'cuddly pooch' than the rottweiler he was portrayed as
> being.
>
> (*Guardian* 21.5.92)

Just as vicious new breeds have converted the British to a
dog-fearing nation, the cosy certainties of British policing are
under assault, and 'police culture' is no exception in this regard.
Policing is marked by an assertive working culture displaying
significant similarities in different societies. The archetypal police
perspective is hard-bitten, cynical and drawn to rigid in-group/
out-group distinctions. Until recently, the relationship between
these cultural values and gender has passed unremarked outside
feminist thought. Indeed, research suggests that the values of
female police converge with those of the dominant male
occupational culture (Fielding and Fielding 1992; Brewer 1991).
However, that American policewomen are an exception suggests
that *structural* features of the occupation, such as equal
opportunities policies, can impact on culture (Heidensohn 1989).

The resilience and solidarity of the occupational culture has
long been implicated as a prime force in undermining organisational innovation, with resistance greater the more innovations
threaten established working practices. This chapter assesses
police occupational culture as a gendered social institution, and
the 'masculine' and 'feminine' overtones of routine police work,
while acknowledging that gender inequality in the police is
compounded by racism and heterosexism (Renzetti and Curran

1992). Yet the occupational culture is not monolithic, and there are policies and individuals which challenge its dominant form.

It is almost a cliché that policing is a 'macho' occupation. Both academic (Smith and Grey 1985) and journalistic (Graef 1990) studies have referred to the centrality of masculine values in the internal culture of the police. Yet the matter cannot rest there. The key question, as in other domains of social life, is the relationship between culture and action. Further, we must not only pursue the impact of values on behaviour, but consider whether police culture is responsive to, or at odds with, changes in wider society.

CHARACTERISTICS AND VALUES OF COP CANTEEN CULTURE

The stereotyped cultural values of the police canteen may be read as an almost pure form of 'hegemonic masculinity'. They highlight (i) aggressive, physical action; (ii) a strong sense of competitiveness and preoccupation with the imagery of conflict; (iii) exaggerated heterosexual orientations, often articulated in terms of misogynistic and patriarchal attitudes towards women; and (iv) the operation of rigid in-group/out-group distinctions whose consequences are strongly exclusionary in the case of out-groups and strongly assertive of loyalty and affinity in the case of in-groups.

Some see in the culture's machismo similar qualities to those of criminal offenders. Ryder (1991) argues that conformity to peer group values of machismo, not deviance, chiefly motivates teenage offending.

> To gain the respect of your peers you have to prove you are tough. This means doing dangerous things which in your heart of hearts you would rather not be doing, such as burglary or joyriding. By doing these things you prove to others and to yourself that you are *hard*. Tough is good.
>
> (ibid.: 12)

The stereotypes of machismo are perhaps too well known to require much illustration. Nevertheless, as it is indeed a stereotype, it is worth exploring to what extent it is a useful means of making sense of police culture. The stereotype revolves around the physical resolution of direct, violent confrontations construed in highly personal terms and justified by Levitical notions of punishment, qualities particularly apparent in the control of major public disorder and also apparent in other forms of uniformed service cast in a similar role. The following justification by a paratrooper of his regiment's application of 'street justice' while in a policing role in County Tyrone is not untypical: 'They [Republicans] are downright bastards. You are constantly jeered at and spat at. The blokes have just said enough is enough and gone in a bit hard' (*Guardian* 19.5.92). Regimental friends told him the rampage in a bar was triggered when local Republicans boasted that a soldier whose legs were blown off by a bomb had also lost his genitals in the blast. Paratroopers found it hard to adhere to tight guidelines on their behaviour because, as a rapid reaction force, they had been trained to 'go in and smack 'em on the nose and get out quick' (ibid.). This example conveys a sense of competitive conflict, expressed in direct physical terms and only to be resolved by aggressive action. Similarly, when Derbyshire Police lost their central government 'certificate of efficiency', officers interviewed about the consequences of underfunding highlighted problems relating to their manly pride. Joint exercises in riot control had been a humiliating experience: 'you see these guys from Manchester and Leicester in their Robo-cop gear, and then we appear with shin pads and hockey players' arm protectors . . . it's unfair on the lads' (*Guardian* 20.6.92). That the 'inferior' equipment might encourage the use of negotiation rather than force is an argument that, one imagines, would get short shrift.

Ryder (1991) draws parallels between the culture of offenders, especially youths, and that of the police. Perhaps it is no coincidence that urban disorder has developed a strongly 'tit for tat' quality, with both sides depicting riots in a contest vocabulary. One young rioter in Coventry commented, 'I've been out there doing the damage with the other lads this week because the police are out of order. They come on here harassing people and dragging them off to jail for no reason. There'll be more aggro if they don't pull out of our turf' (*Guardian* 15.5.92). Recent riots have been marked by youths monitoring police messages, explicit admissions of tactics to tempt police on to estates so as to ambush them, and driving 'displays' where stolen cars were driven hard to 'entertain' bystanders and demonstrate the inadequacy of law enforcement.

Meanwhile, in its first debate on the death penalty for twenty-two years, the Police Federation overwhelmingly endorsed its longstanding policy to resume hanging. A constable attacked the 'liberal, wet policies of do-gooding politicians' who, unlike him, had not 'looked down the barrel of a shotgun'; 80 per cent of his force allegedly favoured hanging (*Guardian* 22.5.92). The extent of belief in 'physical' resolutions of conflict is conveyed by this superintendent's comment on the limitations of recruit training:

> Some basic police training does try to build you into these difficult situations where people won't talk to you. The unfortunate thing is that training doesn't allow you to do what you do in reality, which is act outside the law, which can at times be making threats which you know are unlawful. They won't let you do that in training. I joined the Hong Kong police and I was trained there, then I joined the British police and I went through basic training there. So I have seen the training [as] . . . an officer with experience and I was saying 'No, this is unreal,' because I know I wouldn't do this. I know that if he tried to walk away I'd have his back up against that bloody wall and he'd talk to me one way or another. So training is a bit unreal and I don't see how you can get around that because the Training School cannot encourage you to do that which is unlawful.
>
> (research interview 1986)

While Ryder argues that macho values are increasingly dysfunctional, he concedes that:

> of course it is useful in a warlike society which must defend itself against attack from wild animals or tribal enemies, and it is an especially important quality where hand-to-hand conflict and extreme physical hardships need to be endured.
>
> (1991: 13)

It is common to encounter police who depict their working world like that, despite evidence that police spend much more time in social service than fighting crime (Punch and Naylor 1973).

It is also clear that policemen often treat policewomen with disdain. The Metropolitan Police recently felt obliged to issue a handbook advising its officers on sexist and racist language. It referred to 'name calling in derogatory terms, for example, Doris and Plonk' (*Guardian* 23.7.92; for less restrained epithets, see Young 1991) and asked 'what is the effect of constantly referring to female police officers as girls but to male officers as men?' A chief constable cited several instances of discrimination: a Catholic policewoman was told she could not become a detective unless she could prove she was on the Pill. A WPC was told she had to lift a 1000cc motorbike with its panniers loaded to qualify for a police motorcyle course, a test not applied to males. Another was repeatedly refused a truck driving course but allowed to work as a police truck driver after she qualified outside the force (*Police Review* 27.3.92: 569). Anderson *et al.* (1993) found that nearly all policewomen experience some form of sexual harassment from policemen, and at a significantly greater rate than that to which other women working within the police were subjected. Three in ten policewomen had been subjected to unwanted touching and some 6 per cent reported having been seriously sexually assaulted. Research on female officers' career aspirations indicates they are often inhibited from applying for specialist duties or believe they are thwarted, because of male prejudice (Coffey *et al.* 1992). A survey of Scottish police found that only 39 per cent of male respondents thought women should have a fully integrated role, compared with 77 per cent of female respondents (Centre for Police Studies 1989).

These problems are related to cultural mandates within the police and society at large. Excitement and status attached to physical danger are crucial in policemen's self-image and lifestyle, fuelling occupational imageries featuring exaggerated stories of violence and sexual conquest amounting to a 'cult of masculinity' (Smith and Gray 1985), and a culture Holdaway (1989) describes as hedonistic, tough and adventuresome. Women threaten this by inhibiting use of 'raunchy' language and exposing the reality that most policing does not involve fights and physical danger (Martin 1989).

A final insight on police culture comes from an officer who 'came out' as homosexual after 17 years hiding it from his colleagues, including marriage and fathering two children to cement his 'normality'. 'I called it the canteen culture. Heavy drinking, womanising, and doing all the things that heterosexual males are expected to do' (*Guardian* 21.11.91). Yet this officer served for seven years on the vice squad, enjoying success in operations against gay men meeting in public places to have sex because 'I know what to look for and what sort of places to investigate'. The implication is that the contest between occupational demands and personal qualities is chiefly marked by the accommodation of the latter to the former.

OCCUPATIONAL CULTURES OF POLICING

While the stereotyped qualities of hegemonic masculinity present in police culture have been highlighted in the preceding discussion, there have also been hints at important sources of variation and ambivalence, such as the sexuality of officers. This section will argue that police culture is not monolithic, that the way policing is administratively organised and legally regulated has an impact on the translation of cultural values into action on the street, and that the function of macho talk in promoting solidarity in the 'off-stage' areas of policing establishes a vocabulary of motives which may help officers to legitimate street justice and other malpractice.

Although the characteristics and values of canteen culture are familiar to any police officer, not all officers – male or female – ally to them. There is reason to argue that the values of canteen culture have higher salience in some sections of the police community – such as among police in inner urban stations, among young, male recruits, and among relief constables rather than community constables – than in others. The values of canteen culture pose one particular style of policing and are associated with one particular construction of masculinity, but they compete with others (and may indeed vary over time in their bind on particular individuals). It is also possible to specify the circumstances which enhance the scope for prejudiced policing, whether the basis of that prejudice is machismo, racism or some other bias.

Police constantly display an orientation to their occupational group as a collectivity, for instance, in emphasising experience on 'the street' in order to understand policework. Managers are apt to base their claim to lead on credibility as operational 'street' officers rather than 'desk' officers. To be 'good with the troops' means public loyalty to values depicted as binding on all officers and grounded in common experience of beat policing. The constant orientation to occupational culture is marked by direct appeals to what 'we' as a collective group think, referring both to the equality of those present and to 'our' connection with others elsewhere. There is also continual reference to 'the job' as an entity, invoking the organisation as a solidary whole with intentions and personal characteristics. It would be easy, then, to treat unswerving adherence to the cultural belief system as the *sine qua non* of organisational membership. Yet this collective emphasis also permits a sharper differentiation of members one from another than in public contacts (where the uniform obviates differences of rank or gender; people sometimes say they were dealt with by 'a woman policeman'). The discussions which occupy police in 'home' settings like the canteen or patrol car are often highly competitive.

Thus, we must not only acknowledge masculine values in the occupational culture but remember that different circumstances and demands bring the culture's different, sometimes contra-dictory elements, into and out of prominence (Reuss-Ianni 1983: 9). Another significant source of differentiation is the local milieu in which officers operate (Hobbs 1991a: 606).

Since there are several variants of culture, the obvious question is whether there is an occupational culture of female police. Martin (1989) maintains that lack of patronage inhibits development of women's networks in the police; their dispersion in the organisation may also feature. There is little evidence of a female occupational culture among British police, so it cannot be empirically established whether it would be characterised by distinctive, 'feminine' adaptations to the role, though there is evidence that female police differently prioritise offences like domestic violence (Lunneborg 1989). In any case, this begs the question whether qualities associated with 'masculinity' and 'femininity' are rooted in gender or are responses to demands made by the occupation. We do know there is a strong connection between men's friendships and social structure (Nardi 1992), a point relevant to men in occupational cultures and hierarchies like the police.

Emphasis on assertive, 'red-blooded' values and unquestioning loyalty echoes the traditional relationship between male friendship and the achievement of goals in the working world. Wellman (1992) argues that men's friendships were formerly about accomplishing important things, like economic survival. The growing dominance of the service sector over manufacture has shifted emphasis from the comradely virtues of practical skills and towards friendship as an end in itself. Consequently, 'men do not routinely rely on their friends to accomplish important tasks outside of the household' (ibid.: 74–5). Policing's assertion of traditional values of crime and punishment, order and subordination to the state, is reflected in assertion of traditional male bonds, to be found in the working world, not at home. It is not just a matter of culture but the way policing is organised, on a model decreasingly characteristic of work in general, lending new nuances to the description of the organisation as a police *force* rather than a police *service.*

The crucial matter is the relevance of cultural beliefs to actual behaviour. When Cruse and Rubin observed 1,059 police/citizen interactions they found 'a wide difference between attitude and behaviour, particularly in racial differences and attitudes. . . . [W]hile policemen might express highly prejudiced attitudes, they were rated as having behaved in an even-handed fashion with citizens' (1973: 18–19). Research on police decision-making highlights situational features, which alert officers to the need to attune action to context. Further, officers do not have complete autonomy. The organisation's administrative rules, and the law, may not always be followed, but this does not mean that action is not orientated to them. They limit action by restricting the range of legitimisable discourse; only certain justifications and kinds of evidence may be used. Nor is this merely an instrumental perspective. Officers invest meaning in organisational symbolism. The imagery attaching to enforcement not only communicates instrumental messages but 'expresses selves' (Manning 1980: xii).

It is here that we would expect to 'read off' action from attitude: when the organisation's mission is taken to heart by officers and relates to an 'action opportunity' (Defleur and Westie 1958). It is also here that we should be most concerned by 'macho' values. While police do many things, most see their primary role as law enforcement, and believe this is what the organisation wants them to do. When officers feel there is justification to 'go in hard' or 'bend the rules', prejudice may well influence their actions. If they are presented with circumstances where law enforcement is thwarted by uncooperative citizens or a lack of evidence, they may feel that aggressive enforcement is justified. There are numerous reported cases where police have proceeded on concocted evidence, or engaged in other malpractice, on the basis that the system's rules had to be bent to secure its larger objectives. The Court of Appeal was told in 1992 that police in Manchester supplied an armed robber with heroin to persuade him to implicate another man as his accomplice; it was further alleged that police later assisted his escape from prison (*Guardian* 19.5.92). In another case, experts maintained that officers doctored statements by an armed robbery suspect by double spacing his original remarks and making incriminating additions between the lines (*Guardian* 30.4.92).

Here the notion of a 'vocabulary of motives' is helpful. It was developed to explain how individuals justify actions which they know to be illegal or deviant (Matza 1964). Like a deviant subculture, occupational cultures can warrant self-serving practices by such techniques. In primary groups, talk can serve as an exclusionary device. The purposes are several, including for example, to keep some circumstance from the view of supervisors while a protective line is concocted.' The closed and loaded meaning of talk between officers permits the matters being negotiated to be rendered using established interpretive repertoires and standardised devices. When formulating their claims, officers have available the interpretive forms of the legal repertoire, which enable them to translate their experiences into the impersonal linguistic currency of 'legal evidence'. This permits officers to construct versions of events apparently founded on privileged access to the legally salient features of the everyday world. The generation of in-terms among officers also provides a further prop to occupational culture.

The vocabulary-of-motives idea carries us some way in the argument that tenets of occupational cultures may help police to warrant action at odds with the law to citizens and colleagues, and provide them with organisationally plausible justifications for doing so. Canteen rehearsals of macho action also function as pep talks, and hasten the prospect that the story will again be made real in the future actions of officers. Such influences are powerful because, unlike training, codes of practice and exhortations by senior officers, the occupational culture is there every day.

The recent Metropolitan Police 'Statement of Common Purpose and Values' advised that 'we must be compassionate, courteous and patient, acting without fear or favour or prejudice'. One constable reported that 'the second day in our canteen, it appeared upside down. People got the hump with it, they saw it as an affront' (*Guardian* 4.9.91). It was part of an initiative including seminars on responsiveness to the public. Asked to describe the ideal colleague, participants cited 'supporting, loyal, friendly, reliable, discreet, honest, sense of humour', mostly qualities relating to taking cooperative roles in stable in-groups. While there has been a change in emphasis at senior levels to one which promotes a service ethos, the remarks quoted here suggest that this has to date had limited impact on occupational culture.

CRIME-FIGHTING, SOCIAL SERVICE AND GENDERED POLICE WORK

Cousins (1980) suggests that we should consider masculinity and femininity as a continuum, in line with the primacy of socially constructed gender over biologically determined sex. Gelsthorpe and Morris (1990) argue that criminology has ignored the role of stereotyped ideas of masculinity in deviance. Rice (1990) maintains that the analysis needs to examine historical, economic and political influences, and incorporate cultural ideologies, geographical location, age, race and class. While these arguments have been put in theorising female deviance, the idea of gender characteristics as a continuum, the negative consequences of stereotypes, and the concern to bring 'culture' and 'situation' into relation with 'structure', are consistent with the analysis of police culture.

Stereotypical machismo is unlikely to find much room for expression within the 'social service' aspects of policing. Yet the bulk of police work is apparently of this type. Until recently, a clear consensus existed that most police work had little to do with law enforcement (Sherman 1973: 240) and that this came about because most calls for service did not refer to crimes (Reiner 1992a: 460). However, it may be more accurate to describe most police work as 'peacekeeping' or 'order maintenance', rather than as either social service or law enforcement. This change in thinking comes about because researchers have increasingly re-cognised that, 'while most calls do not unequivocally refer to a crime and although the standard police reaction is not to invoke their legal powers, most incidents dealt with do involve an element of, at least, latent conflict and the potential ingredients of a criminal offence' (ibid.). It is also plausible that changes in police organisation and increasing responsiveness to the demands made by victims have increased the proportion of crime-related calls.

What this shift in academic thinking highlights is the definitional contingency in 'reading' police action, and if researchers have to negotiate it then so do the police themselves. That is, the same event can be seen by the officer as a crime-related conflict requiring an aggressive response or as an interpersonal dispute requiring informal conflict resolution. In other words, the character of the incident is (often) in the eyes of the beholder, and the nature of the demand for service is shaped by how officers wish to respond. In this view, police forces are sites for competing ways of being a man and expressing masculinity. Since an orientation to crime control is one widely remarked characteristic of role concepts held by police, it is likely that many incidents will be read by police as crime-related but not appear so to outsiders. But stereotypical aggressive machismo (or hegemonic masculinity) is but one way of expressing masculinity. The definitional ambiguity may also help account for the competition to join units such as Criminal Investigation Departments or the riot squad. Their concentration on 'real crime' or 'real disorder' may attract those wishing to appear as 'real (police) men'.

Until quite recently, female police officers were confined to a separate women's section. Equal opportunity legislation put an end to this and women theoretically could participate in the range of police duties. Our characterisation of the 'canteen culture' as informed more by values and qualities associated with masculinity than femininity relies on evidence that women are still effectively 'ghettoised' in particular duties (and take on values of masculine police culture rather than substituting their own). They are *kept from* some duties and *kept for* others. The EOC (Equal Opportunities Commission) (1990) reported that women in the Metropolitan Police were excluded from specialisms like dog handling, mounted branch and firearms duties. They were unlikely to be employed in public order duties while more likely to be assigned to station duties, communications and work with children and women, results consistent with Jones's (1986) study of a provincial force.

The argument will be pursued with regard to criminal detection and routine beat patrol. After two years of 'probation', recruits seek to accumulate a good record of activity, usually arrests, with which to make their claim for promotion. A very popular form of horizontal promotion is transfer to the CID, customarily enjoying the highest status within the police. But the two sexes do not compete equally. There is a pecking order among arrests; a 'good crime arrest', e.g., of a residential burglar, is better than arresting a drunk for obstruction. While WPCs certainly walk the beat, they do so less than their male counterparts, because women are thought to be better at clerical and administrative work and are more often deployed in the station. There is also evidence that, regarding offences of public order, they are pushed to the rear by male constables at disturbances, and excluded from the frontline when deployed against pickets. It follows that it is harder for women to collect a portfolio of good arrests and thus to become detectives.

But let us say an individual succeeds. Some female detectives have always been recruited. Before equal opportunities legislation they worked on cases involving women and children, chiefly sexual offences. There is little reason to suppose this has changed. My research on the investigation of child sexual abuse suggests that female detectives are especially likely to be assigned to specialist training in child protection and consequently to be used in such work. Indeed, many victims and their mothers indicate a preference for female officers. This work is, of course, valuable, but in terms of advancement within CID it is not accorded the status of homicide and other 'major' crime. The thinking of senior detectives may well reflect gendered assumptions. The EOC (1990) found that unofficial quotas operated in departments like CID, with recruitment often by word of mouth. The Centre for Police Studies' survey (1989) of deployment found women less likely to have experience of CID work. Brown and Campbell (1992: 328) reported that 'whilst numerically represented in CID operations . . . for practical purposes deployment is made on the basis of gender in that a female officer is assigned to a squad as *the* woman detective'. Differential deployment was most likely to apply to experienced female officers, so lack of representation in specialist roles cannot simply be due to length of service. If women find it difficult to gain entry to CID, and those that do succeed are largely confined to stereotypical 'women's work', then it follows that the predominant source of the branch's ethos will be masculine. '[B]ias in deployment . . . serves to buttress stereotypic beliefs about the skills and abilities of policemen as well as policewomen' (ibid.: 332). Detectives remain the least-studied segment of the police. What is known is that detectives form a tight-knit in-group who are reluctant to cooperate with uniformed officers, reflect some characteristics of local criminals, such as heavy drinking (Hobbs 1988), and that their stock methods include the application of pressure in various ways to those with information, rather than the classic intellectual deductions of a Sherlock Holmes.

Routine, uniformed beat patrol is conducted largely by constables and pursues three broad functions: law enforcement, order maintenance and social service. Social service accounts for the largest share of an officer's time, for example, providing crime prevention advice. Next comes order maintenance, e.g., mediating domestic disputes. Yet while law enforcement is the least encountered demand, and passive interventions like compiling reports greatly exceed active interventions like chasing suspects and 'feeling their collar', crime-busting remains central to constables' preferred image of the role.

The masculine qualities of this image and working style – the quest for excitement, aggressive interventions, winning a contest between 'us' and 'them' (Reiner 1985) – are obvious in the contrast between relief-based and community patrol. 'Relief' policing is the dominant form. Here, constables respond to calls from despatchers relaying demands for service. This is 'reactive' or 'fire brigade' policing. It features short-term interventions anywhere in the division which are concluded by arrest, taking crime reports, or advice that the matter is not police business or requires no further action. Minimal information is available before arrival, so officers may respond in haste and in force. Relief officers despise community constables, who work regular hours rather than round the 24-hour shift system. Community police are seen as 'hobby bobbies' who are unconcerned with crime and spend their time kissing babies and chatting to pensioners over tea. But community policing's rationale is that crime-relevant information will flow from close community contact resulting from long-term assignment to one beat. Officers who know the area can diagnose problems and pursue long-term solutions, working in an incremental, 'proactive' fashion and cooperating with other agencies. They will be more responsive to local priorities because they face the same public every day.

The contrast between relief and community policing is bold. Reliefs rush to problems, often in cars, often with their radio squawking, terminate interventions as quickly as possible, have no concern with the long-term resolution of problems, indulge in minimal community contact. For them, being in the police is being among police. When they are not at a call they are in a car or the canteen. Community constables are free of the despatcher and exercise considerable autonomy. They seek solutions to problems about which they have background knowledge and they maximise community contact. For them, being in the police is being among the public. When they are not at an incident they are on patrol (since they are on foot its harder to get back to the station). Moreover, their long-term relationship with the public means they may prefer negotiated, informal responses because these better resolve problems than simply making arrests.

THE CRISIS OF LEGITIMACY AND CHANGING OCCUPATIONAL CULTURE

Miliband (1978) described declining deference by social groups as a process of 'de-subordination', identifying it as a characteristic of contemporary society. Reiner (1992b) has linked this to declining public consent to policing. The police are not alone among social institutions in falling under greater scrutiny and scepticism, but the forces of change have been most restrained there. The collapse of police evidence in numerous widely reported cases, televised applications of 'street justice', and the continuing decline in crime clear-up rates, have recently prompted official inquiries and new thinking. Community policing is seen as one means to bring the police closer to the public.

The Home Office, and some senior officers, are keen on community policing. In 1992 the Chief Inspector of Constabulary called for forces to devolve more responsibilities to local commanders and reflect community priorities. The Home Secretary gave forces two years to shift more control to local areas (Home Office news release 5.3.92). There would be more flexible working patterns with a move away from the eight-hour shift and more officers were to be available when demand was high. However, 'traditional elements feel that the "thief-taking" role is being submerged in public relations' (*Guardian* 14.2.92). Several forces have already attempted to switch from relief mode to 'area' or 'sector' policing, taking officers from the reliefs and making them responsible for one area. There are signs of great resistance:

> Asking street-hardened coppers, whose self-respect is defined by the approval of their peers, to take on the morality and ethos of community policing is like expecting them to police in drag. For a softer style of policing to be endorsed in the canteen, the need of young police officers for war stories, to see themselves

as always on the verge of another episode of a real-life television cop show, will have to change.

(Graef 1990: 4)

It is interesting that Graef chose a word play on men wearing women's clothes to express his view.

Another challenge to the elements in police culture which tend towards hegemonic masculinity may be posed by the advancement of female officers, provided they do not fall prey to 'masculine' qualities while negotiating their way to the top. A graduate who attended a special course normally leading to promotion in three years found herself stalled as an inspector for seven years and cited problems about operational command experience, without which senior rank cannot be gained:

> Women often do paperwork very well. There are a lot of good women around and so there's a temptation to get them to do these administrative jobs, because they're going to do them well – only then to criticise them for lacking operational experience. And then, if they start pushing hard to get involved with operations, you find people saying they're just trying to be macho.
>
> (*Guardian* 2.6.90)

Thinking which gives rise to a dual labour market for men and women is not confined to the worlds of commerce and industry.

Despite an overall doubling of women in the police, the percentage above the rank of constable fell from 11.2 in 1971 to 5.8 in 1988 (survey by Z. Adler reported in *Guardian* 12.3.92). In 1987, Alison Halford wrote:

> there are so many reasons why the male is preferable to the female in the eyes of male selectors. Will the woman rock the boat, can she carry a shield, is it not 'odd' – in every sense of the word – that she wants to progress in her career?
>
> (Halford 1987: 2019)

Eventually suspended as Assistant Chief Constable of Merseyside, having been the first woman to reach that rank, Halford claimed she was denied promotion nine times because of her sex. She initiated an industrial tribunal case in 1990. Soon after, a member of the police authority reportedly said he thought she was a lesbian and should never have been appointed ACC. A few weeks later she was suspended for swimming in her underwear with other officers at a businessman's house while on duty; the others were not suspended.

Sexuality appeared to feature in the thinking of those allegedly opposed to Halford's advancement. As well as the lesbian allegation and the mildly risque pool incident, Chief Constable Kenneth Oxford reportedly accused her of improper spending on an academic consultant and subsequently asked if she was having an affair with him (*Guardian* 3.6.92). Lady Simey, former chair of the police authority, said whenever Oxford was challenged 'it was as if you had opened the front gate and gone into a garden where a dog was loose – barking, shouting, denigrating. I put it down to the fact that being challenged by a woman was quite outside his experience' (*Guardian* 14.7.92). Halford discovered that a job reference by a subsequent chief constable queried her personal suitability, her judgement over the *Police Review* article quoted above, and her operational experience. The lawyer acting for the chief constable asked, 'He thought your operational experience was somewhat limited, and you think that is discrimination?' to which she replied 'It is unfair compared to others', (*Guardian* 30.6.92). This point about operational experience again echoes the distinction made in the hegemonically masculine version of police culture between crime fighting as men's work and social service as women's work. At the industrial tribunal Halford was questioned about alleged 'familiarity' with a chief constable at a conference. The tribunal also heard allegations that Halford drank heavily. As one officer put it, 'if you don't have a drink with them you're a lesbian, if you do you're an alcoholic' (*Guardian* 22.7.92). In July 1992 the tribunal hearing was abandoned. Halford agreed to retire on medical grounds and withdraw her allegations of sex discrimination, and disciplinary charges against her were dropped. While the case might have been inconclusive in terms of sexual discrimination, it revealed much about the culture of very senior officers.

THE FUTURE

The changing style and identity of British policing has at least partly been prompted by the crisis in legitimacy facing the police. If aggressive, competitive, 'win-at-all-costs' values are associated with the values of hegemonic masculinity then its consequences have become increasingly clear to the general public in the train of *causes célèbres* such as the cases of the Guildford Four and the Tottenham Three. It is at least worth speculating how these and other discredited investigations may have been conducted had they not been led by male officers.

In 1988 the Metropolitan Police received a report on its corporate identity which advised that, while 'massive' organisational changes had occurred, it now needed cultural change. Culture cannot change overnight. What can change quickly is the environment in which culture operates. Recent policy initiatives challenge the environment which has permitted police culture to operate on masculine precepts. A 1992 circular introduced annual appraisals as a basis for 'administrative dismissal', while acknowledging that 'some officers feel it's more macho just to bark out instructions [and] others feel it's demeaning to have to report on their colleagues' (*Guardian* 29.1.92). In 1992 officers in six forces gained the opportunity to work part-time. An explicit aim was to encourage 'women returners', largely those on maternity leave. Job-sharing also became available. In 1990 the Met dropped height requirements in a bid to increase minority recruitment. An assistant commissioner said height was no longer essential to officers' effectiveness (*Guardian* 23.1.90). In the first such case, a sergeant was dismissed from the Met for sexual harassment in 1992 (*Guardian* 9.6.92). A woman officer complained after repeated comments, and other officers gave evidence on her behalf. The Met also made discrimination against officers on grounds of sexual orientation an internal offence, following two other forces, although the 500-strong Lesbian and Gay Police Association, set up in 1990, felt it would take more than equal opportunity statements to quell the homophobic element in canteen culture.

Graduate recruitment may also challenge established practices. A chief constable said his degree taught him that 'we do not operate in a hermetically sealed environment' and that there were 'external ideas and concepts' he could usefully apply (*Guardian* 2.6.90). But it is not easy to challenge culture. A graduate joined with social service ideals and, using his discretion, preferred to warn 'mildly errant motorists' than apply formal means. But his sergeant entered 'not firm enough with offenders' on his file, which stopped him applying for graduate promotion courses because 'I didn't feel I'd made a good enough start to stand a chance'. The graduate wastage rate is over double that for non-graduates (ibid., quoting a University of Manchester survey).

We might ponder whether Jones's (1983) still-contemporary list of problems undermining police/public relations – 'fire brigade' policing, the complaints procedure, misuse of discretion, racial bias and distancing of police and public by technology – could be overcome if there were more female police. Women are outside the male 'club' and may be better able to expose malpractice (Hunt 1990). There are facets of the feminist movement which have affected women's role in policing, and policing in general, such as the higher priority given to domestic violence, rape and child abuse. These link to broader demands for a different style of policing, which would be more aware of victims' needs and place more emphasis on social service and cooperation with other agencies (Heidensohn, 1992). The argument that policing is imbued with the values of masculinity is not perfect but is eased by the fact that readers would find utterly improbable the argument that policing is imbued with the values of femininity. Yet the research on police decision-making suggests that neither legal nor cultural influences fully explain decisions, that situational factors interact with 'structural' features. While we may characterise an occupational group by simple bi-polar distinctions (is not canteen culture also a 'white' culture?), it must not become a caricature.

NOTE

1   The author gratefully acknowledges the comments of Dr Jennifer Brown, Research Manager, Hampshire Police, and of the editors.

Chapter 4

Young black males
Marginality, masculinity and criminality

Jewelle Taylor Gibbs and Joseph R. Merighi

INTRODUCTION

Since the earliest days of slavery, young black males have been the symbol of sexual aggressiveness and explosive violence in American society (Baldwin 1963; Frazier 1949). This link between sex and violence has gradually evolved through political demagoguery, social exclusion, and media caricature into an extremely negative stereotype of young black males who have been stigmatised and demonised as inherently deviant and dysfunctional (Gibbs 1988; Madhubuti 1990). Viewed by the dominant society as victimisers, these young black males have themselves become victims of persistent poverty and racial discrimination in a self-fulfilling cycle of deprivation, denied opportunities, and deviant behaviour (Gibbs 1988; Glasgow 1980).

Young black males, aged 15 to 24, occupy a very marginal status in American society that has projected upon them its own anxieties about power, its economic insecurities, and its moral ambivalence. Their black skin, their poor families, and their deteriorated neighbourhoods are constant reminders of the gap between democratic rhetoric and demographic reality, the legacy of generations of discrimination and exploitation, and the intractable social problems of ethnic minority groups in American society (Farley and Allen 1989; Gibbs 1988; National Research Council 1989).

In a society that values wealth, power and achievement, and measures adult males by these yardsticks, minority males recognise very early that their marginal status creates nearly insurmountable barriers to success through the traditional avenues of business, the professions and government service (Perkins 1975; Stafford 1991;

Staples 1982). Since these legitimate routes of success have been historically blocked for low-income inner-city black youth, their survival instincts lead them to seek alternative avenues to play out their masculine roles in their own communities. Not surprisingly, these alternate routes to economic independence and mobility are rather limited and circumscribed, but may include the world of sports, entertainment, or small ethnically oriented business ventures. Since relatively few black males are blessed with the abilities of a world-class athlete or the talents of a gifted entertainer, many will gravitate towards the 'underground sector' of the economy and will gradually become involved in the world of crime (Glasgow 1980; Schulz 1969; Wilson 1987). This world is attractive to inner city black youth because it provides them with three major sources of affirmation: a 'masculine' sociocultural role; a source of occupational income; and a route to social mobility within their community. In reality, these sources of affirmation reflect a skewed conception of appropriate 'masculine' sociocultural roles, a distorted assessment of occupational risk, and a false perception of mobility processes.

In order to elucidate these themes, the authors of this chapter have three goals: (1) to describe the involvement of young black males in the criminal justice system; (2) to demonstrate the relationship between racial marginality and antisocial or criminal activities in these youths; and (3) to explore the relationships between marginality, racial and sexual identity, sense of masculinity, and criminal behaviour in these youths.

Black youth in the criminal justice system

In 1990, black males aged 15 to 24 constituted about 15 per cent of the total youth in that age cohort in the United States' population. Nearly one-third live in families whose income level is classified below the poverty line. The majority have been reared in single-parent families, usually headed by a female. One out of seven has dropped out of high school and nearly half have never held a full-time job (US Bureau of the Census 1992). They reside primarily in substandard housing in inner cities that are besieged by crime, drugs, and urban decay. Their daily lives are punctuated by acts of random violence, police brutality and countless minor indignities. They are society's outcasts, its surplus labour, and its urban underclass (Glasgow 1980; Wilson 1987).

Despite their small proportion in the youth population, black males accounted for over one-third of all juvenile and all adult male arrests in the United States in 1990 (US Department of Justice 1992). Black male juveniles, under the age of 18, were more likely than their white peers to be arrested for violent offences such as homicide, robbery, aggravated assault, and forcible rape (US Department of Justice 1992). They also had high rates of arrest for drug violations, especially for heroin and cocaine, and for weapons violations.

Since 1980, the black youth arrest rates for violent crimes have increased by 19 per cent, with much of that increase due to a rapid rise in homicide, aggravated assault and drug-related offences (US Department of Justice 1992). Cited most frequently as the major factors contributing to increased levels of violent crimes in this group are: the proliferation of 'hard' drugs in urban areas; the spread of gangs to control the drug trade; and the easy access to guns (Marwick 1992; Roper 1991). The combination of drugs and guns is not only linked to crimes of violence against people and property, but also to an increase in family violence, suicide, unintentional injuries, and random violence (Centers for Disease Control 1992; Gibbs 1988; Rose 1986).

To be arrested and to spend some time in jail has become a rite of passage for all too many young black males in the inner cities of America (Brown 1965; Monroe 1988; Stafford 1991). 'Doin' time' for inner-city black males is analogous to joining a fraternity for college-age white males; that is, it provides an instant peer group with a special bond, a special set of initiation rites, and a special identity as brothers. In the absence of socially sanctioned paths to manhood, the inmate identity for these black males conveys validation of an introjected negative identity while simultaneously enhancing their sense of masculinity as 'tough guys' and 'jailbirds'. First-person accounts of imprisonment by well-known black authors reveal both anger at the isolation, degradation and violence, countered by pride in their ability to survive the dehumanisation, to endure the humiliations, and to become inured to the brutality (Brown 1965; Cleaver 1968; Haley and Malcolm X, 1964). The triumph of their survival over inhumane prison conditions is frequently couched in terms of discovering or asserting their manhood, where 'manhood' is equated with stereotypical notions of masculinity, aggressiveness, and manipulation of the system. These traits are further reinforced by the status and privileges accorded to them as leaders while they are incarcerated (Cleaver 1968; Haley and Malcolm X 1964).

A recent report estimated that nearly one in four black American males, in the 20 to 29 age group, was involved in the criminal justice system either in prison, on probation, or on parole (Mauer 1990). These national estimates are reflected in similar rates in various states and metropolitan areas of the USA. However, there is an ongoing debate about whether these figures represent a valid reflection of crimes committed by blacks or whether they reflect selective biases at every stage of the criminal justice system (Hindelang 1978; Krisberg *et al.* 1986). Due to the disproportionate rates of incarceration of black and Hispanic males, the United States holds the unenviable distinction of having the highest incarceration rates of any country with the exception of South Africa.

Unfortunately, jails and prisons rarely rehabilitate prisoners, so black youth has high rates of recidivism – over 60 per cent will return to custody within two years (Hawkins and Jones 1989). More importantly, staying out of jail does not necessarily indicate an absence of criminal behaviour but may reflect the effect of more sophisticated knowledge and techniques of crime that enable ex-convicts to avoid detection and arrest. Developing a reputation as someone who can outsmart the police lends special cachet to a young black male, who may be an unskilled school drop-out, and enhances his stature as a 'real man', a dude to be reckoned with, a macho male to be respected (Brown 1965; Haley and Malcolm X 1964; Majors and Billson 1992). Although this invincible male status allows young black males to establish themselves within their community, it is seldom the strategy that is needed to penetrate the barriers to mobility and the feelings of marginality imposed by the majority culture.

Marginality and barriers to mobility

The 'marginal man' has been described by Stonequist (1937) as a person

> who is poised in psychological uncertainty between two or more social worlds, reflecting in his soul the discords or harmonies, repulsions and attractions of these worlds, one of which is often 'dominant' over the other; within which membership is

implicitly based on birth or ancestry (race or nationality); and where exclusion removes the individual from a system of group relations.

(1937: 8)

Although later social scientists criticised Stonequist's rather negative views and proposed alternate conceptions of marginality as a social status and as a personality type, certain aspects of this early definition of marginality provide an apt description of the status of young black males in American society – they are marginal by race, by socioeconomic status, and by age. Their marginality is fully documented and delineated in several recent works which present a comprehensive profile of black youth social indicators, ranging from family income and family structure, school drop-out and unemployment rates, delinquency and drug use, to homicide and suicide (Gibbs 1988; Farley and Allen 1989; Majors and Billson 1992; National Research Council 1989).

More than half of all black youth growing up in low-income families live in 'hypersegregated' neighbourhoods where they are isolated from the dominant white community, neglected by the political bureaucracy, exploited by the business community, and underserved by educational, health and social service systems (National Research Council 1989). As they grow up, black youths are further marginalised by their experiences in the educational system where they are often mislabelled as educationally deficient, disproportionately punished and suspended or expelled, so that school becomes a punitive and painful experience until they either drop-out or are pushed out (Kozol 1991; Ogbu 1978; Reed 1988).

When young black males enter the labour market, they are forcefully confronted with their marginality as they face persistent and often blatant discrimination in their search for jobs (Freeman and Holzer 1986; Larson 1988; National Research Council 1989). Their rates of unemployment are twice as high as their white peers (38 per cent versus 17 per cent in December 1992); they tend to be concentrated in jobs at the lower end of the wage scale; and they have higher turnover rates and less job stability than their white counterparts. It has been shown that level of education is not a confounding factor since black male high school *graduates* had higher unemployment rates in 1988 than white male high school *drop-outs* (Children's Defense Fund 1991).

By the time they reach young adulthood, black males have had ample feedback from every major institution in American society that they are inherently unequal; that they cannot fully avail themselves of this society's rights and privileges; and that they will be characterised by the gatekeepers of society and by the mass media which guards those gates as 'disadvantaged, deprived, deviant, disturbed and dumb' (Gibbs 1988). Consigned to second-class status by these self-fulfilling stereotypes, young black males perceive fairly quickly that they will be denied access to traditional channels of economic and social mobility such as good schools, high-salaried jobs, attractive neighbourhoods and investment opportunities (Majors and Billson 1992; Stafford 1991). At some time between early adolescence and young adulthood, many black males face the painful dilemma of either challenging these barriers with only a slim chance of success or of seeking alternate illegitimate routes to mobility, which pose a high risk of danger and criminal prosecution. We propose that a major element in this choice is the black youth's need to seek affirmation for his self-esteem, his sense of personal and racial identity, and his need to assert his masculinity, all of which are inextricably linked to his psychosocial and psychosexual development.

Before explicating the complex links between marginality, masculinity and criminality, we will briefly review findings from ethnographic and clinical studies of young black males who express their own feelings of marginality in a variety of responses, on a range of measures, and in different research settings.

Ethnographic studies afford the most comprehensive portrait of the marginal status of young black males in American society and culture. These studies provide a variegated window on both the experiences of marginality and its behavioural consequences, from such pioneering works as *Black Metropolis: A Study of Negro Life in a Northern City* (Drake and Cayton 1945) and *Talley's Corner* (Liebow 1967) to the more recent contemporary descriptions in *Cool Pose* (Majors and Billson 1992) and *The Truly Disadvantaged* (Wilson 1987). These studies portray low-income black youth realistically but sympathetically as captives of their impoverished environments, developing strategies of adaptation, survival and even empowerment. As these and other studies clearly capture the impact of discrimination and structural barriers on the abilities, aspirations, and options of black inner-city youth, the reader is amazed at the resilience of the majority of black youth in coping with their disadvantaged status and in developing innovative strategies to 'get over' and outsmart 'Mr Charlie' (Glasgow 1980; Majors and Billson 1992; Schulz 1969; Staples 1982). In fact, it is surprising that the greater part of black ghetto youth do not succumb to a life of crime despite their exclusion from the mainstream, yet it is important to identify those risk factors which increase the vulnerability of those youths who do become involved in antisocial activities.

In clinical studies of young black males in college and community settings, mental health professionals have reported widespread feelings of social alienation, social marginality and rejection of the dominant Anglo culture (Franklin 1982; Gibbs 1975; Grier and Cobbs 1968). These young men also reported concomitant feelings of anger, hostility, irritability, depression, and somatic symptoms. Some had been referred for treatment due to acting-out behaviours, inappropriate aggression, delinquent behaviours, and self-destructive or antisocial behaviours intended to defend against the anxiety generated by their inner feelings of marginality.

Clinical vignettes of black youth often illustrate quite dramatically their ambivalence towards the dominant society as well as their overwhelming feelings of anger, depression and despair (Franklin 1986; Gibbs 1992; Grier and Cobbs 1968; Poussaint 1972). They often speak of feeling emasculated, of not feeling that they have achieved full manhood, and of being deprived of their masculinity due to societal oppression that denies them equal opportunity, equal justice, the right to develop their full potential, and to provide adequately for their families.

In treatment of these young men, one of the central issues to address is their deep-seated sense of inadequacy and devalued sense of self that may be expressed through self-derogation, lack of self-confidence, fear of failure, depression, and dysfunctional behaviours (Grier and Cobbs 1968; Poussaint 1972). There is always an underlying sense of hopelessness and helplessness that seems related to a narcissistic injury. The narcissistic wound, in turn, threatens the young man's sense of masculine sexual identity and consequently his sense of masculinity (Franklin 1986; Staples 1982).

Finally, black novelists and essayists have created an excellent body of literature describing the psychological and phenomenological perspectives on marginality from the views of fictional characters and autobiographical experiences. From the cynical musings of the protagonist in Ellison's *Invisible Man* (1947) to the angry rhetoric of Richard Wright's *Black Boy* (1937) or Eldrige Cleaver's *Soul on Ice* (1968), black males have expressed their pain and rage at their treatment in American society; their feelings of being alternately ignored and harassed; their chronic anxiety about overstepping invisible but symbolic boundaries; and their frustration over insults of inability to compete on a level playing field with their white peers (Baldwin 1963; Brown 1965; Wright 1937). While it is not prudent to condone the antisocial behaviour of the youth in these stories, it is possible to gain more empathetic insights into the causes of these behaviours from those who can write so eloquently about their slide into delinquency and criminality after a childhood of deprivation, abuse, discrimination, and denied opportunities. Through their perceptive visions of their own marginality, these authors have communicated to others their struggles to define themselves as ethnic minorities in a majority society, their frustrations in seeking outlets for their abilities and aspirations, and their temptations to acquire money and status through criminal activities. In the following section we will explore the relationships between marginality, identity, and masculinity; between sexual identity and masculinity; and between marginality, masculinity, and criminality.

Marginality, identity, and masculinity

Erikson (1959) has proposed that the central task of adolescence is to develop a cohesive personal identity, which includes a commitment to a sexual orientation, vocational choice and autonomy from parental control. In his few observations about minority youth, he underscored the difficulties encountered by black adolescents in developing a positive personal identity in the face of consistent negative messages about their membership of a devalued and marginal minority group (Erikson 1964, 1968). Despite the persuasiveness of this theory, it was not congruent with results of a number of empirical studies which reported high levels of self-esteem among black children and adolescents (Gordon 1980; Porter and Washington 1979; Powell 1985; Rosenberg and Simmons 1970).

In a comprehensive view of the research on self-esteem and self-concept among black youths, Cross (1991) points out that researchers have shifted from a deficit unidimensional model of black self-esteem to a more complex multidimensional model of diverse aspects and sources of self-esteem. His historical review of these studies between 1939 and 1980 found a distinct shift towards more positive self-esteem levels after the civil rights movement of the early 1960s.

Several other researchers have proposed theories of identity development in minority youth which take account of the apparent inconsistency between achieving positive ethnic identity and positive personal identity (Arce 1981; Kim 1981; Phinney 1989). Cross (1991) has proposed that identity can be conceptualised as a composite of group identity and personal identity, thus black adolescents could have a positive personal identity while feeling somewhat negative about their ethnic group identification. Cross (1978) has proposed a model of racial identity development that progresses through *four* stages until the youth accepts and internalises a positive black identity. The more general models of ethnic identity development, as noted above, share certain common features, i.e., they all recognise that there is a greater challenge for minority adolescents to achieve an integrated identity and that this process may occur at a different pace and in different stages than with white teenagers.

From her observations of developmental processes in black children, Spencer (1982) has proposed that low-income children are more likely than their middle-class peers to experience an 'identity imbalance' due to the discrepancies between their actual negative experiences and feedback from a hostile and unstable environment and the idealised values and goals to which they are exposed in school and other social institutions. This early identity imbalance may develop into an identity diffusion in late adolescence, when young black males begin to comprehend more fully the societal barriers to their legitimate mobility aspirations. In their reanalysis of the data from the large-scale study of self-esteem in black and white youth by Rosenberg and Simmons (1970), Hunt and Hunt (1977) found that higher levels of self-esteem in black youth were not as firmly integrated into a coherent sense of personal identity as they were in white youth by the end of high school, thus they concluded that this differentiated identity 'would permit black boys to deal with cultural "dualities" by avoiding clear withdrawal from conventional values and identity options while moving partially in the direction of accommodation to restricted opportunities to achieve these goals' (p. 554).

Findings from some recent studies of young black males suggest that those from low-income, father-absent homes feel more negatively about themselves in terms of self-esteem and sexual identification than those from upper-income, intact families (Moss 1991; Taylor 1989). For the inner-city youth in Taylor's sample, the lack of a positive male role model hampered their ability to develop a strong sense of masculine identity and a positive sense of personal identity. Combined with their low socioeconomic status, they also reported negative feelings of racial identity which was reflected in their lack of trust of significant others and their inability to make a firm commitment to school or to work. Taylor also concluded that this behavioural pattern could be viewed as a form of

> identity diffusion, characterized by a lack of commitment to a set of self-definitions, values, and plans for the future. Their approach to life tends to be haphazard and disorganized, their role model identification shifting and tenuous. The general pattern here is one of varying degrees of confusion and lack of integration and wholeness in personal organization.
>
> (Taylor 1989: 167)

Racial identity and sexual identity

The connection between disturbed sexual identity and disturbed racial identity is consonant with psychoanalytic theory which posits that a boy's failure to make an appropriate same-sex identification with his father during the phallic phase of psychosexual development will result in a conflicted gender identity and sexual orientation (Rosenberg and Sutton-Smith 1972). For a black male child, failure to make this proper identification at this early stage may result in the rejection of his father's racial identity as a devalued and powerless adult male. As an adolescent, these conflicts will reemerge and he would be likely to exhibit confusion both in sexual identity and racial identity. In a recent study of biracial adolescents, Gibbs and Hines (1992) found that racially mixed teenagers who exhibited more conflicts about their racial and sexual identity were those who failed to identify positively with the same-sex parent who was black. It has also been established by developmental psychologists that children begin to understand racial and colour distinctions at about age three, a time that coincides with the phallic period of development and when a black child is trying to sort out both the racial and sexual aspects of his or her parents which the child wishes to incorporate into his or her identity (Spencer 1982). This is a particularly crucial period for the black male child since it is the period during which the ground-work is formed for later racial and sexual conflicts in adolescence.

Sexual identity and masculinity

According to developmental theorists, an appropriate male sexual identity is a precursor to the development of a sense of masculinity and a feeling of male gender identity (Rosenberg and Sutton-Smith 1972). This sense of masculinity is also shaped by social and cultural factors, so there are expected differences between various cultures and social groups. In a homogeneous society one would expect these variations in masculine attitudes and behaviours to be minor, primarily due to personality and situational variables. Conversely, in a heterogeneous society, the range of socially acceptable masculine behaviours would be much broader, but they would be expected to conform to some normative standards and boundaries.

The definition of masculinity has undergone much change during the last two decades and has been strongly influenced by the feminist movement (Kimmel 1986; Steinem 1974). Tradition-ally, the role of the male 'involves self-reliance and autonomous inner structures, and relationships that are characterized by domination, control, aggressiveness, taking charge, and taking over' (Zuckerberg 1989: 21). According to Kimmel (1986), 'although American men have hardly shed many of the constraining features that have [consistently] defined masculinity they may be expressive and emotionally available husbands and lovers, warm and compassionate friends, and devoted and involved fathers' (p. 518). Recently, there have been empirical efforts to examine some of the components of masculinity. For instance, Mishkind *et al.* (1986) reported that men exhibit preoccupations with body image and a perfect body type or 'muscular mesomorph'; Herek (1986) suggested that homophobia is a vital part of heterosexual masculinity; and Gray (1986) underscored the importance of race in defining masculine roles and predicting interpersonal conflict. It is not surprising, given the changing roles of men and the effect of cultural norms on these roles, that masculinity is not a universal concept; rather it is constantly reshaped in accordance with prevailing social influences and norms.

In his review of theory and research on black masculinity, Franklin (1986) points out that black males in American society are expected to conform to three different sets of role expectations: a societal male role which emphasises 'competitiveness, aggressiveness, the work ethic independence', a black male Afrocentric role which emphasises cooperation, group cohesiveness and survival, and an amorphous black male cultural role which emphasises 'sexism, irresponsibility, violence . . . and dysfunctional . . . elements' (1986: 162–3). While delineating the structural and societal constraints on the ability of black males to assume a 'traditional' masculine sex role in this society, Franklin also explores the psychological factors which impinge on this process and contribute to confusion, ambiguity and dysfunction in the socialisation of black males to appropriate sex role behaviour. His analysis of these constraints and dynamic processes finds substantial support in the work of a number of other social scientists who have investigated the phenomenon of black male sex roles in the inner city (Anderson 1989; Cazenave 1981; Hannerz 1969; Majors and Billson 1992; Perkins 1975; Rainwater 1970; Schulz 1969; Staples 1982).

In the case of young black inner-city males, conflicts in their sexual identities due to the absence of positive male role models have often resulted in a confused sense of sexual identity, accompanied by a distorted sense of masculinity. Their ideas about appropriate masculine behaviours are not drawn from older adult males who are effective and productive members of their families and communities, but rather from young adult males who have adopted a set of exaggerated 'pseudomasculine' behaviours to compensate for their lack of education, their marginal employment status, their inability to support families, and their lack of stability. These behaviours include hanging out on street corners and in bars, transient sexual relationships with women, a 'hip' style of dressing, walking and talking, 'playing the dozens' with their peers, and manipulating family, friends, and acquaintances for economic, social and sexual favours (Majors and Billson 1992; Schulz 1969; Staples 1982). These pseudomasculine behaviours may also include out-of-wedlock paternity of several children, dependency relationships with various relatives in exchange for minor services, physical or verbal abusiveness in sexual relationships, driving flashy new cars, confrontational behaviours with police and community leaders, high-risk and self-destructive behaviours such as gambling, drug and alcohol use, and street hustling in petty crime (Anderson 1989; Majors and Billson 1992; Schulz 1969; Staples 1982). To describe this constellation of pseudomasculine ghetto-specific behaviours in his study of black males in a large midwestern city, Hannerz (1969) coined the term 'compulsive masculinity', an alternative compensatory pattern of adaptation emphasising sexual aggression, hustling, toughness, and frequent involvement in criminal activities.

In the next section we will show how this set of pseudomasculine or 'macho' behaviours, developed to compensate for the inability to fulfil the traditional functions of an adult male role due to social and economic exclusion from mainstream society, are often a precursor to more serious involvement in crime and a criminal lifestyle.

Marginality, masculinity, and criminality

In the foregoing discussion we have attempted to demonstrate the links between racial identity, sexual identity and feelings of masculinity in young black males, particularly in those from economically disadvantaged backgrounds. We have proposed a possible developmental progression which begins with a black male child who has an absent or inadequate adult male father figure with whom he is unable to form an appropriate same-sex identification during the phallic stage of libidinal development. Whether this partial or complete failure to incorporate elements of a positive sexual identity is due to the rejection of the father's racial identity or to other negatively perceived characteristics, it will result in a conflicted sexual and racial identity and will re-emerge in adolescence as a confused (diffused) or negative identity. If sexual identity is conflicted and racial identity is diffused or negative, the possibility of developing pseudo-masculine behaviours would seem to be more likely for the young black male as he searches to establish strategies of self-esteem management and adaptive behaviours to compensate for his devalued marginal status and his lack of strong male sexual identity (Goffman 1963; Hannerz 1969; Majors and Billson 1992; Perkins 1975).

The final link in this developmental scheme is the connection between pseudomasculinity and antisocial behaviour. The relationship between race and crime has been of interest to lawyers and criminologists for many years. Theories have ranged from the erroneous assumptions that certain groups possess inherent criminal tendencies (Lombroso 1911) to more contemporary theories that underscore the influence of poverty on criminal involvement and behaviours. According to Staples (1982), 'Crime, economic deprivation and masculinity are all intertwined. . . . The masculine ethic of success leads [black males] to commit illegal acts when the dominant culture restricts access to socially accepted ways of attaining [cultural] goals' (p. 52). Although Staples' interpretation of the masculinity-race-crime interface is based on colonial theory, it is a laudable attempt to explain the motivations and impact of societal influences on the development of criminal behaviours. As noted earlier, many descriptions of young black inner-city males have emphasised the importance of self-presentation through a set of elaborate behaviours, attitudes and values (Hannerz 1969; Majors and Billson 1992; Schulz 1969). Many of these attitudes and behaviours can be characterised as pseudomasculine because they caricature traditional behaviours of males in the dominant Anglo society. Moreover, since many of these black youths are poorly educated, unskilled and unemployed, in order to maintain their 'cool pose' they soon drift into street hustling and gradually become involved in more serious crimes, including the drug trade, burglaries, car thefts, and violent offences.

This progression from minor delinquency to serious criminal activity has been described in a number of ethnographic and empirical studies about inner-city communities (Hannerz 1969; Perkins 1975; Rainwater 1970). It has also become one of the major themes of black exploitation films, novels, and television programmes over the past two decades. These films and novels have graphically portrayed the limited options available to young black males in American society, where crime is an equal opportunity employer and the drug trade is one of the major industries in the ghettos.

Adolescents most at risk for becoming involved in antisocial and delinquent activities are those from low-income, female-headed families and who are failing in school and associate with peers of similar characteristics (Dembo 1988). Black males in their late teens and early adulthood who are school drop-outs, unemployed, and have a history of drug use are particularly vulnerable to the lure of street crime and involvement in the drug trade. Joining a gang in a large city further increases the risk of a black male engaging in violent felony offences and more sophisticated criminal activity such as extortion, pornography, and prostitution (Hawkins and Jones 1989; Lemelle 1991).

The journey from minor hustling on a street corner to major crimes of burglary and car theft may take place within a few months or a few years. 'Car-jacking' by young black males began in Newark, New Jersey in 1989 and has now become a very popular activity in cities and suburbs across the country. Although a number of very young teenagers have been killed or seriously wounded by pursuing police officers while joy-riding, they continue to steal cars simply to demonstrate that they are courageous enough to defy the police and to prove their manhood to their peers. As long as they perceive that they can gain respect and status from stealing a car, the fear of arrest and even disability or death will be eclipsed by the anticipation of notoriety as a 'bad brother'.

The drug trade is another example of criminal activity that provides illegitimate income to young black males, who weigh the risk of arrest from the police or violence from competitors against the promise of quick profits (Brunswick 1988). The drug trade, especially in 'crack' cocaine, has spawned an industry in the ghetto, providing jobs for spotters, pushers, distributors and wholesalers. Despite the inherent dangers of selling drugs and handling large sums of money in frequently tense situations, some drug merchants express feelings of omnipotence and power over their ability to manipulate people and to exploit their weaknesses for a quick fix. Those feelings are analogous to the sentiments expressed by stock brokers and bankers who control financial markets and access to economic resources in the legitimate society, yet these avenues are blocked for young black males who may display excellent financial and organisational skills in managing their drug operations.

Owning a gun is another potent symbol of masculinity for young black males, who are increasingly likely to use a gun in the commission of a crime and most at risk from being killed by a gun (Centers for Disease Control 1992). Not only does the gun give them a sense of power and invincibility, but it also provides them with a sense of control in situations that are ambiguous or potentially dangerous. Carrying a gun for an inner-city black youth can be compared to carrying a briefcase for a young white corporate lawyer – it is a statement of his status, a symbol of his manhood, a sign of his strength. The gun is a 'piece' for which he may have paid a cheap price, but it affirms his masculinity and confirms his identity as a black male who will take care of business, no matter how difficult or dangerous the assignment (Fingerhut *et al.* 1992). It is this intense attachment to guns and the willingness to commit violence to prove their masculinity that is one of the most disturbing trends among young black males in today's inner cities.

Finally, criminal activity has traditionally been one of the avenues of mobility in America for ethnic minorities who were excluded from mainstream economic systems (Davis 1976; Wolfgang and Ferracuti 1967). While white ethnic minorities gradually became assimilated and were able to follow legitimate routes to mobility, blacks at the end of the twentieth century are still the victims of poverty, discrimination and economic exploitation. This persistent marginal social status has fostered feelings of exclusion, rejection and rage in low-income black male youth; increased their distrust of the legal system and the legitimate institutions, norms and values it represents; and reinforced their involvement in dysfunctional, antisocial and criminal activities (Hindelang 1978; Oliver 1989; Staples 1982).

SUMMARY AND CONCLUSIONS

In this chapter we have discussed the complex interrelations between marginality, racial and sexual identity, masculinity and involvement in criminal behaviour. While some of these relationships have been proposed in the literature and documented in empirical research, other relationships are suggested by theoretical, descriptive and clinical linkages that are clearly speculative. We have proposed a series of developmental events and processes which may occur in certain groups of young black males, resulting in later conflicts in their racial and sexual identities. These identity conflicts are more likely to arise in low-status black males with inadequate models of identification and they, in turn, will develop pseudomasculine behaviours in an attempt to overcompensate for their feelings of racial inferiority and sexual confusion. Pseudomasculinity is thus conceptualised here as a mediating factor between marginal social identity and criminality; that is, the young black males who develop 'macho' behaviours as a defensive strategy to counter their feelings of marginality will be at greater risk for antisocial behaviours than those who deal with marginality with more pro-social adaptive strategies (Gibbs 1974, 1975).

In an effort to test these propositions we suggest the need for more empirical research to investigate different subgroups of black males under varying social and economic conditions. As the number of minority youth increases in the population of the United States and other Western industrialised nations, it will be extremely important to tease out the relationships between structural factors in the economy, social and cultural factors in the family and community, individual development and psychological characteristics, and situational factors in the rising crime rates of minority youth. Similar trends occurring in England have been well-documented by a number of British scholars of race relations (Bhat *et al.* 1988; Gilroy 1987; Solomos 1988). In a recent study of black youth in England, the senior author found that their socioeconomic status and their negative social indicators (school drop-out rates, juvenile delinquency, unemployment, and drug arrests), relative to their white counterparts, were remarkably similar to those of black youth in America (Gibbs 1993).

In conclusion, future researchers should focus on identifying the protective factors as well as the risk factors in order to make more reliable predictions about which black youth will be most vulnerable to involvement in crime (see Rutter 1987). Research strategies should include intraethnic and interethnic differences as well as cross-national comparisons with minority youth in other countries. Through such research efforts, we may eventually move beyond theories and predictions of criminal behaviour towards developing improved programmes of prevention and early intervention to divert vulnerable youth into pathways towards productive adulthood.

Chapter 5

Schooling, masculinities, and youth crime by white boys

James W. Messerschmidt *

The two most significant and tenacious features associated with crime are age and gender. For example, young men account for a disproportionate amount of crime in all Western industrialised societies (Beirne and Messerschmidt 1991; Chesney-Lind and Shelden 1992). Moreover, although Albert Cohen's (1955) thesis on 'delinquent boys' can be legitimately criticised for a number of reasons (see Messerschmidt 1993), his awareness of a relationship between the school and youth crime should not be discounted. Research has shown that youth crime declines drastically when state schools are not in session and that young people who leave school during the academic year engage in less crime than those currently enrolled (Elliott and Voss 1974; Messerschmidt 1979). Yet schooling is one of the chief social milieux for the development of youth crime and also a social setting that has institutionalised gender and, therefore, patterned ways in which femininity and masculinity are constructed and represented. School, then, does not merely adapt to a natural masculinity among boys. Rather, it constructs various forms of masculinity (and femininity) and negotiates relations among them (Connell 1987: 291–2).

Similarly, there is a strong relationship between youth group activities and youth crime (Morash 1986), and youth groups are an important social setting for the accomplishment of gender. Accordingly, in this chapter I examine the reciprocal relationships between schooling, youth groups, masculinities, and crimes and attempt to illustrate how all of these are constituted through structured social action. More specifically, I explore the way social action is linked to structured possibilities/constraints, identifying in particular how the class, race, and gendered relations in society

* For helpful comments on earlier drafts of this piece I am grateful to Piers Beirne, Bob Connell, Tony Jefferson, Nancy Jurik, Gray Cavender, and Meda Chesney-Lind.

constrain and enable the social activity of young men in the school and the youth group and how this structured action relates to youth crime.

'Boys will be boys' differently, depending upon their position in social structures and, therefore, upon their access to power and resources. Social structures situate young men in a common relation to other young men and in such a way that they share structural space. Collectively, young men experience their daily world from a particular position in society and differentially construct the cultural ideals of hegemonic masculinity. Thus, within the school and youth group there are patterned ways in which masculinity is represented and which depend upon structures of labour and power in class and race relations. Young men situationally accomplish public forms of masculinity in response to their socially structured circumstances; indeed, varieties of youth crime serve as a suitable resource for doing masculinity when other resources are unavailable. These forms of youth crime, as with other resources, are determined by social structures (this perspective is spelled out in Messerschmidt 1993).

SOCIAL STRUCTURES, MASCULINITIES, AND CRIME IN YOUTH GROUPS

Research on youth groups indicates that what young men and women do with the group tends to mirror and recreate particular gender divisions of labour and power and normative heterosexuality. This appears to be so regardless of class and race position. From Thrasher's (1927) early research to the works of Cohen (1955), Cloward and Ohlin (1960), Short and Strodtbeck (1965), Klein (1971), Miller (1980), Quicker (1983), Schwendinger and Schwendinger (1985), Harris (1988) and Fishman (1988), women have been found to take on secondary or 'auxiliary roles' in the group if, in fact, they are involved in the group at all.

Anne Campbell's (1984) important ethnographic study of lower working-class racial minority youth groups in New York City found that both men and women assume positions within the group that might be available to them in society at large.

In straight society the central, pivotal figure is the male. His status in the world of societal and material success is the critical factor, while the woman supports, nurtures, and sustains him. The gang parodies this state of affairs, without even the economic infrastructure to sustain it, for the male rarely works and often it is the female who receives a more stable income through welfare. Nevertheless, the males constitute the true gang! Gang feuds are begun and continued by males; females take part as a token of their allegiance to the men.

(Campbell 1984: 242–3)

Campbell argues further that specific girl groups:

exist as an annexe to the male gang, and the range of possibilities open to them is dictated and controlled by the boys. Within the gang, there are still 'good girls' and 'bad girls', tomboys and fallen women. Girls are told how to dress, are allowed to fight, and are encouraged to be good mothers and faithful wives. Their principal source of suffering and joy is their men. And though the girls may occasionally defy them, often argue with them, and sometimes patronise them, the men remain indisputably in control.

(Ibid.: 266)

What Campbell's research indicates is that the gendered social structures of labour and power shape interaction in youth groups, affording young men the opportunity to arrange social life to their advantage. Although these opportunities vary by race and by class, young men exercise authority and control in terms of gender, at least relative to young women of the same race and class. The youth group, then, is unmistakably a domain of masculine dominance, a domain that reflects the gender structures of labour and power in society and the related practices by which they are reproduced.

Besides overall dominance in youth groups, normative heterosexuality is a decisive 'measuring rod' for group participation. Indeed, young men often control and exploit the sexuality of young women. Campbell (1984: 245) reported that in one particular group, heterosexuality was so crucial to young women's group membership that when 'dykes' were discovered, they were 'multiply raped and thrown out of the club'. Similarly, the Schwendingers (1985: 167) found that 'sexist exploitation of girls is common to all stratum formations', from middle- to working-class youth groups.

Suspicion and jealousy being one of the most disruptive practices inside youth groups, serial monogamy is demanded and enforced. The jealousy of a young man is often interpreted by a young woman as evidence not of his lack of self-control, but of his passionate attachment to her. Similarly, 'the beatings that she may receive at his hands when he believes that she has been unfaithful are interpreted as a direct index of his love for her' but 'his infidelity is blamed upon his desirability to other women, rather than seen as evidence of his less-than-total commitment to her' (Campbell 1990: 174–5). Campbell (1990: 180–1) adds that both the young men and young women see the men as being:

> by nature, unable to refuse an offer of sex. Consequently, it is not the boy's fault when he strays but rather the other woman's. The confrontation is recast as between the girlfriend and her rival, rather than between the girl and the boy. Consequently, sexual betrayal is terminated by an attack on the rival, not on the boyfriend, who simply was following his nature.

Other research suggests similar heterosexual relations in lower working-class (Fishman 1988), working-class (Willis 1977), and middle-class (Schwendinger and Schwendinger 1985) youth groups. Accordingly, normative heterosexuality is constructed as a practice that helps to reproduce the subordination of young women and to form age-specific heterosexual styles of masculinity, a masculinity centring on an uncontrollable and unlimited sexual appetite. Normative heterosexuality, then, serves as a resource for the situated accomplishment of gender in youth groups.

Regardless of the degree of participation in youth groups by young women and the nature of youth sexuality in such groups, research clearly shows that various masculinities (as well as femininities) are constructed within these groups and, thus, the various forms of youth crime associated with those masculinities. William Chambliss's (1973) classic study 'The Saints and the Roughnecks' is notable in this regard. The Saints were 'eight promising young men – children of good, stable, white upper middle-class families, active in school affairs, good pre-college students' (1973: 24). They were successful in school, earned high grades (two boys had close to straight A averages), and several held student offices. At the end of their senior year, the student body selected ten seniors as 'school wheels'; four were Saints.

As for youth crime, the Saints were involved primarily in practices that 'raised hell', such as travelling to nearby cities on weekend evenings (often under the influence of alcohol) to vandalize property, engage in a variety of 'pranks' and forms of 'mischief', and commit minor forms of theft. The Saints, however, never fought; in fact, they avoided physical conflict both inside and outside of their group. Chambliss points out: 'The boys had a spirit of frivolity and fun about their escapades. They did not view what they were engaged in as "delinquency"' (1973: 26).

Although the Roughnecks attended the same school as the Saints, they were six lower working-class white boys. The Roughnecks avoided school as much as possible because they considered it a burden. They neither participated in school affairs, except for two who played football, nor earned good grades, averaging a C or lower. Moreover, these boys were involved in more serious forms of delinquency. In addition to drinking, truancy, and vandalism, they engaged in major forms of theft and violence. The Roughnecks sometimes stole as a group (coordinating their efforts) or simply stole in pairs, rarely stealing alone. Regarding violence, the Roughnecks not only welcomed an opportunity to fight, but they went seeking it, frequently fighting amongst themselves; at least once a month the Roughnecks would participate in some type of physical fight (1973: 27–9).

Chambliss's study is important for showing that within this particular social setting, the same school, the Saints and the Roughnecks both used available class and race resources to shape particular types of public masculinity. It is not that the Roughnecks were masculine because of their violence and that the Saints were not masculine because of their pranks. Rather, the Saints and Roughnecks were constructing different personifications of masculinity and drawing on different forms of youth crime (i.e., pranks vs. violence) as resources for that construction.

Other research indicates similar processes occurring among masculine-dominated youth groups, enabling us to build on Chambliss' data. For example, Herman and Julia Schwendinger's (1985) study, *Adolescent Subcultures and Delinquency*, attempts to explain the forms of youth crime that emerge at the group level and, in so doing, identify two types of group formations that young men dominate: the 'socialite' and 'street-corner youth'. The Schwendingers' data shows that both groups construct different forms of masculinity and, therefore, exhibit varying types of youth crime. Yet the middle-class 'Socs' (socialites) and the lower working-class 'Eses' (street-corner youth) both marshal gender and class resources in their struggle for power and status in the adolescent world.

Like the Saints, the Socs are 'less likely to be involved in the most serious violent and economic forms of delinquency' (1985:

56), drawing on school resources and various forms of vandalism, drinking, gambling, petty theft, and truancy to construct a specific type of public masculinity. Although the Eses engage in the same types of delinquent activities, other more extreme forms of violence are found among these street-corner youths. In other words, both groups of young men pursue gendered strategies of action that reflect their relative class and race/ethnicity position. Again, like the Saints, Socs have specific potentials and opportunities that help construct less violent forms of masculinity. As the Schwendingers point out:

> the Socs control the student organizations in their high schools, and the payoffs from this control are considerable. These advantages do not merely mean unique experiences, such as trips and contacts with prestigious youth in other schools, but also large and pleasant facilities in which to hold dances. Furthermore, their frequent control over the student council, cheerleading squad, and student monitor system reflects their integration with prevailing systems of institutionalized power and enables them to establish an authoritative position in the eyes of other youth.
>
> (1985: 208)

Eses have no access to such resources and power, and thus accomplish gender in a different way. For the street-corner youth, masculinity does not derive from competition for school office but from violent conflicts with other street-corner men. Carlos, a member of a street-corner gang, told the Schwendingers (1985: 171), 'In my territory that's the way they are now. That's the way we are. It seems to be the neighborhood that is the thing. You want to prove yourself to nobody but these people.'

For both the Saints/Roughnecks and Socs/Eses, the youth group is a critical organising setting for the embodiment of public masculinity. It is within this group that young men's power over young women is normalised and that youth crime, as a social practice within the group, constructs gendered differences, weaving 'a structure of symbol and interpretation around these differences that naturalises them' (Messner 1989: 79). Yet, simultaneously, these findings exhibit clear differences in 'doing gender' (West and Zimmerman 1987) for middle- and working-class boys. In fact, the above findings require a more rigorous examination of class and race distinctions.

In what follows, then, I attempt to identify certain of the chief class and race junctures in the social construction of youthful public masculinities and crimes – in particular, the important relationship between youth crime and school. The focus is on how some young white men come to define their masculinity against the school and, in the process, choose forms of youth crime as resources for accomplishing gender and for constructing what I call *opposition masculinities*. I begin with white, middle-class boys.

WHITE, MIDDLE-CLASS BOYS

Given the success of the middle-class Saints and Socs in school, it is this very success that provides a particular resource for constructing a specific form of masculinity. In this type of masculinity, the penchant for a career is fundamental: a 'calculative attitude is taken towards one's own life' and the crucial themes are 'rationality and responsibility rather than pride and aggressiveness' (Connell 1989: 296–7). Throughout their childhood development, white, middle-class boys are geared towards the ambiance and civility of the school.[1] Within the school environment, for these boys, masculinity is normally accomplished through participation in sports and academic success. This participation in (or at least avid support for) sport creates an environment for the construction of a masculinity that celebrates toughness and endurance, incessantly advocates competitiveness and shame of losing, and 'connects a sense of maleness with a taste for violence and confrontation' (Kessler *et al.* 1985: 39). Yet, in addition to creating this specific type of masculinity, sport is so revered and glorified within the school that it subordinates other types of masculinity, such as the sort constructed by the 'brains' who participate in nonviolent games like debate (p. 39).

Over and above sport, white, middle-class masculinity in the school is typically achieved through a reasonable level of academic success. As Tolson (1977: 34–6) argues, the middle-class family supports this trajectory: 'books in the home and parental help with homework provide a continuous emotional context for academic achievement'; moreover, middle-class families also tend to emphasise the importance of obtaining the appropriate qualifications for 'respectable careers' that guarantee the security of a profession. As Heward (1988: 8) noted in an English boarding school, white, middle-class parents 'planned their sons' futures carefully and then pursued their plans very actively, with the aim of placing them in suitable occupations and careers'. For the white middle class, then, manliness is about having a secure income from a 'respectable' professional occupation. Thus, there is an important link between school and family in middle-class life, and both transmit class-specific notions of hegemonic masculinity to white, middle-class boys – a particular type of work in the paid-labor market, competitiveness, personal ambition and achievement and responsibility.

Accommodating and opposition masculinities

None the less, hegemonic masculinity also involves practices characterising dominance, control and independence (see Messerschmidt 1993). Such masculine ideals are, however, the very qualities that schooling discourages. Although white, middle-class youth generally exercise greater authority and control in school than do the youth of other class and race backgrounds, research on secondary schooling reveals that adaptation to the social order of the school requires that all students, regardless of their class and race, submit to rock-hard authority relations in which students are actually penalised for creativity, autonomy, and independence (Bowles and Gintis, 1976; Greenberg 1977; Messerschmidt 1979). In other words, white, middle-class boys, like other boys, experience a school life that is circumscribed by institutionalised authoritarian routine.

In spite of this constraint, within the school most white, middle-c lass boys conform, since proper credentials are necessary to attaining careers. As Greenberg (1977: 201) notes, students 'who believe that their future chances depend on school success are likely to conform even if they resent the school's attempt to regulate their lives'. Within the social setting of the school, then, white, middle-class boys accomplish gender by conforming to school rules and regulations and by dominating student organisations, reflecting a wholehearted obligation to the school and its overall enterprise. White, middle-class boys 'accept' school values and there-fore the school exercises a prominent and influential restraint on these youth, at least within its own boundaries (Tolson 1977: 39).

Because masculinity is a behavioural response to the particular conditions and situations in which we participate, white, middle-class boys thus 'do masculinity' within the school in a specific way that reflects their position in the class and race divisions of labour and power. Their white, middle-class position both constrains and enables certain forms of gendered social action, and these boys monitor their action in accord with those constraints and opportunities, thus reproducing simultaneously class, race, and gender relations. Moreover, this particular masculinity is sustained as a type of collective product in a particular social setting – white middle-class schools.

However, because the school is 'emasculating' in the fashion discussed earlier, white, middle-class boys who join a youth group act outside the school in ways that help restore those hegemonic masculine ideals discouraged in school. In this process of 'doing gender' (West and Zimmerman 1987), these boys simultaneously construct age-specific forms of criminality. Youth crime, within the social context of the youth group outside the school, serves as a resource for masculine realisation and facilitates (as do such other practices as school athletics) 'dominance bonding' among privileged young men (Messner 1989: 79).

Successful 'pranks', 'mischief', vandalism, minor thefts, and drinking outside the school validate a boy's 'essential nature'. Such behaviours reflect an age-specific attempt to reestablish a public masculine identity somewhat diminished in the school, behaviours that are purposely chosen and manipulated for their ability to impress other boys. Moreover, outside the confines of the school, white, middle-class boys' masculinity is still held accountable, not to school officials, but to other white, middle-class boys. These behavioural forms help a white, middle-class boy to carve out a valued masculine identity by exhibiting those hegemonic masculine ideals the school denies – independence, dominance, daring, and control – to resolve the problem of accountability outside the school, and to establish for himself and others his 'essential nature' as a male. Indeed, most accounts of these forms of youth crime miss the significance of gender: it is young men who are overwhelmingly the perpetrators of these acts (Chesney-Lind and Shelden 1992: 7–18). Accomplishing gender by engaging in vandalism, 'pranks', and 'mischief' (as an age-specific resource) incontrovertibly provides a public masculine resolution to the spectacle of self-discipline and emotional restraint in the school.

Thus we see that white, middle-class, youth masculinity is accomplished differently in separate and dissimilar social situations. For white, middle-class boys, the problem is to produce configurations of masculine behaviour that can be seen by others as normative. Yet, as the social setting changes, from inside the school to outside in the youth group, so does the concept-ualisation of what is normative masculine behaviour.

Through class appeal for educational credentials, white, middle-class boys are drawn into a different masculine construction within the school: they develop an *accommodating masculinity* – a controlled, cooperative, rational gender strategy of action for institutional success. The white, middle-class boy's agenda within the school, then, is simply to become an accomplice to the institutional order, thereby reaping the privileges it offers – access to higher education and a professional career (Connell 1989: 295–7). In other words, as white, middle-class boys accomplish gender in the school setting, they simultaneously reproduce class and race relations through the same ongoing practices.

Being a man is about developing the essential credentials to obtain a suitable middle-class occupation. However, because the school both creates and undermines hegemonic masculinity within the company of peers outside the school, some white, middle-class boys draw primarily on nonviolent forms of youth crime, thus constructing an *opposition masculinity* – a masculinity based on the very hegemonic masculine ideals the school discourages. In short, white, middle-class boys are forming different types of masculinity that can be assessed and approved in both social settings (inside and outside school) as normal and natural. Through this specific type of youth crime in the peer group, middle-class masculinities are differentiated from one another.

The case of white, middle-class youth demonstrates how we maintain different gendered identities that may be emphasised or avoided, depending upon the social setting. White, middle-class boys construct their gendered actions in relation to how such actions might be interpreted by others (that is, their accountability) in the particular social context in which they occur. White, middle-class boys are doing masculinity differently because the setting and the available resources change.

School success, masculinity and youth crime

Social control theorists argue that the youth who develop close bonds to the school are the least likely to engage in youth crime

(Hirschi 1969; Wiatrowski *et al.* 1981). Yet the considerable amount of youth crime committed by the Saints and the Socs (who were the school 'wheels' and high academic achievers) outside the school justifies reasonable concern regarding this argument. Nevertheless, middle-class schools, like schools in other social settings, develop a status system based on academic success. Research has consistently shown that students who fail academically (for whatever reason) and/or who occupy the lowest status positions in school, exhibit the highest rates of youth crime. (See Messerschmidt 1979 for a review of this research.) Consequently, for white, middle-class boys who are not successful at school work and who do not participate in school sports or extracurricular activities, the school is a frustrating masculine experience as a result of which they are likely to search out other masculine-validating resources.

This view was demonstrated in one study of an upper middle-class, white neighbourhood, described by the authors as an 'environmental paradise' that 'harbors mansions and millionaires as well as deer and raccoons' (Muehlbauer and Dodder 1983: 35). The particular neighbourhood youth group, which called itself 'the Losers', was composed primarily of boys who did not do well in school and who demonstrated little athletic interest or ability. The Losers spent considerable time 'hanging out' together in the town square, but were not at all fond of interpersonal violence and controlling turf. Rather, they engaged chiefly in acts of vandalism – such as breaking streetlamps, making graffiti, destroying traffic signs, and doing donuts on the lawns of the more affluent members of the community – as well as organising drinking parties at public beaches and parks. Indeed, the only serious violence committed by the Losers was the firebombing of the personal automobiles of two representatives of 'emasculating' authority: the chief of police and the vice-principal of the school. Thus, the specific types of youth crime engaged in by the Losers served as a resource for masculine construction when other types of class-specific resources were unappealing and/or unattractive (e.g., academic success).[2]

Although this opposition masculinity outside the school is clearly not the only version of white, middle-class youth masculinity, nor perhaps the most common version, it differs considerably from that of white, working-class youth, especially because of its reduced emphasis on the public display of interpersonal aggression/violence. It follows that we must consider more closely how this type of youthful, white, middle-class, masculine construction and its attendant youth crime differs from that of youthful, white, working-class men.

WHITE, WORKING-CLASS BOYS

As exemplified by the Roughnecks and the Eses, white, working-class boys engage in such acts as vandalism, truancy, and drinking because, as demonstrated more precisely below, they also experience school authority as an 'emasculating' power. Not surprisingly, many of these boys also turn to this age-specific resource for 'doing gender' outside the school. And yet, they define their masculinity against the school in a different way than do white middle-class boys, a way that nevertheless leads to an in-school opposition masculinity as well.

'The Lads' and the 'Ear'oles'

Paul Willis's (1977) classic study *Learning to Labour* demonstrates how a group of white, working-class British boys ('the Lads') reject both schoolwork and the 'Ear'oles' (Earholes, or other young men who conform to the school rules) because the Lads perceive office jobs and 'bookwork' as 'sissy stuff'. The Lads come to school armed with traditional notions of white, working-class masculinity: the idea that 'real men' choose manual, not mental labour. Because of this particular gendered strategy, schooling is deemed irrelevant to their working-class future and 'emasculating' to their conception of masculinity. In other words, schooling is unmanly in a different and broader way for these boys than for the white, middle-class boys discussed above. Accordingly, the Lads evolve into an unstructured, counter-school group that carves out a specific masculine space within the school, its overwhelming rules, and unnerving authority.

In resisting the school, the Lads construct behaviour patterns that set them apart from both the Ear'oles and also the school. Because the Ear'oles are enthusiastic about schooling and support its rules, they are a major conformist target for the Lads.[3] One such practice for opposing the school and the Ear'oles is 'having a laff', that is, devising techniques to circumvent the controlled environment of the school. Willis (1977: 13, 31) describes some of these:

Settled in class, as near a group as they can manage, there is a continuous scraping of chairs, a bad tempered 'tut-tutting' at the simplest request and a continuous fidgeting about which explores every permutation of sitting or lying on a chair. During private study, some openly show disdain by apparently trying to go to sleep with their head sideways down on the desk, some have their backs to the desk gazing out of the window, or even vacantly at the wall. . . . In the corridors there is a foot-dragging walk, an overfriendly 'hello' or sudden silence as the teacher passes. Devisive or insane laughter erupts which might or might not be about someone who has just passed. It is as demeaning to stop as it is to carry on. . . . During films they tie the projector leads into impossible knots, make animal figures or obscene shapes on the screen with their fingers, and gratuitously dig and jab the backs of 'ear'oles' in front of them.

Another activity that distinguished the Lads from the Ear'oles is fighting. The Lads exhibited 'a positive joy in fighting, in causing fights through intimidation, in talking about fighting and about the tactics of the whole fight situation' (Willis 1977: 34). Constructing masculinity around physical aggression, the Lads – eschewing academic achievement – draw on an available resource that allows them to distance and differentiate themselves from the nonviolent Ear'oles. As Willis points out, 'Violence and the judgement of violence is the most basic axis of "the Lads" ascendance over the conformists, almost in the way that knowledge is for teachers' (1977: 34). The Lads reject and feel superior to the Ear'oles; moreover, they construct such practices as having a laff and fighting to demonstrate their perceived masculine eminence.

In this way, then, the Lads accomplish gender in a specific relational way by opposing both the school and its conformists. Whereas white, middle-class boys are more likely to oppose school outside its boundaries but conform within school, the social setting for the Lads is different. *They are the opposition both inside and outside the school.* Understandably, there is no accommodating masculinity here. Because schooling is conceived as unnecessary to their future while simultaneously encompassing effeminate endeavours, the Lads earn symbolic space from the school by engaging in different forms of 'pranks' and 'mischief' within the school itself. Such behaviours help transcend the 'sissyish' quality of the school day while simultaneously distancing the Lads from the conformists.[4]

But the Lads also draw on forms of physical intimidation and violence to differentiate themselves from the Ear'oles and the girls. For the Lads, the fight 'is the moment when you are fully tested'; it is 'disastrous for your informal standing and masculine reputation if you refuse to fight or perform very amateurishly' (Willis 1977: 35). In fact, physical aggressiveness seems to be an institutionalised feature of the Lads' group. As Willis notes, 'the physicality of all interactions, the mock pushing and fighting, the showing off in front of girls, the demonstrations of superiority and put-downs of the conformists, all borrow from the grammar of the real fight situation' (1977: 36). These activities provide the fodder with which to accomplish their gender and to establish (for the Lads) their 'essential male nature'. They are designed with an eye to gender accountability and resultingly construct inequality among boys by attempting to place the Ear'oles masculinity beneath their own within the public context of the school. The Lads are constructing an opposition masculinity as a collective practice; notwithstanding, this specific type is significantly different from the white, middle-class in school accommodating masculinity and gains meaning in relation to the masculinity of the Ear'oles.

Outside the school

It is not only conformists to the school whom white, working-class youth, like the Lads, attempt to subordinate in the process of doing gender. In Western industrialised societies, what have become known as hate crimes – racist and anti-gay violence – are disproportionately committed by groups of white, working-class boys, crimes that can also be understood in the way discussed above (Beirne and Messerschmidt, 1991: 562–3; Comstock 1991: 72–92).

For some white, working-class boys, their public masculinity is constructed through hostility to, and rejection of, all aspects of groups that may be considered inferior in a racist and heterosexist society. For example, the Ear'oles are considered inferior and subordinate to the Lads because of their conformity to, and seeming enjoyment of, effeminate schooling projects. But other groups outside the school are also viewed as inferior by many white, working-class boys. Willis (1977: 48) found that different skin colour was enough for the Lads to justify an attack on, or intimidation of, racial minorities. Indeed, the meaning of being a 'white man' has always hinged on the existence of, for example, a subordinated 'black man'. Thus, a specific *racial gender* is constructed through the identical practice of racist violence; a social practice that bolsters, within the specific setting of white, working-class youth groups, one's masculine 'whiteness' and, therefore, constitutes race and gender simultaneously. White, working-class, youthful masculinity acquires meaning in this particular context through racist violence.

Moreover, for some white, working-class youth, homosexuality is simply unnatural and effeminate sex, and many turn this ideology into physical violence. As one white, working-class youth put it, 'My friends and I go "fag-hunting" around the neighbourhood. They should all be killed' (Weissman 1992: 173). Gay bashing serves as a resource for constructing masculinity in a specific way: physical violence against gay men in front of other young, white, working-class men reaffirms one's commitment to what is for them natural and masculine sex – heterosexuality. In other words, the victim of gay bashing serves, 'both physically and symbolically, as a vehicle for the sexual status needs of the offenders in the course of recreational violence' (Harry 1992: 15). Accordingly, gender is accomplished and normative heterosexuality is reproduced.[5]

White, working-class boys such as the Lads construct public masculinities outside the school in other ways as well. As with the Roughnecks and the Eses, the Lads also occasionally participate in various forms of theft. Because they want to take part in the youth culture (go to pubs, wear the 'right' clothes, date, and so on) shortage of cash becomes 'the single biggest pressure, perhaps at any rate after school, in their lives' (Willis 1977: 39). Through contacts with family and friends, many of the Lads acquired part-time, after-school, and summer jobs; in fact, Willis found that it is not uncommon for these youths to work over ten hours a week during the school year. Consequently,

> this ability to 'make out' in the 'real world' . . . and to deal with adults nearly on their own terms' is seen by the Lads as evidence of their 'essential nature' as 'males' – a practice that reproduces this specific type of white, working-class masculinity.
>
> (Willis 1977: 39)

In addition, because of their access to paid employment, the Lads involvement in theft is irregular rather than systematic, providing a little extra pocket money when needed.

Mercer Sullivan's (1989) analysis of a white, masculine-dominated, working-class youth group from 'Hamilton Park' suggests the presence of analogous processes in the United States. Most of the boys in this group are from the more established and better employed white, working-class households where the 'man of the house' is the 'head of the house' as well as the principal wage earner. The working-class jobs held by these men have been passed down from generation to generation through masculine-dominated, family networks. The boys from these families view schooling in the same way that Willis's 'Lads' in Britain viewed schooling, and racism is pernicious and widespread among these boys. Indeed, the violence committed by these youths is based on ethnic boundaries between the predominantly white neighbourhood of Hamilton Park and the adjacent African American and Latino areas.

Sullivan did not examine interpersonal violence in depth and he disregarded whether or not these youths engaged in 'pranks' and 'mischief' in school; rather, he concentrated on property crime outside school. Sullivan found that by the age of 14, the Hamilton Park boys began working steadily in part-time jobs during the school year and in full-time jobs during the summer months. This regularised work came to them in the same way work came to the Lads, through connections. Sullivan found that because of these links to paid employment, the Hamilton Park youths had far less involvement in street crime than youth from lower working-class, racial minority neighbourhoods who had no such connections. Although during their early and mid-teen years the Hamilton Park youths engaged in factory burglary, shoplifting, and joy-riding, none of them later engaged in systematic theft as a primary source of income. By their mid-teens, most worked at jobs paying better than the minimum wage and, therefore, 'wages, not theft, provided their primary source of income during those years' (1989: 179).

Because of their attachments to paid employment and a future in manual labour, periodic property crime was an important practice in the construction of their specific type of masculinity for both the Lads and the Hamilton Park boys. The way they committed theft reflected their lack of dependence on stealing for income, which in turn provided a resource for constructing their 'essential nature' in a specific way. As Willis (1977: 40) recorded for the Lads:

> thieving puts you at risk, and breaks up the parochialism of the self. 'The rule,' the daily domination of trivia and the entrapment of the formal are broken for a time. In some way a successful theft challenges and beats authority.

In this specific context, then, intermittent theft is a resource that helps construct an 'out-of-school', autonomous, independent, and daring opposition masculinity. And with part-time work available as a masculine resource outside the school these white, working-class youths only sporadically turn to theft as a resource to accomplish gender. Thus, theft not only provides these youths with a resource for doing masculinity in the specific social setting of the group, it also helps construct a gendered line of action in which future gender accountability may be at risk. That is, it contributes to the wherewithal for adequate masculine participation in the youth culture.

Yet while the part-time workplace and youth group are initially seen as superior to the school – a milieu where masculinity as they know it is accepted – these working-class boys eventually find themselves locked into dead-end jobs, making less money than those who did not participate in the group and who conformed to the school. In this way, Willis's book shows how white 'working-class kids get working-class jobs'. The initial context, and ultimate result, of the Lads' opposition masculinity in the school was an orientation towards manual labour. Through their specific construction of masculinity, the Lads themselves (and, similarly, the Hamilton Park boys) thus reproduced class, race, and gender relations as the structures constituted in those relations constrain and enable their collective social action.[6]

CONCLUSION

White, middle- and working-class boys, produce specific configurations of behaviour that can be seen by others within the same immediate social situation as 'essentially male'. As we have seen, these different masculinities emerge from practices that encompass different resources and that are simultaneously based on different collective trajectories. In this way, then, class and race relations structure the age-specific form of resources used to construct specific opposition masculinities. Young, middle-class and working-class men produce unique types of masculinity (situationally accomplished by drawing on different forms of youth crime) by acknowledging an already determined future and inhabiting distinct locations within the social structural divisions of labour and power. Collectively, young men experience their everyday world from a specific position in society and so they construct differently the cultural ideals of hegemonic masculinity.

Opposition masculinities, then, are based on a specific relation to school, generated by the interaction of school authority with class, race, and gender dynamics. For white, middle-class boys, a nonviolent opposition masculinity occurs primarily outside school; for white, working-class boys, a specific type of opposition masculinity prevails both inside and outside school. Yet for each group of boys, a sense of masculinity is shaped by their specific relation to the school and by their specific position in the divisions of labour and power.

Social structures are constituted by social action and, in turn, provide resources for constructing masculinity. And the particular type of youth crime, as one such resource, ultimately is based on these social structures. Thus, social structures both constrain and enable social action and, therefore, masculinities and youth crime.

NOTES

1   Research in this section concentrated on the white middle class. Although it is conceivable that middle-class racial minority boys may emphasise similar masculine patterns discussed here, there is no reason to assume that this specific type of masculinity speaks for all racial and ethnic groups of boys, even though they may be from the same class. In the same vein, the type of masculinity discussed here is not the only version of masculinity within a given population of young white, middle-class boys.

2   The English boarding school study referred to earlier evidenced that 'school failures' were the most likely to be 'rebellious pranksters', whose pranks occurred primarily outside the school and were nonviolent in nature (Heward 1988: 54, 139–40). See also Cookson and Persell (1985) for similar evidence in a US boarding school.

3   Within the same working-class school, the Lads and the Ear'oles construct different types of white masculinity. The latter comply with school rules and do well academically, constructing an accomodating in-school white masculinity similar to white, middle-class boys. That is, the Ear'oles are constructing a different gendered strategy of action than are the Lads. The working-class school itself fosters this

differentiation among boys and masculinities through such institutionalised processes as tracking and grading systems. In other words, the Ear'oles are the white, working-class high achievers and do well academically, while the Lads are the opposite. The result is a 'contest of hegemony between rival versions of masculinity' (Connell 1989: 295) and those who adopt the accomodating form – as school status evidence shows (see Messerschmidt 1979) – are the least likely to engage in youth crime both inside and outside the school. Since academic achievement is unattractive to the Lads, they search out other resources for masculine accomplishment, such as youth crime. Notwithstanding, the focus in this chapter is on boys who engage in youth crime and how these boys, by reason of their social structural position (race and class), view the school differently and primarily (but not always) make use of different forms of youth crime to construct different types of masculinities. And although adversarial masculinities clearly develop within the specific social setting of the school (e.g., accomodating vs. opposition), among youth who specifically engage in youth crime we can observe (by race and class, for example) distinct types of opposition masculinities. For excellent work on the construction of different masculinities by working-class boys originating from the same class and race position, see Connell (1989, 1991).

4   Many working-class girls also oppose school. Although opposition among boys, in the manner of the Lads, can be understood as a practice that attempts to confirm specific notions of hegemonic masculinity, similar behaviour among girls actually violates stereotypical femininity. Because convention maintains that girls are to engage in practices that express courtesy, docility, and refinement, contradictory practices are seen as a project protesting conventional femininity and, as Kessler et al. note, 'a genuine challenge to their subordination as women' (1985: 38). Yet these young women are by no means masculine in style or outlook. As in other avenues of everyday life, they reproduce conventional notions of femininity. Similarly, McRobbie's (1991: 45–51) sample of white working-class girls opposed the school in specific ways (e.g., smoking in the lavatory), yet accepted unquestioningly conventional femininity within the school. Thus, considerable evidence suggests that white, working-class girls – like white, working-class boys – construct specific styles of gender (femininity) within the confines of the school and draw on forms of youth crime as a resource for that femininity.

5   Clearly, most white, working-class boys do not engage in such behaviours and boys from other class backgrounds may indeed engage in such behaviours. My argument is simply that the combined class and race social setting of these youths increases the likelihood of this type of violent behaviour.

6   I do not suggest that 'reproduction' is simply automatic. Reproduction of class, race, and gender relations must constantly be realised through social action that depends upon the collective efforts of the specific participants.

Chapter 6

Tougher than the rest?

Men in prison

Joe Sim *

[Power] manages to persuade us that what it censures as
deviance is actually deviance from its norms, when in fact the
censured activities or demeanours are usually well within the
terrain of the dominant norms.

(Sumner 1990: 39)

The recent upsurge in the analysis of men as a gendered class and the
specific debates concerning the social construction of hegemonic
masculinities has added a significant new dimension to sociological
theory. As David Morgan has noted, this development stems directly
from feminist and gay studies both of which have put 'the critical
studies of men and masculinities on to the agenda' (1992: 2). Such
studies have been important both in demonstrating the deeply
rooted, structural imbalance in social power at all levels of state and
civil society and its often devastating impact on the personal identities
and lived experiences of women, as well as turning the sociological
searchlight onto the behaviour of men as 'gendered individuals
rather than as ungendered representatives of humanity' (Morgan
1992: 2). The influence of this work on the sociology of the prison has
however been less dramatic. Prison studies, despite taking male
offenders as the 'primary subject matter' rarely 'focus on *men* and
masculinity' (1992: 3). Instead they have created 'theories about
criminals without a conceptualisation of gender' (Gelsthorpe and
Morris 1990: 3–4, emphasis in the original).

Close scrutiny of prison research supports Gelsthorpe and
Morris's position. Since the 1950s there have been numerous
studies of male prisoners which have traversed theoretical and

* Thanks to Anette Ballinger, Susan Barlow, Jenny Burke, Gillian Hall, Tim
  Newburn and Betsy Stanko for their helpful supportive comments on earlier
  drafts of this paper. The title comes from a song by Bruce Springsteen.

methodological positions as far apart as positivism, functionalism, interactionism, Marxism and abolitionism. From the analysis of inmate normative structures and the adaptive roles taken by male prisoners in the struggle to survive the pains of imprisonment, through to the role of the institution in the regulation of the detritus generated by advanced capitalist social formations and the demand for its abolition, these studies have produced a rich and often compelling body of work on penality and its historical and modern consequences.[1] In addition, since the late nineteenth century numerous autobiographies have been published which have also generated immensely powerful and moving accounts of the pain of men in prison.

However, while many of these studies have been academically sophisticated and theoretically advanced they have concentrated on *men as prisoners rather than prisoners as men.* In this chapter I shall focus on the latter phenomenon and sketch some of the implications that a gendered reading might have for the sociology of British prisons.[2] To achieve this I shall utilise the conceptual framework developed by Bob Connell in analysing state institutions. Connell has argued that a gendered reading of these institutions involves four dimensions: the persistent and general use of force by men against men, the institutionalisation and control of hegemonic masculinity, the development of relationships between different masculinities and the exclusion of women from positions of authority (Connell 1987: 125–32). This framework is useful for laying a conceptual base from which to launch an exploratory study of prisoners as men. As I shall indicate, it is also useful for allowing the analysis to move beyond individual behaviour and to raise broader sociological questions about the role and goals of imprisonment for men. Finally, the chapter will argue that while individual acts in prison are sustained by a powerful culture of masculinity, this culture is not homogeneous but contains internal contradictions and fissures out of which other, empowering and positive patterns of behaviour have developed as a challenge to the networks of domination and subordination engendered by male and penal power behind the walls.

MEN IN PRISON

The experience of men in prison has traditionally been tied to understanding the hierarchical arrangements of the institution.

These arrangements have been built on the complex horizontal and vertical links established between prisoners and prison officers and between these groups and the white, male technocrats who occupy powerful positions as governors, area managers and state bureaucrats in the Home Office. While this work has generated a number of important sociological insights it has, like the majority of organisational studies, ignored the dialectical relationship between gender and power in prison (Savage and Witz 1992). In particular, it has failed to consider how the social order of the institution has been sustained and reproduced not only by organisational demands and individual personalities but also through deeply embedded discourses around masculinity and femininity. In other words, the daily experience of prisoners can be seen to be consistently and continuously mediated, not simply by their status as numbered and packaged individuals within the formal organisation of a state institution, but more fundamentally, by their relationship with, and expectations of, the other prisoners and their guards as men. A central dynamic of this daily experience and structured within these relationships is the question of violence and its place in reinforcing the hierarchical arrangements inside.

Attempting to understand the mobilisation of violence in prison and its relationship to strategies of domination and subjugation from a gendered perspective requires moving beyond commonsensical, state-defined and, indeed, many sociological explanations which have focused on the role of inadequate individuals, psychopathic personalities or 'bad apples'. Instead a critical analysis means 'drawing distinctions between different situations, which, taken together, comprise a violent institution' (Scraton *et al.* 1991: 66). At the same time, it also means recognising that:

> the acts of violent men in prison, sustained by a culture of masculinity, which idealises and equates personal power with physical dominance, reflects the world outside. Inside, the dominance can be total with nowhere to hide from the bullying of other prisoners. It is concentrated within a totality of masculinity, the ground-rules heavily underlined by official male authority. Prisoners' violence is often part of the symbol, ritual and reality of a hostile male environment.
>
> (ibid.: 67)

It is important to recognise that the culture of masculinity which has developed inside varies between different prisons. The hegemonic masculinity and the controlled use of violence which prevails in open prisons with its population of older men, middle-class offenders, convicted police officers and those completing their sentences, is of a very different order to the dominant, and often uncontrolled masculinity which operates systemically in young offenders' institutions and detention centres. Here physical violence, psychological intimidation and constant bullying provide the chilling and stark context in which everyday decisions are made, lives controlled and bodies and minds sometimes broken and destroyed. For many young men in these places, and the older men who staff them, violent behaviour is not abnormal but a normal, 'legitimated part of the taken-for-granted' (Morgan 1987: 183–4). This process of normalisation and routinisation underpins and gives meaning to the self-perception of the individual and the perceptions of the significant others in the power networks of the institution. As the account below makes clear, the institution sustains, reproduces and indeed intensifies this most negative aspect of masculinity, moulding and re-moulding identities and behaviourial patterns whose destructive manifestations are not left behind the walls when the prisoner is released but often become part of his 'taken-for-granted' world on the outside:

Violence. I was thinking about it afterwards the other night. Either you understand it or you don't. If you understand it, you find it hard to explain to somebody who doesn't. You've never questioned it, you've always taken it for granted, part and parcel of everyday life. It's normal: what would be abnormal would be if violence wasn't in your life. . . . Before I stopped at the DC [Detention centre]. Now that is violence, real violence a detention centre is. They do things to you at a detention centre, mentally and physically, as bad or worse than anything you could have got sent there for in the first place. Beatings, kickings, humiliations: they heap them on you one on top of another. The idea's to break your spirit, to show you violence doesn't pay, that if you give it out you'll get it back ten times over. So what do you learn? If you haven't got it already, you learn hatred of authority and determination you're not going to let it break your spirit. You're not going to let it win, you're going to show them you're stronger and tougher than they are. If you don't you go under. You come out looking back on it with pride. They didn't break me. I won, I won. It's like graduating from an academy, it's a great feeling. Stay violent you say to yourself; stay violent and you'll win out in the end. You come out bitter at them and what they tried to do, but proud because you didn't let them. You could really call yourself a fully fledged hard man.

(cited in Parker 1990: 86–7)

Confronted by such institutionalised violence, the consequences for individual prisoners can be profound. In March 1992, it was reported that forty prisoners were attempting suicide each month in Feltham young offenders' institution where an 'atmosphere of terror' prevailed. In addition, four prisoners had killed themselves in seven months. One prisoner provided a vivid description of the atmosphere:

About 70 or 80 boys arrive each day in big buses. You are stripped, given a number, a box of clothes. You are put in a large room with 60 other boys, big guys staring at you. There's a lot of friction when you arrive and you've got to front it out. If you sit in a corner with your head down they will pick on you for sure . . . if you show fear your card is marked. I've seen guys with fear in their eyes. . . . You get smashed around the head, sent to hospital and you're back on the wing the same night. . . . Some of the boys are so frightened they won't come out of their cells.

(*Observer* 22.3.1992)

In adult, male, long-term prisons there is also a clear hierarchy which has been widely documented in social science and is well established in popular culture. Within both discourses the construction of this hierarchy has been understood less in terms of masculinity and more in terms of organisational demands or the 'natural' differences between offenders. The armed robber and the professional criminal, the epitomes of masculinity, stand at the apex while their antithesis, the child sex murderer, flounders at the bottom. Normal manhood and abnormal perversion live together in the same institution. Understanding the dynamics of this hierarchy from the perspective of prisoners (and prison officers) as men again provides a different analytical starting point. To paraphrase Max Weber both groups are trapped within an iron cage of masculinity which secures not only the reproduction of the material domination of the body but the continuation of oppression within and beyond the walls of the penitentiary:

> All male prisons house men who settle their arguments through fear, intimidation and fighting. Many are convicted for violent assault and present a no-compromise, hard-man image. They gather around them a network of support based on their coercive influence within the prison. Protection rackets, dealing, settling scores and victimisation are the ingredients of the institutionalisation of male violence. The culture of masculinity which pervades male prisons is all-inclusive and reinforces hierarchies based on physical dominance. . . . While the prison authorities denounce publicly the activities of a hard core of pathologically violent prisoners, their officers utilize privately the full potential of control which is rooted in their violence. This quite different expression of violence, which dominates interpersonal relations within prison, is also implicitly condoned, if not actively supported and exploited. A clear example of this is the brutal treatment suffered by sex offenders. Their institutionalized brutalisation reinforces their damaged personalities and does nothing to alleviate the oppression of women. Yet it consumes the energies and reinforces the aggressive masculinity of many prisoners
>
> (Scraton *et al.* 1991: 66).

Violence and domination in prison can therefore be understood not as a pathological manifestation of abnormal otherness but as part of the normal routine which is sustained and legitimated by the wider culture of masculinity: that culture condemns some acts of male violence but condones the majority of others. It will be condemned only if it transgresses the acceptable limits of masculinity. State servants, for example, will focus their gaze on uncontrollable prisoners who in their view use force indiscriminately, the 'ballbuster' in American prison literature. Such prisoners pose problems for the normal running of the prison and challenge what the official rules call 'good order and discipline'. Seen from a gendered perspective they can be understood quite differently. First, they reinforce popular and professional discourses which equate male violence inside and outside, with individual pathology. Second, they allow the state to maintain that something is being done about violence inside through the removal of these prisoners from normal circulation and into solitary confinement. Third, they normalise violence in that the concentration on these prisoners allows other forms of prison violence to be seen as legitimate, a normal if regrettable part of prison life. In this way the debate on prison violence is constructed on the narrow terrain of psychopathic personalities while the everyday normality of domination, control, humiliation and violence is continually reproduced. These prisoners:

> become the living proof of the assumption that the troubles in British prisons are derived in and orchestrated by the words and deeds of a handful of pathologically violent men. This enables the authorities to affirm the commitment to the traditional criminological classifications of inadequate and violent personalities and to reject the charge of institutionalised violence within harsh regimes. The very celebration of masculinity, then, reduces its most violent manifestations to the level of opportunism and restricts its analysis to the psychologies of a few men. The culture and cult of masculinity which permeates all aspects of life in male prisons . . . remains dominant and reinforced.
>
> (Scraton *et al.* 1991: 77)

A good example of this point can be seen in relation to the issue of sexuality in prison. A number of recent studies have rightly moved away from the positivist emphasis on the forensic basis of rape in prison to a position which emphasises the relationship between institutional and sexual violence and broader cultures of masculinity. Robert Dumond (1992: 138), for example, has noted how in American prisons highly sexualised terms such as 'Gorilla', 'Daddy', 'Kid', 'Fag' and 'Queen' have become 'sexual scripts which help to define an inmate's orientation within a society which values aggression, power and loyalty – many of the attributes of traditional masculinity in society'. While it is important to focus on the often immense physical and psychological emasculation that is generated by male rape both inside and outside the walls (McMullen 1990) it is also important to recognise that rape behaviour is only one aspect of a broader process of sexual exploitation and coercion which as Betsy Stanko has noted:

> serves to enhance heterosexual masculinity. Inmate power and

control can be gained by treating other inmates 'like women', essentially keeping the fear of sexual danger associated with being female. By turning some men into 'women' these inmates use sexuality to dehumanise and degrade fellow inmates. To safeguard an inmate's manhood and manliness an inmate must fend off sexual attacks and be wary of sexual approaches.

(Stanko 1990: 123–4)

The influence that sexually predatory prisoners have is often disproportionate to their numbers in the system. They will generate a deep fear among younger prisoners in particular whose masculinity is kept both under constant surveillance and threat. Jimmy Boyle has described how young prisoners arriving in Peterhead in the mid-1970s would be terrified by the activities of one particular prisoner to the point where:

> some of them would ask for 'protection'. The screws of course thought this all very funny, but personally I felt deeply humiliated that another prisoner could allow himself to be 'used' in this way by them. In his own way he was policing the prison for them and the fact that he was causing conflict amongst the prisoners meant that pressure was taken off the screws. He didn't get away with it completely as some individual prisoners would have a go at him, including some of his group. But he had a frightening effect on prisoners in the main and this gave him some measure of control.

(Boyle 1977: 196)

The organisation and broader power structures of the institution legitimate and facilitate this coercion. At this level many prison officers, for example, will fail to challenge sexual exploitation not only because it divides the prison population against itself (although that is clearly one major benefit for them) but more fundamentally because such exploitation in the words of Bob Connell 'is a form of person-to-person violence deeply embedded in power inequalities and ideologies of male supremacy. Far from being a deviation from the social order, it is in a significant sense an enforcement of it' (Connell 1987: 107). To concentrate on deviant individuals therefore misses this more fundamental sociological point.[3]

A similar critique can be made of the traditional and ungendered perspective on prison officer violence. The popular

and professional distinction between legitimate and illegitimate
violence is often constructed around those few officers – the 'dogs'
– who, like the 'ballbusters', step beyond the normal, clearly
defined manifestations of maleness in relation to violence and
domination. Such officers are again symbolically important in
focusing attention on the 'bad apples' of the prison service.
However, as with prisoners, the distinction between normal and
abnormal manifestations of male behaviour is much less clear cut
when seen through the lens of gender; the behaviour of the 'dogs'
is only a matter of degree rather than of substance when compared
with the majority of state servants. As the prison officer Paisley
points out in the play *The Hard Man*:

> [screws] know what this prison would be like if we didn't get
> tough from time to time . . . they tolerate me. I'm *their* hard
> man. And they feel a wee bit guilty about me because I'm an
> aspect of themselves they don't like to admit to . . . dirties like
> me . . . we're a necessary evil. Very necessary.
> (McGrath and Boyle 1977: 57, emphasis in the original)

A gendered reading of the social order and hierarchies of the male
prison therefore moves the analysis beyond organisational
imperatives and individualised profiles. This reading points to how
the maintenance of order both reflects and reinforces the
pervasive and deeply entrenched discourses around particular
forms of masculinity. To speak in terms of normal and abnormal
men – as the vast majority of state and sociological studies have
done – is to miss a fundamental point, namely that normal life in
male prisons is itself highly problematic – it reproduces normal
men. The mortification which male prisoners undoubtedly
experience in their daily lives does nothing to alleviate the
problems that the majority will face on their release in terms of
their structural location as class and racial subjects. Nor does it
alleviate, change or challenge their self-perception as gendered
individuals, as men. Rather in its very 'celebration of masculinity'
(Scraton *et al.* 1991: 70) the prison, like other state and cultural
institutions, materially and symbolically reproduces a vision of
order in which normal manhood remains unproblematic, the
template for constructing everyday social relationships. How far
the goals of the prison contribute to this process is the subject of
the next part of this chapter.

THE PRISON'S GOALS: A GENDERED READING

The traditional goals of the prison have been built around the institution's power to combine punishment, deterrence, prevention, incapacitation and rehabilitation. The critical socio-logical response which developed in the 1970s pointed not only to the inability of the institution to do much about crime but also to its role in maintaining and reproducing wider social divisions (Mathiesen 1990). While both positions have generated a range of important work, when scrutinised in terms of gender the differences between them are less apparent than first appears. For example, if the prison was to succeed in its classical liberal goal of rehabilitating male prisoners it could be argued that the definition of success is conceptualised on the narrow terrain of rescuing male law-breakers from behaviour conventionally defined as antithetical to the criminal law and preparing them to live 'a good and useful life' when released. Close links with the family are regarded as central to their rehabilitation. And yet reforming the prisoner so that he can return to normal family life – whatever that means given the breakdown of the traditional nuclear family – fails to take account of the nature of power and its distribution in these micro situations. Deconstructing what a 'good and useful life' means for the women and children in the lives of male prisoners therefore provides a very different perspective on rehabilitation. It should be stressed that this is not an argument for defending the often appalling arrangements for personal contact which currently prevail, nor is it an argument which underestimates the intolerable and harrowing psychological pain that male prisoners feel at particular moments during their confinement (Scraton *et al.* 1991: Ch. 5). It is, however, a position which recognises that the success of the prison is being measured on a narrow philosophical and sociological terrain devoid of gendered power relationships. Similar questions can be asked about deterrence, incapacitation, prevention and punishment.

Radical critiques face similar problems. For example, the correlation between rates of unemployment and rates of imprisonment which has been identified in critical studies since the 1930s is a correlation which is discussed almost entirely in terms of male unemployment. Similarly, the theory that prison distracts attention away from crimes of the powerful and symbolically constructs discourses around good and evil is highly plausible until it is genderised. As a number of feminist writers have noted, powerful men are not necessarily those who occupy the economic and political positions as classically defined in Marxist and Weberian sociology. Those who are the most economically and politically powerless often exert a profound material and ideological influence over the women in their lives through utilising 'everyday violence' (Stanko 1990). Who are the powerful and from what crimes are individuals being distracted therefore become significant theoretical questions when the distraction function of the prison is genderised.

The liberal and radical demand for community alternatives is another area which is also problematic when genderised. As Jill Box-Grainger has noted, the idea of community which has dominated both positions, has assumed a homogeneity of monolithic values within the society in general and working-class communities in particular. This conceptualisation has serious implications for women:

> [community] has always involved the re-assertion of the role of the family, the basic unit of the community and ultimately the containment of women in the home. That in the short term the interests of a son may be in conflict with a mother's own interests is not only a theoretical problem but potentially a barrier against 'community' support for radical alternatives.
>
> (Box-Grainger 1982: 16)

Once again, this is not an argument which underestimates the contribution made by liberal and radical scholars in uncovering the daily brutalisation of men in prison and the will to power inherent in the discourses operating within and without the walls of the penitentiary. Much of this work has been inspired by what Maureen Cain has called 'practical humanitarian concerns which most of us have about what goes on' in state institutions which are 'worthy of our political or reformist zeal' (Cain 1990: 10). But as she also notes, there may be a need to displace traditional criminological accounts of penal and state practices and to ask different theoretical questions which:

> in their very formulation connect these practices with the rest of the lives of the people passing through as staff or offenders, questions which are thus concrete and specific but which also make possible abstract formulations and therefore comparisons and generalisations (Cain 1990: 10).

CHALLENGING HEGEMONIC MASCULINITY

While the analysis in this chapter has pointed to the usefulness of hegemonic masculinity as a theoretical tool for analysing the particular form of gendered order found in male prisons, it is important to recognise that the material and ideological network of power generated by and through hegemonic masculinity inside has not been without its own internal contradictions and challenges. As Bob Connell has pointed out, utilising hegemony as a theoretical concept involves recognising that the relationship between, and the politics of, domination and subordination is very often an incomplete process. Alternative definitions of reality, other strategies and ways of behaving are not simply obliterated by power networks. They are 'subordinated rather than eliminated' (Connell 1987: 184). Thus, while physical and psychological violence might be a cornerstone of male imprisonment which support dominant cultural patterns and ideologies, they are utilised within a balance of forces in which there is an everyday contestation of power and where there is always the possibility for individual, social and historical change (Connell 1987: 184).

Connell's point is an important one. It is also one which is often forgotten when Gramsci's concept of hegemony is utilised theoretically. Domination is emphasised at the expense of contradiction, challenge and change, both at the level of individual identities and social formations. This position has particular relevance for the study of men in prison, for despite the domineering brutalisation which underpins and reinforces the culture of masculinity inside, this culture has often been undercut by individual and collective strategies of dissent and sometimes by alternative penal policies which have provided a glimpse of the possibility for constructing social arrangements which are not built on violence and domination. I want to explore some examples of this in the last part of this chapter.

First, it is necessary to recognise that not all prisoners are fearless, manipulative and violent hard-men. Fear is a constant factor in the daily lives of the majority of prisoners. In a recent study of Peterhead prison, 86 per cent of prisoners interviewed stated that they did not feel safe in prison while 62 per cent indicated that fear was a 'predominant factor' in their daily lives (Scraton *et al.* 1991: 68). While a number of writers have rightly pointed out that the male experience of fear outside prison is very different compared with women (Stanko 1990: 126) and that this fear will often leave men 'isolated and unable to ask for support' (Stanko and Hobdell 1993: 27) it is also important to recognise that frightened prisoners are not always exploited by their fellow inmates. Prisoners who have been beaten or who are frightened of being beaten, will often generate gentler and softer feelings in those observing these events. Interviews with prisoners in Peterhead provided 'poignant accounts of suffering in which the most hardened man identifie[d] with the anguish of another but remaine[d] frustrated and angry at the indifference of the institution and its officers' (Scraton *et al.* 1991: 75). Two accounts illustrate this point:

Of all the liberties I witnessed among them was one assault on a young cripple. This particular day his sticks were at surgery being adjusted. He intervened in a slanging match on behalf of another prisoner, the officer seized him by the throat and punched him 3 times or so in the face, the officer said later that he had hit him with a stick. [The prisoner] got 14 days for assault.

The guy has slashed his own face twice in the past couple of weeks. What state of mind is the poor guy in? Not one person has lifted a finger to help him.

(both cited in Scraton *et al.* 1991: 74–5)

Second, some male prisoners make conscious decisions to utilise non-coercive strategies to deal with the encroachment of male and penal power into their lives. These prisoners pose different problems for prison managers. They stand at the opposite end of the masculinist continuum from the 'ballbuster'. Pursuing education classes, attaining an intimate knowledge of prison rules, regulations and standing orders, becoming a 'jailhouse lawyer' and categorically refusing to engage in violent or coercive behaviour are all examples of strategies developed by prisoners which do not necessarily derive from the culture of masculinity inside. This argument also applies to those few prison officers who refuse to work within the bounds of accepted practices organised around discourses of power, authority and domination which underline, underpin and give meaning to the working lives of the majority of prison workers both on the ground and within the bureaucracy of the state. The ideologies and behaviour of these officers can be contrasted with the 'dogs' who work at the opposite end of the masculinist continuum. Attempting to step outside the swamping disciplinary culture can result in alienation, stress, lack of promotion and overt hostility from the majority. As Ken Smith has noted:

> There are officers who are well-intentioned and take what they do seriously, working at the thin end of the seam of hope . . . . others nurse the sick or find some niche within the system running a little workshop or a library. Some who begin as idealists soon get beaten down by the overriding ambience, and are pushed out. Among the governor grades there seems to be frequent interchange between the Prison Service and the priesthood. Some become disillusioned and turn cynical; some question their role and their task. For those with any sensitivity, looking for long into the heart of horror sours them. All face pressure to conform to the status quo.
>
> (K. Smith 1989: 65)

A third example of this process can be seen in a number of the small units established in British prisons in the last two decades. Space does not allow for a full discussion of these units and the politics behind and within them. I do, however, want to look at them through the lens of gender in order to pinpoint what they can offer as a challenge to the dominant discourses inside. In particular, I want to focus on the Barlinnie Special Unit, opened in February 1973 as perhaps the clearest example yet of the challenge to masculinity in prison.

From the outset the philosophy and practices of the Unit were diametrically at odds with those prevailing in the traditional system where interpersonal confrontation was a daily event. Some of the Unit's prisoners had previously been detained in the notorious segregation unit, the Cages, at Inverness prison where conditions were brutal:

> The caged area is approximately 9ft by 6ft. The only moveable objects besides the human body are a small plastic chamberpot – lidless, a woollen blanket and one book that is issued each week. Human contact is made three times a day when the 'screws' enter to search the body of the prisoner. . . . There is no communication between the 'screws' and the prisoner. . . . Brutality and abuse of human rights is rife. If a prisoner is particularly awkward then punishment takes the form of leaving his food just out of reach behind the cage bars until it is cold, or he receives it with spittle in it.
>
> (MacDonald and Sim 1978: 23–4)

This regime can be contrasted with that operating in Barlinnie. The most significant aspect of the Unit's work lay in the decentring and deconstruction of violence as central to the repertoire of responses which staff and prisoners had utilised to defend their respective positions in the traditional system. Both groups responded to the others in the Unit not through physical violence and psychological intimidation but through the 'community meeting' where each man was encouraged to examine and articulate his feelings about himself, his life inside and his actions outside the walls (Wardrup 1982: 26). For the prisoners this was a particularly painful experience. They had never been encouraged to shine the searchlight of scrutiny on themselves as individuals or more fundamentally as men. Nor had they been encouraged to take personal responsibility for their actions. According to some accounts this philosophy which demanded personal as opposed to interpersonal confrontation, generated more psychic pain than the physical and psychological brutality they experienced prior to entering Barlinnie.[4] Jimmy Boyle has provided a powerful and highly perceptive account of the pain involved in shedding the layers of psychological skin from his past and the implications this might have for dealing with violent men:

> I have entered a world that has dyed and cast me, like so many others, where certain parts of myself have not been allowed to express themselves; a world that didn't allow my mother to kiss and cuddle me; a world where natural affection was seldom shown. To the present day I am labelled 'Killer' when in fact parts of me were done to death and only now am I discovering them . . . to think I am labelled 'Scotland's Most Violent Man'. Is it right that I should think these thoughts or should I do as I have done in the past and fulfil people's expectations of me? Am I doomed to eat raw meat and live in a Cage to satisfy the masses? I come to the present day and watch those very same people who gave me that label say that I am a 'con-man' who is trying to work his ticket out of prison – such versatility I must possess. Could it be that the consequences of someone like me changing would be too much for the establishment to accept?
> (Boyle 1984: 148–51)

Another prisoner has also provided a graphic illustration of the internal conflict he endured:

I was creating crisis after crisis and becoming more hostile towards the community confrontations as they grew more intense in a concentrated effort to modify my behaviour. At this point four of the more experienced members of the community began to work on what can be described as a crash course in maturing me. The understanding and total honesty demonstrated by these men rocked me on my heels and at times became very painful, because each of them in his own way stripped away the masks until I was standing before them, naked in a primitive sense that left me feeling very vulnerable. My values altered to a degree, and while recognising the futility of submerging myself within the false security of the prison subculture I realised that this was only my first step in what was going to be a long, hard struggle with much more pain to come.

(cited in Carrell and Laing 1982: 25)

Similar views have been expressed by prisoners in Grendon Underwood whose regime emphasises:

the responsibility of prisoners to explore their criminality, to share and express their feelings. To be answerable to each other as individuals and as a community, is we believe a valuable feature and most significant it is social as opposed to anti-social.

(Newman 1991: 21)

While it is important not to underestimate the problems faced by these institutions and to be aware of what Rebecca and Russell Dobash have called the 'therapeutic discourses' (Dobash and Dobash 1992: 248) which often underpin many progressive programmes, it is equally important to recognise that the examples above illustrate the complex and contradictory nature of masculinity in prison and the possibilities for empowerment and change within an often overwhelming network of male and penal power. This approach can be contrasted with the traditional methods utilised in dealing with offenders in general and conventionally dangerous offenders in particular. Incapacitating rapists for example, has not guaranteed an alleviation of violence against women either at an individual or collective level. Such men are likely to be confronted by a culture of masculinity which will do little to change their behaviour, heighten their consciousness or the consciousness of those in the wider society concerning the 'intimate intrusions' which collectively face women on a daily basis

(Stanko 1985). This argument is supported by the first major study of rapists in the UK which showed that only thirty-two out of 142 believed that raped women had been harmed while less than half displayed any compassion for their victims (*Guardian* 5.3.1991).[5]

These findings are hardly surprising given the nature of most penal regimes and the discourses surrounding sexuality, masculinity and femininity that prevail within and without the prison walls. In that sense, even allowing for their obsessive secrecy, prisons are not as removed from the body of the wider society and as has previously been argued. They are linked to that society by the umbilical cord of masculinity where similarities between prisoners and men outside may be more important than the differences between them in explaining sexual and other forms of violence against women. As one sex offender has noted:

> The most common accusation I get is that I've committed my crimes because I like doing them – because . . . that's the way I get my kicks. But I ask who's getting the real kicks? My case got a centre-page spread in the Sunday newspapers, thousands of extra copies were printed, *and* they exaggerate it for the delight of their readers. And the worst element is that, all the way through, no one asks you why. Oh they'll ask, 'Why did you do this?' But all they're looking for is an explanation which will make sense in their own terms.
>
>   (cited in Campbell 1986: 117, emphasis on the original)

CONCLUDING REMARKS

This chapter has considered the sociological and political implications of a gendered reading of the literature on male prisons. I have concentrated on a number of specific areas but clearly there is scope for developing this analysis through focusing on a range of other areas that are directly related to the micro and macro politics of confinement including: the place of the body in prison culture and hierarchies; sexuality, masculinity and confinement; race and hegemonic masculinity, violence and domination in women's prisons; masculinity, militarisation and the state; the relationship between state violence and male violence and the use of violence as a strategy of resistance. Taken together, these issues raise fundamental questions about the conceptualisation of male imprisonment within social science and the need to reconstruct and transgress the orthodox study of penal power.[6] Such a theoretical shift can provide a more analytical starting point for understanding the behaviour of prisoners as men. At the same time it may also generate strategies for changing their behaviour both within and without the walls of the penitentiary where the culture of masculinity casts a long and profoundly damaging shadow of patriarchal domination over the hearts, minds and bodies of the many women and children whose lives are eclipsed and diminished by its impact.

NOTES

1   Space does not allow me to list all of the studies about men in prison. For a good early summary of the literature on prisonisation and the inmate normative structure see Edwards (1975). I am grateful to Jeff Hearn for pointing this article out to me. For the abolitionist position see Mathiesen (1990). For the relationship between prisons, the state and social authoritarianism see Sim (1987).
2   This chapter deliberately focuses on British prisons. While there has been an enormous amount of research and writing conducted around American prisons, consideration of this work is beyond the scope of this chapter. There are very important cultural differences with respect to the history and contemporary role of prisons in America and elsewhere which have important implications for the study of masculinity. In order not to do a sociological disservice to the full complexity of these issues I have omitted them from this chapter.
3   It is worth noting that the symbolic attack on the individual's masculinity through sexual exploitation makes it very difficult to gather data on the full extent of this exploitation. Between 1988 and 1993 there were seventeen alleged rapes of juvenile prisoners but as the Prison Reform Trust has noted the shame felt by those subjected to such attacks undermines the gathering of evidence. These reported rapes are therefore likely to be the tip of the iceberg (*Observer* 4.4. 1993).
4   The history of the Barlinnie Unit remains to be written. There has been no serious sociological study of its genesis and consolidation or of the antagonism, both official and unofficial, which was directed towards it. The accounts I am referring to come from my personal discussions with staff and prisoners during my visits to the Unit in the mid-1970s.
5   Scully (1990) found similar views in her study of convicted rapists in American prisons.
6   This reflects Cain's (1990) call for the reconstruction and transgression of criminological theory in general.

Chapter 7

Mannish boys
Danny, Chris, crime, masculinity and business

Dick Hobbs

Sex status is of greater statistical significance in differentiating criminals from non-criminals than any other trait. If you were asked to use a single trait to predict which children in a town of 10,000 people would become criminals, you would make fewer mistakes if you chose sex status as the trait and predicted criminality for the males and non-criminality for the females.

(Sutherland and Cressey 1978: 130)

After I got my first few bucks and the nerve to go shopping without my mother, I went to Benny Field's on Pitkin Avenue. That's where the wiseguys bought their clothes. I came out wearing a dark-blue pinstriped, double-breasted suit with lapels so sharp you could get arrested for just flashing them. I was a kid, I was so proud. When I got home my mother took one look at me and screamed, 'You look just like a gangster!' I felt even better.

(Pileggi 1987: 24)

This chapter will examine the lives of two men, Danny and Chris, for whom crime is a central prop of their masculinity. It is based upon fieldwork carried out during the period 1982–92 as part of a study of professional crime (Hobbs, forthcoming).

It is naïve and somewhat arrogant of criminologists to study criminality in splendid isolation both from other forms of action and from other social processes. It is impossible to comprehend the lives of Danny and Chris without piecing together the complex relationship between their identities and structural arrangements. Crime for Danny and Chris is no more an important mediating methodology with these components than entrepreneurial competence. Indeed within the specific shadows of these imposing structures, hierarchies of competence are constructed by imposing a historically forged template upon a cognitive map.

This cognitive map will be constantly updated. Craft skills and traditional trades which have been crucial in defining and shaping images of masculinity, may no longer contrive to create viable gendered careers for men. Most crucially, unskilled opportunities have also been affected. For instance, the building industry has declined, so employment, particularly unskilled employment in that sector, fades along with associated criminal opportunities. Similarly the nature of dockwork, in particular containerisation and mechanisation has led to a decline of traditional forms of theft, which are as crucial as alterations in the patriarchial base upon which recruitment, work practices and neighbourhood ecology were grounded (Cohen 1972). In addition, changes in youth culture created a demand for recreational drugs, and the subsequent market place was exploited by a new intake of youthful entrepreneurs, as well as their older brothers and fathers. Knowledge of markets both legal and illegal is directly related to the exercise of power, and in the case of working-class entrepreneurship, the exercise of power is often inextricably bonded to violence or violent potential. In this respect working-class entrepreneurship of the type described by Danny and Chris represents a 'gendered life course' (Morgan 1992: 45) *par excellence.*

The effectiveness of entrepreneurial reproduction is closely linked to the inevitability and consistency of structural components that, within the social sciences, are traditionally regarded as restraining. Entrepreneurial reproduction, of which crime is an integral component, is bonded to family life and the duplication of traditional roles that are tailored to both negotiate structural arrangements, and exploit ever shifting markets.

The exclusion of women from the subsequent emergent discourses is an essential constituent, for in this manner a mental landscape that is both consistent with the past yet compatible with seemingly fickle markets can be formed. The pace of change within a crime market that is rapidly becoming, for the first time, dominated by the rationality of a single commodity (Hobbs, forthcoming) has been mirrored in the legitimate market, and tended to render many features of the traditional working-class family redundant (Parker 1989). Notably, labourist assumptions regarding the gendered inevitability of modes of production and the employment options that they generate.

Although the market is the enemy of conformity (Bauman 1992: 52) certain aspects of the traditional family are ideally suited to exploit the market place and consequently to generate new markets. The irony here is to be found in the strain that is produced by attempting to foster traditional social forms within a post-traditional order that is by definition hostile to modes of authority based upon the eternal recurrence of male hegemony.

As traditional male employment has, in its working-class manifestation, all but disappeared, the cultural authority of men is established by emphasising those key elements of their cultural inheritence that remain crucial for continuity (Hobbs 1988: Ch. 7) Violence is one such way of establishing cultural authority and as Bauman indicates: 'Cultural authorities turn themselves into market forces, become commodities, compete with other commodities, legitimise their value through the selling capacity they attain' (Bauman 1992: 452).

Violence was a crucial and consistent theme of the childhoods of both Chris and Danny, and both men have utilised violence as an essential tool in structuring their identities. Their identities as violent men enable them to occupy a bridge somewhere between the market place and a moral vacuum beyond utilitarianism and instrumentality (Hobbs and Robins 1991: 571). They are as likely to resort to violence over their slice of the market as they are over a game of pool, a personal slight or a challenge from one another.

Masculinity has always been a vital resource of working-class culture. Working-class communities, despite de-industrialisation, often cling to a muscular or highly specialised imagery in order to define essences perceived as essential for the maintenance of internal hierarchies. However, as these essences, having lost their transformative capacities, are identified as redundant, so traditional strategies that have some potential for market leverage are thrust to the forefront of the practical consciousness of agents.

Violent potential has long been a 'cultural expectation' (Wolfgang 1959) of working-class men. Indeed it 'runs like a bright thread through the fabric of life' (Sykes 1958: 102) and Danny and Chris are culturally obligated to engage in combat, as their locations within the market place have been enhanced both by their perceived abilities as fighters, and by their willingness to fight. Their utility of a traditional masculine strategy within the arena of the contemporary market indicates that there is a power-ful sense of continuity with their inheritance of male identity. The disruption of the iconography of working-class labourist identity, and in particular the sell-by-date now reached by images of muscular, yet essentially altruistic, artisans, has left us with few contemporary images that have any resonance with past eras; the fighter is one.

However, the working-class entrepreneur is a rather more ambiguous icon (Hobbs 1991b). He bestrides formal and informal economies and is vulnerable to the whims of the market. His dependency upon the market is limited to the destruction of traditional skills and strategies, for the logic of the market under-lines the fact that contemporary society is not a version of some previous era (Bauman 1992: 111), but a confirmation that bourgeois rational controls in the form of education and welfare are exposed for what they are – mechanisms that prevent most of the population from gaining sight of the trough. The ability of individuals to engage with the market in an entrepreneurial manner will be limited by the opportunities that remain in the form of the debris of industrial society. Further, the abilities of individuals to exploit these remnants will often depend upon the cultural inheritance that has been forged in the local economy. Therefore opportunities and competencies within the market place will coincide due to the manner in which working-class male culture is shaped by the nature of the local formal and informal economies.

The reproduction of traditional working-class strategies within the agency of the market, suggests that the structural elements that secure and shape the various commercial practices that go to make up the market's enacted environment, are at some point transformed into enabling devices. The emergent 'dialectic of control' (Giddens 1981: 63) reproduces and exaggerates those aspects of traditional working-class culture that have some viability, no matter how ambiguous its application. Masculinity is one such aspect of working-class culture that emerges as an enabling strategy adhering both to the market place, and to the moral economy of commercial practice (Hobbs 1991a)

The market is a more attractive place than the portraits of heroic proletarian relics as painted by history-conscious bourgeois admirers (Bauman 1987) would suggest. The inconvenient truth is that Danny and Chris maintain their identities by plucking violence out of a catalogue of culturally defined precedents from the past, and re-working them in conjunction with business. Business above all serves as a master metaphor for the competent application of money-making strategies syphoned through a fine gauze of manly pursuits. While the future for Danny and Chris is uncertain, Chris's six-month-old son has a brand new building society book and a tiny pair of red leatherette boxing gloves.

Danny is 44 years old, 5ft 6ins–5ft 7ins tall, balding, about 15 stone with tattoos on both forearms, a scar under his left eye and multiple indentations on his forehead. Chris is 23 years old, 5ft 6ins–5ft 7ins tall, about 14 stone, with a rapidly receding hairline, a crescent shape scar on his chin and a woman's name tattooed on his left forearm. They are father and son.

Danny: He is like me and he knows it, plays on it since he was a babe. Copied everything. When I had the fucking hump so did he! So I come in, got the fucking hump with Sheila then he turns round, little kid I'm talking about here, he throws his dinner up the wall and bowls out. Then he starts coming out with me – I'm doing a little deal like a delivery or that and it's all 'Look at him, chip off the old block, don't he look like his dad?' You know, play with him, sweets, fucking cakes the lot. He walks like me always has . . . and I showed him things, told him don't take liberties but don't take any shit, you gotta be first, if there's gonna be a ruck, just go straight in steam in and fucking hurt them. . . . I used to train him up, put a bag up, old kit bag full of rags and teach him how to punch. Could punch and all, always had a dig on him . . . I got him one of those punch balls that you stand on and a pair of gloves, sparring with him, hands up elbows in.

Chris: Loved it, going out with the old man in the van, he had a lorry too, big Volvo Unit. The best was a long run out Southampton or Tilbury to pick up a trailer. We'd stop off at café's, big breakfasts. He knew all the people, the drivers and the people who ran the places. . . . It was great, like when all the others was at school I was out in a unit and seeing all the countryside. The punchball, Christmas present, red plastic thing with like a stand you stand on to keep it up. I'd box with him, he would go down on his knees and spar around. If I fucked it up, he'd give me a slap. Never really let me give him a good slap and that's all I wanted to do – hit him. I am like him, I look like the old photos but he was so over the top it wasn't true. . . . Once I was outside playing kicking a ball about or something, after school, and he pulls up in the van, runs in the house, comes out with a handful of knives. Mum tried to stop him, gets in the van and drives off fast like. Then one of me mates says that your dad's been in a fight. I was having me tea and a knock on the door, this bloke near us says to Mum that Dad's been stabbed, he's in hospital. He come home next morning, stitches in his arm and a lump on his head, that was the end of it. But he could be evil, he was always having a ruck. When we moved there was all this stuff on the pavement, boxes and that. He reckoned that somebody had his records. This is the first day we got there so he's gone next door with this long screwdriver, put their windows out. Always rucking.

Danny: There was no peace. I'd come home, had the lorry and that and sometimes I'd be gone two to three days wheeling dealing, earning, and then I'd come home and the fucking noise, he's done this, she's done that. I'd sit there with a cup of tea and the noise would just build up, you know what kids are like, and I just want some peace. Sooner or later I'd just blow. I'd whack Chris, not whack just slap 'im, tell 'er to fucking button it, get a bath and go and have a drink. I wasn't violent, he says I was, I fucking wasn't. Now you know me, if I want to have a ruck I will have one. I was gonna be violent, I'd kill him. But it wasn't like that . . . I just wanted some quiet and it would start, I'd tell him to shut up and he would give me some lip. Always up front he has been. I'd say 'Did you do that? and he'd say 'Yeah, so what?' I'd give him a dig and he'd say 'One day I'll be bigger than you and I'll beat you up.' Fucker is big now and strong, I mean if I can lift 200 lbs then he can do 250. But I tell him don't mess about with me boy, I'm in my prime. [laughs]

Chris: I know I fucking hated him. He'd give me a slap then just stand there and look at me. Put me across the fucking room sometimes then stand there giving it the big 'un. So when I was about 14 I thought that's it so I hit him hard, punched him in the face. Shouted 'I'm a man now' or something fucking stupid. He walked out the house, just went don't know where, just went. I went to bed shitting myself. Next morning he never come back. That night he comes in like nothing was on, just normal like sits down. Then when I was having my tea he just punches me in the head. I thought he was going to kill me. I was on the floor and he's hitting me with a chair. Mum got him off. He was saying 'Wanna be a man, I'll treat you like a man.'

Danny: I remember I walked out 'cos I would have killed him. Stayed out, away just didn't want to know. But inside I was boiling. I can't stand anybody raising their hands to me. It was teatime and I just went. . . . That's it really, Tom and fucking Jerry, that's us. Always a war going on.

Chris: What do you do, you want to be one of the boys so you do all the usual stuff, running with hounds, getting in bits of shit here and there, you start feeling your way and all right, I was a bit lippy but there was no room at home and we started getting in each other's way. I didn't like being hit by him all the time. He'd come in when he had a drink and Mum would start saying he's done this and that. I never hung about – went out the back way over the wall. Caught me once – threw a dustbin at me, full fucking bin, hit me in the back up the wall. I scratched his car – never told him that [laughs], went right outside and scratched his car.

D.H.: At 13, Chris joined the pool team of the local pub, and Danny took a great deal of pride in his son's skill. Pool was important to Danny for a number of reasons. It was a sport that he could play when four or five stone overweight and there was a great deal of status to be derived from being a good pool player. Yet, most importantly, pool playing creates and demands a most specific economy of movement and style, an aggressive yet quite discreet catalogue of stalking and striking poses that are theatrically designed for maximum drama derived from what is essentially an elaboration of masculine urban street style.

Chris: I was good – fast. Quick weren't in it. I could play. They used to see this little kid and be all nice, you know there there sonny. . . . Then I clear the table and they go well, quiet, I suppose.

Danny: He was so out of order. Good, very good, he learnt quick. I used to take him in the pub and he would play the machines, game of darts, whatever. Then they got the table and he was at it all the time, all his money went in it. Sometimes he would just stand like a little puppy dog with a cue in his hand waiting for some poor wanker to pity him and give him a game. But as he got better he got fucking murder, he started winding people up. Like he'd miss a pot or something and he'd scream 'Oh unlucky!' top of his voice. Wind people up terrible – I had a word in his ear lots of times, 'Don't wind people up, you gonna get a slap off someone soon.' Trouble was when he was playing for the pub he's got everybody shouting, 'Go on Chrissie, do 'im!' and laughing when he fucks about.

Chris: I was a mouthy fucker but I loved it. . . . The old man, all the pub in there watching. I just showed out, just put on a show. Then we got barred. It wasn't me, well it was a bit, but the old man he just blew and that was it.

Danny: We had a match against the 'Carpenters'. We know them all don't we, I mean they are just round the corner, most of them drink in the Bulldog anyway. They all knew Chrissie from a kid, but he still takes the piss on and on. In the end Peter comes up, their captain like, and just asks me to calm him down. If it stayed like that then it would have blew over, but right after one of theirs comes over and says something about whacking him and don't care if he is a kid. So I captures him (Chris) pulls him outside and gives him the fucking news. Tells him stop taking the piss. I slaps him about a bit, let him know I fucking mean it, then goes back inside. Dick, I stewed on it. We are into afters now, the match is finished but he was there, the one who said he would give Chrissie a whack and I went just did him.

D.H.:   Danny hit the man several times with a heavy ashtray before he was pulled off. However, in extricating Danny from the maul a female supporter of the opposing team had her handbag trodden on, which in turn led to punches being thrown by her companion, an elderly man who had recently suffered a stroke. When he was knocked to the floor, the intensity of the fracas escalated and bottles and pool cues were wealded. The fight spilled out into the street and both Danny and Chris were slightly injured in a fight that involved over twenty men and women.

Danny: Old Bill turns up and it stopped like it does. The geezer I whacked was still out and when they were seeing to him Chrissie and most of the others pisses off. I got pulled along with my mate Billy, but it comes to fuck all. I get out next morning, usual thing, very polite, sign here sir, no charges, have a nice fucking day and piss off.

Chris: When he came back he knocked the shit out of me. Why? I suppose as I was getting too leery like. It was nothing, just a ruck, just another ruck, but he could have a ruck, the old man.

CRIME AND BUSINESS

D.H.: Danny was sent to a special school at the age of 12 after his widowed mother remarried.

Danny: My old man was without a doubt a diamond. Everybody knew him. We used to go out totting and I would go with him, had this old horse at the back of the prefabs pulling a cart and I would trot along the street knocking on the doors while Dad would shout and sing, yeah sing, like opera – [sings] 'Have you got any rag and bone or mangles, woollens or cottons? I give you best prices!' He boxed as well in the army . . . all England knew him. Died when I was 9 or 10 I think, he was only about 40, not that probably, nearer 35. When Mum got married it didn't seem right. See Dad never hit me, he would have a row with anybody like anybody but he wasn't what you would call a hard man. He was a singer. On a Sunday morning he would do the breakfast and I would lay in bed waiting and he would just make up these songs. I dunno – (sings) 'Get out of bed and getta your double egg, bacon, bubble and two fried slices.' He was a good old boy my Dad. Like I said when Mum got married again he would try to make me do things but I just used to go missing. I'd sleep the night in the old buildings. There was an old Anderson shelter at the back of the match factory and that was that. I didn't want to know. Tops up got sent to this school out in the country near ——— . Loved it, nobody hit nobody else, the teachers they were your friends. I had girlfriends, played guitar, sort of place you don't want to leave. But you do like, when you leave school and that was it. [stepfather] got me a job as a van boy. I never minded it really, got enough to get by. But it meant living at home so I just got out when I could.

D.H.: Danny became part of a slightly older group who frequented an illegal drinking club in Stepney.

Danny: I was just sort of around the edge. 'Cos I was a few years younger than the others money was easy, like they would always buy. And this will shock you, I wasn't a drinker, a light ale or two then just coffee. The others was well into drink but they earnt well, all of them. Market porters some of 'em, lorry drivers, plenty of money. And they was all at it, anything, buying, selling. There was an old geezer in the ——, we thought he owned it but he never. He would always buy a piece of tom [jewellery] or a watch, and some of the boys they would do a deal with him over a ring or whatever.

One night there was this geezer, brother of one of the others, been going on about how his firm had a room at the back with gear in it, fuck knows what it was, can't remember. Anyway we went in, got nothing out of it, but we was off then. God's truth, up to then nothing, I was not interested, never done a thing. Then after that happened I was well at it, good an' all.

D.H.: Danny changed jobs many times between the ages of 15 and 17 and criminal activity took up an increasing amount of his social and working life.

Danny: I was a grafter, I loved to graft. . . . Over a wall, back of a lorry, didn't matter and work too, I just chased money. I did van jobs, buildings, anything, had a pop at scaffolding. Fuck that. I did a couple of days and nearly went over the edge of a roof in Bermondsey. That was it, no more after that, you never get me up a ladder, no fucking chance. Call the army, get the fucking Air Force, I ain't going up. But you could change jobs twice a day in them days, lot of work there was and I was earning all the time. Factories, offices, I was about ten stone then. Climb through windows, doors, fucking letter boxes. I was up for anything. . . . We did a deal with a butcher when I was on the vans. Had to pick up all the dirty overalls from —— [supermarket]. We'd go in the back and walk through the warehouse. Geezer there who was in on it, he'd have a lamb or a cotchell of chickens, maybe a few choice joints of beef in our little trolley, cover up with the shitty overalls and away. There was loads of little earners like that all the time. . . . The word got around that I was up for one and I was earning.

D.H.: At the age of 17 Danny became engaged to a local woman a year younger than himself, and just weeks later was arrested following an incident outside a dance hall.

Danny: It was Sunday night at the Palais, remember rocking up the Palais? I never did it. I come out at closing time and there was a fight by the bus stop. I was watching just like you do. Old bill pulls up, everybody does a runner and I get a pull. Turns up six months in —— (detention centre). Best thing that ever happened to me. In there you have to learn you can't just do what you like, you learn 'yes sir, no sir'. You wash the floor and when the screws tread over it you just wash it, don't fucking moan, just do it. Because that's the game. It don't get to you. You just hold it back. Some of the screws were gentlemen, they call you Mr and you called them Sir and it was all right. There was a couple of nasty bastards, like fucking Hitlers, give you a little dig, shout and scream. Just go 'yes sir, no sir' and then flob [spit] on their backs so they never knew. Walk around with a nice flob running down their back.

D.H.: Danny emerged from detention centre a wiser man with a clear view of his future.

Danny: I married Sheil almost straight away. Yeah, she was pregnant like, but we got married anyway . . . I got my licence and was in business straight way. I borrowed a van and just went to work.

D.H.: Danny made deliveries, went totting, cleared gardens, anything to make a living. He also continued his criminal activities, particularly commercial burglaries and stealing from building sites.

Danny: The building was good. In them days there was no security guards, none of that. They might have some old geezer in a little hut, he'd take a stroll round the site then get his head down. There was everything, copper, wood, bricks, paint, if you was careful and took a bit at a time then you could do it easy, gentle, without the scream going up. There was so much building going on they never noticed. We were doing well. We got a house pretty early on and had holidays, the lot. I bought a van [caravan], put it on a site in Canvey. Then later when I got the HGV I really started to earn. I had a regular earner out at Tilbury and I was doing lorryloads moving anything. I went in with Tommy and got a contract with —— [clothing multiple store]. I nicked their received stamp and we moved lorryloads. We made thousands, fucking thousands.

Chris: Well he was only doing what everybody else was. You gotta see it from that. I never thought nothing, I suppose when you think back there was always things piled up in the house, people coming and going. I just thought, well I don't think I did think about it really, it just happened. When you're a kid as long as everything's all right . . . I suppose I did know it was hookey gear, but when I was out and about with him it was cartons and boxes, gear moving about so I never thought about it. What you gotta understand about the old man is he's always said earn money don't be a ponce, earn, and he's always grafted so that's what you see when your a kid and that's what I fucking want – bit of graft some money, fuck it.

D.H.: By the time Danny was in his mid-30s times had become tough. He had been through several business partnerships, was deep in debt, several stone overweight and carried half a dozen minor convictions for assault.

Danny: I had about five really good years but I pissed it up the wall. I had motors, a couple of lock ups [garages], spent money boozing like it was yours. I was at it like a good 'un, always at it. Straight and hookey if there was any dough the carbuncle on the hip [roll of cash] that is what it all was. I got into some debt with a new unit [lorry] but I never thought nothing of it, I was earning so well. Then there was the steel strike – we was doing steel all over the country and it dried up and that – and Andrew [partner] he was selling gear behind my back. I was out looking for him when he got nicked, while he was away I clocked on to what he was doing . . . robbing me blind, robbed me blind, the bastard. We had all this gear for the unit, it went missing. Tools, covers, ropes. I was well stitched up. He did me like a kipper.

D.H.: It was during this difficult period that Chris began to get into trouble. First at school and then on the streets. He became increasingly violent.

Chris: I used to love it [school] I was never no fucking brainbox but first school was nice. The teachers and kids, it was good. Then when I went to the big school it was all 'stand up straight, wear a uniform and do as you are told'. I just couldn't handle it. I just got in rows all the time with other kids as well, but the teachers. . . . There was this big mouthy one, he just got into me all the time. I was always having rows with him. Couple of times I just walked out, went home. Then they sent letters and that home wanting to see Mum and Dad. Then I just went over Wanstead – me and this other kid we camped out and got into the old lighter fluid (laughs). After a bit they had enough got barred, kicked out.

Danny: This school, well you know what it was, he was too up front. Then he fucks off for the night and I have to go down the nick sign him out, turns up he's sniffing lighter fuel. So when he goes to —— [special school] I thought this will be the making of him. All the kids are the same, fucking awkward you know no real villains. Lovely place, had everything, swimming pool, garages for doing up cars. Then he gets in a ruck with a little mob. He gets charged in court. He gets off it but after that he went missing a few times, and I give up. I had it up to here. I get bailiffs coming round then the old bill about him. They loved it 'cos they knew me. It's not you this time Mr —— I'm afraid its your boy again. I never had two halfpennies not a pot. I'm wheeling dealing, nowhere. Nothing went right.

D.H.:   When Chris was 14 and in and out of his special school, Danny left home to live with a woman with whom he had conducted an affair for eight years. Chris immediately returned home and assumed the mantle of 'man of the house'.

Chris: I had enough of school it was so fucking boring all this about 'you break your contract'. Fuck it, I came home got a job at —— the ice cream place, said I was 16. I left after about two weeks, they never found out. I just went on the buildings with Tom [Uncle] took it from there. He was well at it. He knew all the geezers on the council give him contracts. I get all cash in hand. Some lovely little fiddles with the others on site. I could get copper bricks, window frames and I was only 14.

D.H.:   Chris moved from job to job over the next two years. The educational authorities sent him back to his original local school but Chris attended for one day before returning to work. Meanwhile Danny had returned to the family home.

Danny: I just had it when I went. It was like everything got on top of me. There was no peace, I was doing everything – I'd chase a pound note all day and come home with 10p – that's what it was like. So Sandi, like I knew her for years, we had a little thing going and I just was over there more and more. I could go there and sit and watch a bit of the box, go over the boozer, game of pool, darts whatever. Come home no hassle, no screaming. I needed that . . . I needed that peace and quiet. Then I just sort of drifted back. You know where she lives it's just the other side of the square. I mean I never left them really, not really. I just had to get away. But everything was the same. I knew everybody was all right. Then I suppose I just came back. Still see Sandi like but I live here again.

D.H.:   By the time Danny returned, Chris had established himself as a good earner.

Chris: About when I should have left school I had this job as a tyre fitter. Anything not bald with a bit of tread on it I lobbed over the fence, picked 'em up later. You know Alex? He had a car lot on

Leytonstone Road, he'd buy whatever I brought, then he put them on the old motors. . . . When he came back [Danny] it never made no odds. I used to see him in the boozer match night, it was all right. Then when he came home it never mattered. I was always out . . . he had this thing about earning and I was earning. He had bits and pieces then his van got nicked so he was fucked for a bit.

D.H.: Six months after returning home, Danny became seriously ill and was admitted to hospital.

Danny: I shit myself. He (the Doctor) says well Mr —— how much do you drink. I says not a lot. He says 'Do you drink spirits?' I says 'Yeah, vodka', he says, 'How much vodka?' So I says about a half bottle. He says, 'That's too much you must cut it out.' Turns up he thought I meant half a bottle a week. I do that and half a dozen light and bitters a night.

D.H.: On his return after surgery Danny found himself depressed and physically incapable of hustling for a living. He lost over 3 stone in weight and stopped drinking. Trips to the pub became rare and entire days were spent in front of the TV set. Meanwhile Chris's entrepreneurial activities were expanding.

Danny: He stopped getting up in the morning. He was round the house a lot. As long as the dough came he paid his housekeeping. I never bothered. But I knew he was at it like, he had to be. Not a dabble neither cos he's got himself a little motor and that.

D.H.: Tension grew during this period. Chris became more confident as Danny's powers waned, and eventually the source of Danny's income became apparent.

Danny: He's put a pair of jeans in the wash and emptied his pockets out on the table there's a lump of shit (hash) with his money and that. So I goes in his room and has a look there's all these deals on his dressing table about a dozen little parcels in silver (foil). I put 'em down the toilet. He comes in and starts banging around I says 'You looking for something?' He looks at me so I told him I put it down the fucking toilet. He says 'you bastard, that comes to a lot of money.' I like a bit of a blow myself but not in the fucking house. Why? It ain't right. I like a bit of a blow myself but it don't do a right lot. I'd rather have a drink. He starts in the house and that, it's fucking iffy I ain't having it. You know all about the next thing.

D.H.: 'The next thing' was a fight between Danny and Chris.

Chris: I was down a lot of money, I don't know, at least a century [£100] and I was doubling me money then. I just walked away from him but he followed me, he just walked behind me. He's giving me all this 'think you're a big man'. I got by the gate and turned round he just nutted me.

Danny: He was gonna have a go so I got in first, then it was all off. I was still not right, not feeling strong. We whacked each other and fell on the gate, the fucking thing come away from the brick and he hit me with it. I went down and held on to his leg and we finishes up rolling round in the road till the old bill got there. Fuckers take him to hospital, reckons I bit him. Me, I got blood coming out me head, they lock me up for the night.

D.H.: While Danny was in the Police Station Chris broke into his lock up garage and set fire to it. Chris then left home and went to live at his girlfriend's parents' home. While Chris was away Danny was spasmodically employed delivering smuggled tobacco to outlets in the London area (see Hobbs, forthcoming).

Danny: Been going on for years. I could have been at the beginning when I had the business, but I never reckoned driving abroad. I did boozers, clubs, anything, shops. All Old Holborn it was. I did the Police Club at the back of —— nick. Turned up one day about 3 o'clock, they were fucking legless even the steward. It was all right but I knew more about the business than them that was paying me.

Chris: After I did the thing with the garage I never went home for a few days and then just for me clothes. I think he [Danny] knew I weren't no little kid he could whack about like he wanted no more. I went back after about three weeks, I got pissed off round Jane's flat. So I just come home. I just never took no notice of him. Just like before I suppose.

D.H.: While Danny was attempting to impose himself once more upon the market place. Chris continued to earn, albeit haphazardly, from an amalgam of sources. Casual employment as a builder's labourer, various driving jobs, dealing in small quantities of dope and some commercial burglary, combined to make a living for a young man who was gaining an increasingly violent reputation amongst his peers. Several local pubs barred him and he became known to the local police as someone who would regularly feature in fights in and around pubs and clubs. At the age of 20 Chris robbed a warehouse of a large quantity of childrens' clothing.

Chris: I put 'em straight out on the markets and that, and people were just turning up outside the house for it. The old man made more than a few phone calls, moved a load of gear through people he knew. Did a load down to somebody he knew, some woman in Dartford. We knocked gear out all over.

Danny: When I see the cartons and that, had a look at the stuff in them, I thought this is it, and to be fair he never knew what to do with it. I mean on a deal I love it. But he was good, he knew he had more than he could handle so he let me get on with it. Prices – he never had a fucking clue to be honest with you, it was down to me. Like, 'How big's the parcel?' 'Who are they?' 'They done stuff before?' 'Cash? Sale or return?' On this the women were the best 'cos it was all kids gear, they were having big parcels £100 to £150. Night time it's 'Here's the money lets have some more.' They were just terrific.

D.H.: At the time both men thrived on the success of their venture. Their familial bond was sealed by a highly successful entrepreneurial venture that had utilised the resources of youth and maturity to profitable effect. The enterprise boosted Chris's confidence to new heights. He had planned the burglary, paid off accomplices and dealt in large sums of money for the first time. Most importantly however, he had been introduced to the intricacies of disposing of a large quantity of stolen goods. The variety of outlets, variations in the sheer bulk of consignments, and the relationship between the perceived personal qualities of buyers, prices and method of payment were all crucial elements of the enterprise. The profit made from this one act of theft was between £11 and £13,000 and Danny was not slow in suggesting how the money should be spent.

Danny: The lease for the Bulldog [pub] was up and lets face it that had to be mine. It was always coming up. It had a bad reputation, rough pub sort of. But I knew I could turn it round, turn it into a family house. But I couldn't get him to put his money into it. If all the dough from the kids' clothes was put into it we was only what two grand short. I would have fucking got hold of that somehow.

It would have been a pension for him. He could have fucked off and done anything. I would have ran the place. He would have been on wages for fucking ever. No he's 'Mr Fucking Big', he's gotta give it that big 'un. Gotta play gangsters. I know he's not all bad like but this was a chance to do it properly, he could have still ducked and dived but a regular earner on business you can't whack it.

D.H.: Danny paid off some debts and bought a replacement for his stolen van. Chris invested £5,000 into a consignment of amphetamine sulphate. He became the co-owner of a second-hand car lot and a successful dealer in amphetamines and ecstasy. He is currently wanted by the police in connection with a drugs charge and credit card fraud (Hobbs, forthcoming). Chris is believed to be out of the country and Danny has not heard from him for over six months. Chris's girlfriend gave birth to their first child: a boy.

Chapter 8

What's the big deal?

We are men and they are women

Alberto Godenzi

The rape circumstances in Bosnia-Herzegovina make it once again brutally clear: terror and torture by men against women are not actions of individual pathological perpetrators but instead dealings of 'normal' men against women of every age and every origin. Whilst war scenarios are social situations in which violent actions against women are to an exceptional degree legitimated, approved and encouraged, the relationship between the sexes outside of war situations is also 'to a large degree characterised by men's violence against women' (Vranitzky 1992). Because of this, terror against women needs to be understood as a continuum. What degree and what kind of violence men are willing to use depends on internal and external barriers, on social situations and anticipated consequences and finally on social images via the mass media. The normalcy of men's violence against women is an elementary structural and cultural element of a patriarchal society.

How do social scientists react to this destructive characteristic of men's behaviour against women? Feminist authors led the way in discussing the problem of terror and presented the structures and consequences of violence (*inter alia* Brownmiller 1975; Barry 1979; Kappeler 1986) via both theoretical analysis and numerous reports from survivors. Traditional research conceded a certain attentiveness to this phenomenon after a long delay and continuing opposition. It is, however, divided on the one hand in a general framework of inter-personal or domestic violence (Goode 1971; Straus *et al.* 1980), on the other hand the tendency has existed from the beginning to individualise and to pathologise the infringements of violence (Amir 1971; Groth and Birnbaum 1979). The last variation above all concerns the scientific approach with perpetrators. This partial aspect of the violence discussion is the topic of the present article, and the focus remains on sexual violence.

The existence of sexual delinquents is undisputed. However for the most part only a certain group of such offenders are identified as real, namely caught, convicted offenders – men therefore for whom there are case files, men who should reflect on their mistakes while in prison, and who should make amends for the damage they have caused. Convicted offenders are however special cases; they form a small, clearly defined group which seem to present similar characteristic patterns, and offender research has for many years been satisfied with looking at those sexual delinquents who are sitting in prisons. Knowledge from such studies is as a rule then applied to all sexual criminal offenders.

The research concerning victims which is in the main inspired by feminism, questions this order of things, as it confronts a small group of imprisoned offenders with a disproportionately large number of victims of violence (see Russell 1975; Dobash and Dobash 1979; Burgess 1985). The assumption that this disproportion can be explained by the fact that each offender is responsible for an excess of victims by means of a multitude of attacks quickly falls away. Consequently, a hypothesis remains open: there are a far greater number of non-detected offenders than has often been thought. Victim research has however introduced an additional factor. The great majority of survivors of sexual violence document attacks by men inside their own family or circle of acquaintances. Most imprisoned sexual offenders are serving time for criminal acts against women unknown to them. This double absurdity refers to the structural filters which are effective between act and judgement and which allow a great number of the offenders to fall through while a small minority are caught.

How safe men can feel when they rape women is shown by statistics from Switzerland. According to average estimates, approximately every tenth rape is reported. One-fifth of these complaints leads to a judgment by a court of law. In the event that an offender is identified and the case investigated, his chances are 2:1 that he will escape conviction: only one in three is convicted. When this number is compared with the estimated number of rapes it can be deduced that only around 2 per cent of all offenders will be convicted or, in other words, 98 per cent of the cases remain unpunished. In these calculations marital rape is not taken into account because in Switzerland it was only made a crime in 1992. Figure 8.1 presents this unique selection process. It is evident to what degree the justice administration detects, processes and punishes rapes.

Consequently, the minority of offenders who are detected and convicted are far from representative. They are frequently men who due to other factors are already marginal (poor education, no permanent work, criminal career, foreigners, ethnic minority). In addition to being a societal and criminal problem, this has significant consequences for offender research. No longer can researchers be satisfied with the 'comfortable' position of gathering data from that convenient sample of sexual criminal offenders in prisons. They must set themselves the more difficult task of tracking down undetected rapists. The easier solution can only again be used when it is proved that the profile, the experiences and the motives of those convicted match those of the hidden offenders.

CHARACTERISTICS OF TRADITIONAL OFFENDER RESEARCH

Prevailing offender research is distorted by the fact that it is dominated by studies which use classifications derived from samples of convicted offenders – during execution of a sentence or in stationary therapeutic treatment (see Gebhard *et al.* 1965; Groth *et al.* 1977). In the main, violence is not grouped into that within and that outside of the family, although it is assumed that in addition to similarities there are also differences between men who sexually abuse women or children who are strangers, and those who abuse wives, friends or their own children. The clinical-psychopathological anchoring of most of the classification attempts is an additional factor (possibly the clinical view of the researchers makes an impact on the personality profile of the criminal offender). Sexual delinquents are neurotic, psychopathic or sociopathic, they are immature, frustrated, senile or mentally handicapped. The implicit assumption is clear: a normally developed, healthy man cannot be a sexual delinquent. What is to be done then when it is revealed that it is not a small peculiar group who commit sexual crimes but in face a larger number of 'normal' men?

Scully and Marolla (1983) have suggested a pragmatic grouping

Figure 8.1 Attrition process of rape cases, Switzerland, 1986

Source: Official Criminal Statistics, 1986, Swiss Federal Attorney General Office/Main Police Office, Bern and Federal Department of Statistics, Berne

Notes:
* On the basis of an average blind number of 10
** The total of all trials is not available in a national statistic
*** The number of incarcerated rapists is certainly smaller than the number of convictions because only some of the convicted rapists must go to prison

Estimated total *   4000 (100 %)

Official reports   398 (10 %)

Detected offenders   215 (5.4 %)

Trials **   ?

Sentences   79 (2 %)

Incarcerations ***   ?

as a counterpoint to the current offender-classifications. This differentiates the sexual delinquents solely by whether they have admitted or denied the act. The 'admitters' frequently act out of anger, want to pay back something to the woman, especially when she is not the reason for the anger. Sexually violent activity is for them a detestable act which they would not do in normal circumstances. The 'deniers' in contrast do not see any wrong in their actions, they dispute the violent activity and consider such 'sexual interaction' as natural. They identify with a particularly strong masculine image with which they legitimate a certain toughness in dealings with women.

As a result of general criticism of traditional offender research, and in particular its fixation on rape by a stranger, work emerged which investigated sexually violent actions in marital or quasi-marital contexts (see Russell 1982; Finkelhor and Yllo 1985). Research reports with promising titles such as *Rape in Marriage* or *License to Rape* spread the hope that finally the thus far hidden offender would be found. However this was only conditionally true. The information concerning husbands who raped was based almost entirely on reports of victims or third persons, only a few husbands were directly questioned. Groth and Birnbaum (1979) for example investigated 500 imprisoned sexual criminal offenders among whom only a few had raped their wives. This underrepresentation did not prevent the two researchers from deriving general conclusions. In contrast, Russell (1982) for example clearly makes it understood that their representative random sampling of wives would not nor does answer adequately the questions regarding the motives and characteristics of the offenders.

METHODOLOGICAL IMPLICATIONS

With what means and in which ways should violent offenders be studied? What we know about any group of social actors is essentially determined by how we know what we know (Larzelere and Klein 1987). However when we have determined that a great many of this offender group are not sitting in prisons but are running around free and unknown, social research is faced with the task of finding the missing subjects. According to Straus *et al.* (1980), there are above all three barriers to such plans: First, men who rape women must be located, regardless of whether they have been detected, arrested, or convicted. Second, once found, they must be made to reveal information regarding their actions in an ethically responsible manner. Third, information collected must be able to be verified for its truthfulness.

In relation to the first point, why should social researchers succeed where in many cases the police have failed: in the tracking down of sexual criminal offenders? The police lay claim to knowledge about sexual dangerousness, and the legitimacy to prosecute such offenders for criminal offences. Social research does have an important advantage: it is not primarily interested in criminal prosecution and can grant the offender anonymity and confidentiality (as long as the criminal law regulations in the relevant country allow). Its aim is in a certain sense 'neutral': it wants general information about why, how and with what consequences sexual delinquents abuse women. Moral judgment of the informant does not belong to its internal task, and nor does legal judgement (at least, according to classic scientific understanding). Consequently, social research does not involve any direct danger to the group of violent offenders it aims to examine.

Having said that, why should violent men who lead safe lives in the protection of the private sphere feel the wish to speak about their actions? For one primary reason: they want to legitimate themselves. They want their perspective, their interpretation of the event to be made public. They will use the opportunity research offers to make clear to the public that things happened otherwise than the way they were described by the victims or third persons. We, the listeners, should understand their actions. Additionally it must be assumed that many are relieved to speak from the soul about an act of which they feel or know to be condemned by law and on moral grounds. This last motive is visible at any rate in a minority of cases because only a few of the non-convicted offenders have a guilty conscience. As men who have gone unconvicted and unpunished they tend not to feel guilty. Therefore researchers do well with hidden offenders by appealing to justifiable intentions, by claiming: 'We are interested in your perspective.' Furthermore, it is exactly that which the research *is* missing: reports, interpretations, views, processing of the hidden offenders. To know more about it can be of great significance for research regarding motives and prevention.

Ethical responsibility was for a long time the reason for the impossibility of such offender research: social research which searches for undetected violent offenders must inevitably interfere in private lives, in hidden areas of human interaction. The interviewees will be asked to give evidence of intimate events. Thereby experiences through which victims have suffered or could suffer serious sorrow are fetched and pulled into the public domain. In the analysis of ethically responsible action, things are weighed against each other: protection of the private sphere versus exposure of criminal acts; also perhaps the interests of the offender versus the interests of the victim. Where in this conflict the interest of society lies, depends on its respective partisanship (up to now its position was clearly in favour of the private sphere, meaning in favour of the offender). There is not the space here to go into detail about ethical controversies in the investigation of 'sensitive topics', though several points can be noted (for a fuller discussion, see Godenzi 1993).

The first ethical principle, that of informed consent, can be extensively complied with in the practice of data collection. Offenders need only report themselves when they want to. Social research does not slide into the role of police search. Offenders can moreover be informed straight away about the intentions and risks of the research. It is possible at any stage for interviewees to ask questions about the research and if need be to get out of the project.

The second ethical principle, to do no harm, is more difficult to guarantee. The physical and psychical integrity of the participants cannot be guaranteed. Discussions about past violent acts, up to now kept quiet, intrinsically carry the danger of undermining the psycho-physical resistance constructions. At the request of the interviewees, the researchers will arrange addresses which could be helpful to the offenders for the reporting of their actions. However in the end, no guarantee can be given as to what happens to the interviewees after the interviews and there may be concern about endangered third persons.

Closely connected thereto is the third ethical principle, confidentiality and protection of personal data. Contact with the researchers should not lead to any criminal consequences for the participant. This guarantee can be given when the consent of the criminal authorities to the intended investigation has been previously obtained. The researchers must however be aware of the responsibility they accept. For one, it must be ensured that the interviewees remain anonymous, that the data gained remains in the sole possession of the research team which takes care that the name is disguised or, even better, destroyed. On the other hand, the researchers must be prepared for the case in which the perpetrated crime will be recognised, where the information is so complete that the police could potentially track down the offender or where an interviewee reports only a planned act. Again the problem of the weighing of interests arises: the protection of third persons from violent actions versus the development of scientific knowledge (which may also be striven for in the interest of this group of third persons). In addition, it is important to remember in such research that the caller is informed at the beginning that a warranted intervention by the researcher for the protection of others, is not to be ruled out. Whether such a limitation, which amounts to a repeal of the principle of anonymity, closes the research channels which have only just been opened must be examined. At least it would be expected that offenders would no longer give information which could be dangerous for them (which could also be the case without this limitation).

Ethical considerations also affect the question of respect for the private sphere. Protection of privacy is of the utmost value in a so-called free societal order. Citizens prefer to avoid interference in their private matters, perhaps especially by a 'neutral' science. Offender research does not, however, escape from the problem of intruding upon privacy; only exceptionally do men themselves approach researchers in order to talk about violent acts they have committed. Can offender research continue to hide behind the rule of respect of private spheres in the knowledge that in many cases violent acts occur in exactly these intimate spaces which due to their isolated private character have the most difficult consequences for the victim? The right to privacy must not legitimate any violent attack. The risks of investigation of such life circumstances must be made in the interest of those mishandled.

In response to the third barrier, 'How do you know the subjects told the truth?' is a question Gelles has posed (1987: 197) in relation to family violence research. Precisely this question is asked of investigations of sexual delinquents. What are the mountains of detailed reports and structured questionnaires worth when their validity can be put into question? What measures can be taken to check validity? Because violent sexual acts occur for the most part in concealed circumstances, only in a small minority of cases does there exist the chance to check up on information from the persons interviewed against 'objectively' recorded data (police investigation documents, medical files, witnesses statements, and so forth). Here also the proven data is limited to visible facts such as bodily harm, instrumentality of violence, scene and time of the crime. Additionally, the problem is again posed of whether the guarantee of confidentiality will be broken.

A further methodological problem is that of 'response effects'. Questioning men possible violent sexual actions can cause a range of reactions from those interviewed which make a substantial impact on the answers (denial, excuses, making harmless, etc.). These effects which are well documented in social research, impair the degree of validity of the results. The response effects are on the one hand influenced by the characteristics of the interviewees and on the other hand, by reactions to the formulation of the questions, to the specificity of the questions or to the given categories of answers. A related consideration is how strongly the answers of the interviewees are dependent on the trust that they have in the interviewer or on the research project or how much the maintenance of anonymity can matter to those questioned.

In order to offset these methodological considerations which cast doubt on the value of the results, different measuring procedures can be instituted – inasmuch as this is possible – with the same population and the achieved results can thus be compared. Thus questions of reliability of the statements are addressed: how can it be guaranteed that a question addressed by one interviewer will have the same result when addressed by another? Here the demands of scientific methods collide with ethical guidelines. Can a violent offender be repeatedly questioned about a violent action for the reason of reliability alone? Is it not a precondition for such a conversation that the questioner does not give out any feelings of mistrust of the person questioned which could damage the hoped for information? Finally – it seems – it cannot be definitely decided whether a description is valid and reliable. Must this search after 'truth' be given up because it does not exist and is every statement to be understood and interpreted as a self-presentation? It seems important to me to continue to depict carefully contexts in which certain statements are given: answers generated in response to particular questions. Social research lies at the borders of achieveability. For the sake of quality and depth of data, it must be decided, case by case, how it can combine rigorous methods and ethical considerations. The relief of being able to get at data from undetected violent offenders should not be allowed to undermine the validity of this information in question. Precisely because so much external social political relevance is stuck in this research area, methodological considerations must be openly presented, discussed and suitably applied.

RESEARCH DESIGN

Against the background of the above substantive and methodological reflections and objectives, an explorative investigation in accordance with a Los Angeles study by Smithyman (1978) was carried out in Switzerland (see Godenzi 1989 and in relation to non-detected offenders, see also studies with student samples such as Koss *et al.* 1981). It was the goal of the project to reach non-detected sexual delinquents by means of a broad media appeal (contributions in print, word and picture media). In this manner, the research group of the University of Zurich invited men to document verbally their violent actions and promised them anonymity and confidentiality. A telephone number was installed which could be used for fourteen days round the clock by men prepared to discuss the topic. In the 288 hours in which data was collected, 200 calls were received. A small proportion disconnected the line immediately. Some men wanted to talk with the male researchers about sexuality in general or about the relevance of scientific research. Of all the talks, thirty-five reports have been selected which were detailed enough for analytical purposes (Smithyman actually analysed fifty non-detected rapists).

As a comparison group to the non-detected offenders, thirteen in-depth interviews with incarcerated rapists were conducted. As Switzerland is small and crime report files are rudimentary, it was very difficult to locate even these thirteen offenders and finally convince them to cooperate. The interviews with both non-detected and incarcerated perpetrators have all been anonymous, they lasted on average one hour and were recorded on tape. A manual and partially structured questionnaire was the basis for a conversation about the course of the event, the motive and the objective of the perpetrator, the rational and emotional coping strategies and short- and long-term effects on the offender. The central research question has been: what effects does non-detection, and in contrast, incarceration, have in the mind and on the behaviour of sexual assaulters? The data were analysed using qualitative content analysis procedures.

SELECTED RESULTS

> Because we worked in the same place, I knew her in passing. At the company's yearly celebration, we then danced together and later I drove her home. I thought that I could go to bed with her, otherwise she won't have danced with me nor let me in. But then she acted coy and I had to help a little.
>
> (non-detected offender, Godenzi 1989).

Demographic characteristics

In view of the research situation as previously discussed, the statistical information about the offenders can only have an indicatory character. We cannot know, for example, who was reached by the media action, who was out of town at the time of the telephone action, who from the target group was prepared to call or who was discouraged due to an occupied telephone line. Differences from the population of normal prisoners are conspicuous. While in Swiss prisons there are an overproportional amount of foreigners and members of the lower social classes, the Zurich study reveals many Swiss men from the middle- and upper-class segments. These differences are confirmed in relation to schooling and professional qualifications. The Swiss men reported longer periods of education and higher professional qualifications than the prisoners. As a consequence, one might question Wolfgang and Ferracuti's (1967) subculture thesis, for only 30 per cent of the non-detected offenders correspond to the lower stratum. The remaining 70 per cent come from environments and professions which offender studies had previously only discussed in passing.

> I admit I forced her but not like in the movies, brutal with blows and weapons. I simply threatened her with her husband. That was also not new for her, she is after all married.
>
> (non-detected offender)

Differences between non-detected and incarcerated offenders

On the whole, non-detected offenders placed greater emphasis on the sexual motive of their actions. They depict themselves not exactly as sexual offenders but at least as neglected erotics. They feel that they must, according to their own information, help the woman a little so that finally something happens in bed or so that a propitious opportunity does not slip away unused. They describe the violent side of their actions as of secondary importance or as harmless, otherwise they would be arrested. They view themselves as men who act in sexual need and reject the portrait of the violent offender. The evidence found in the Swiss study in regard to the given motivation for the action has already been found by Smithyman (1978) who argued that the feminist thesis of power being the motivation for a rapist could be contradicted. Smithyman, though, neglects any analysis of the meaning of self-presentation of the non-detected offender. To underline their innocence it is central not to stand there as a violent offender.

Convicted sexual offenders in the Swiss study distance themselves from the sexual motivation of their actions in contrast to the non-detected offenders. They attach importance to not being perceived as sexual perpetrators. If they had wanted sex, that would have been no problem for them – that is their message. They do not want to appear as men who can have access to sex with a woman only by means of violence. When they admit to the crime, their admission is in relation to the use of violence. Because the act is known to the public and the man has been convicted, he only has the choice to lie about everything or admit parts. He decides on the label violent offender and against the stigma of sexual offender. This choice is understandable because the sexual offender is placed very low on the status hierarchy of criminal offenders. A man who must force sex by violence isn't a real man, says the unwritten rule. Who wants to be counted in this category?

> The fright of the woman had an effect on me, I was then totally different. Sex was for me not concerned, instead I wanted to humiliate this woman. This force released something in me – that somehow I am practically a man.
>
> (incarcerated offender)

In contrast to convicted offenders, non-detected offenders hardly count on the negative consequences of their act. Their self-image and behaviour seem less affected. Smithyman's interviewees stated how everything happened without a problem, how they were barely in danger of being caught. What they wanted, they achieved – sexual satisfaction and/or a feeling of power over a desired object. The processing task for the offender is thereby essentially simplified because he is the initiator and executor of the violence. He had prepared himself and was willing to go through with the action. Inasmuch as the situation did not surprise him, he had it more or less under control. The worst that could happen is that the woman would behave otherwise than expected.

> A colleague of mine told me that he had also already done that, simply helped a bit. Otherwise nothing happens with women. That he said that, gave me courage.
>
> (non-detected offender)

A non-detected perpetrator must not as a rule process the offence as a kind of trauma. He has thought about all of the possible results before the act and faces the result of his actions 'at a distance'. He did not limit his own radius of action, instead he in contrast expanded himself over the borders of another person. Only then when the consequences of the act become visible, can it also for him become menacing, his freedom then comes into play. This point determines how men as offenders deal with sexual violence, and what consequences the act has for their own lives. The few offenders who have been caught by the police and sentenced by the courts to prison sentences to a certain extent suffer a similar fate as most of the victims: they are deprived of their freedom of action. They are unable to do any more what they want. Their will pushes against walls and bars. Their boundaries are more apparent and perhaps narrower than those of the woman, only she stands in front of a paradoxical situation – to be imprisoned in freedom.

> I thought a long time whether violence is the correct way to make my wife have sex. One day I decided then, I thought it was the right occasion. She could have done it in order to make me happy. It was my birthday.
>
> (non-detected offender)

Non-detected offenders seldom express guilt feelings and when directly questioned, they rarely see a reason to feel guilty. Indeed, 70 per cent of the offenders rationalise their behaviour: guilt for the act lies with the woman; by their behaviour they provoke, above all by their appearance; whoever attracts should carry the responsibility, otherwise violence occurs; women make men dependent because they know that they need sex; this power is used by the woman to realise objectives; men are manipulated by women, they play with them; men are humiliated by women, the weakness of men is exploited; when men defend themselves with violence because they do not have the same means available, it is a form of self-defence. The calculation for the non-detected offender is simple: if they were guilty, they would have been reported and convicted. According to their thinking, women only report guilty men. Incarcerated offenders have it less easy in this regard. The criminal law system has pronounced them guilty. Based on the evidence and a public pronouncement of guilt, and perhaps as a sign of a certain contrition, incarcerated offenders are more willing to take a part, albeit very small, of the blame themselves. They are more reasonable in regard to their behaviour and understand violence as an illegal medium. In contrast, the offenders try to minimalise their guilt, relating their crime to situational and personal factors such as stress or alcohol. Moreover, the majority of them are also convinced that women carry the main blame or at least are jointly guilty.

> Basically the wife enjoys sex. But it was probably painful for her. Perhaps she was hurt but she certainly is sorry that I must be in prison. I went along for the fun, I certainly didn't want to do harm.
>
> (incarcerated offender)

The conviction causes an additional change with the criminals. If before the act their hostility and frustration were mainly directed towards women, being incarcerated shifts the object of their aggression primarily to the criminal justice system. This was particularly noticeable in offenders' emotional responses during interview. Although they do not dispute their violent acts, they do not attach too much importance to them. They do not understand why they are handled by the police and the rest of the justice system as dangerous criminals. The criminal justice system is the representative for the state's principle of atonement, the anger of the one convicted is vented on it. The court has it in its power to say one is guilty or not guilty. For the non-detected offenders the effect is exactly the opposite. The criminal justice system is their guarantee of faultless behaviour because their acts are never identified as illegal. From the view of the violent offender, the police and justice system legitimates their actions. Figure 8.2 shows an overview of the differing effects on the violent offender.

In the upper half of the diagram the stages of both offender categories (incarcerated versus non-detected) are very simply

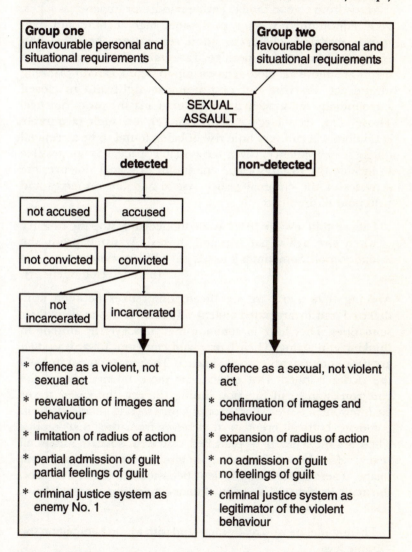

Figure 8.2 Model of differentiating effects of being incarcerated vs. being non-detected

presented. There the probability due to unfavourable and situational requirements (group one) of being caught, charged, convicted and incarcerated is substantially greater than with men from group two. Favourable personal requirements are for example: being a native, having white skin, language of the country, from a good family, having middle- or upper-class status, good education, respected profession, high income and high status, married, children, good reputation, political and economical power and prestige. Favourable situational requirements are above all: close relationship to victim, careful planning of the act, carrying out of the act at night and in closed surroundings, renouncement of apparent, massive use of violence. Those who, to a large extent, can rely on such favourable conditions will run very little risk of being found to be a criminal due to sexual violence. Given the available space, it is not possible to include the macro-societal conditions of sexual violence, the activities of the criminal justice system and the resources and behaviour of the victim.

> I always told my wife that I would immediately stop the violence when she again participated in sex. At some point she understood. Sometimes it needs just a little pressure.
>
> (non-detected offender)

Arguing that there are significant differences between non-detected and incarcerated violent offenders is not to deny their similarities. They have in common their misogynistic attitude in thinking and acting. Their hatred and contempt towards women are basic components of their violence. The more contemptuously the victim is rated, that means, the more unencumbered the conscious mind can function during the act, the easier terror against women is used. Both groups have a second characteristic in common: both differentiate themselves from the 'real' rapists. These are the scum, to be punished, castrated, isolated. Almost all sexual offenders differentiate themselves from this phantom image. Thereby their own violent behaviour becomes innocent, the mode legitimated, as a sign of their continuing status as a 'real' man:

> I hate someone who really rapes and with whom I am put on the same level.
>
> (incarcerated offender)

CONCLUDING REMARKS

Those who wish to study the average rapist must find perpetrators who are not incarcerated, not convicted, not accused and not detected. Sexual assaulters are generally not men with criminal backgrounds, they are proper citizens attacking women not as a result of an emotional eruption but on the basis of a rational decision in order to benefit from the violent act. Mostly they know their victims, frequently they are intimate friends/partners of them (only three of the thirty-five non-detected offenders were unknown to the violated women). If male researchers would focus on non-detected offenders, they would increase their chances of approaching the reality of male violence a bit more and possibly would contribute in an effective manner to feminist research in regard to victims/survivors.

Men's sexual violence against women is sustained and supported through the ruling norms of society and the daily experiences of both sexes. Men are encouraged, or at least not discouraged, from performing or approving sexual violence. Every man knows, consciously or unconsciously, that to a high degree, our societies and their supporting institutions cover men's violence against women. The social framework is the basis for the violent aspirations of men against women. The overall gender inequality, men's privileged distribution of power and prestige in societal subsystems, the patriarchal norms and values, the images of violence and the images of the sexes, are the main societal requirements for these destructive behaviours and are one of the central reasons why men think they have a right to sexually exploit women.

Due to its sampling procedure, the Swiss study does not allow any definitive conclusions. The methods described of contacting the non-detected offender are merely a first step. Social research must develop methodologically creative and at the same time sensitive approaches for the search for the average offenders which hold firm reliability and validity standards. If possible, such studies should be representative, prospective and longitudinal. Good research implies also comparison groups. In the particular case of non-detected offenders, such groups could be non-violent men (difficult to find) or detected, accused, convicted or incarcerated rapists. It would also be interesting to make comparisons with male offenders of other crimes, for instance, those who admit what they have done is illegal.

Social research as a public service business owes it to the survivors of sexual attacks and in general all women (as potential targets of the masculine destructive intent) to fully document men's sexual violence. In this manner it can break through a harmful silent alliance of social institutions which let undetected offenders 'off the hook' and whose costs are primarily carried by abused women.

Eventually, a reevaluation of intervention and prevention programmes and of criminal justice options seems to be necessary. In a situation where non-detected offenders are not only satisfied because they have realised their objectives but also feel that society and specifically the criminal justice system is on their side, a new general policy towards male violence is needed.

I was violent with my first wife. She was my secretary. With my second wife such behaviour seemed to me somehow inappropriate. She is a faculty member like me.

(non-detected offender)

Chapter 9

When men are victims
The failure of victimology

Tim Newburn and Elizabeth A. Stanko

Whilst once it was realistic to argue that 'the victim' was not only the forgotten party in the criminal justice process but also in criminology, the development both of victim services and of academic victimology have drawn attention to this significant oversight. A veritable industry of 'services' has developed and a wide range of academic studies have focused upon these developments and the range of victims that they are designed to support. Indeed, so strong have these developments been, that a number of authors have referred to the emergence of an all-encompassing 'victims movement' (see Pointing and Maguire 1988).

Yet, the criminal justice system remains far from being victim-friendly, and whilst uncovering new areas (see Morgan and Zedner 1992 on child victims), the study of crime victims appears to have reached something of a plateau. One of the reasons that this sub-discipline is fairly stagnant is, we suggest, that, in at least one important respect, criminologists continue to treat the notion of 'the victim' as if it were a 'given', i.e. as if it were unproblematic. More particularly, insufficient attention is paid to the complexity of criminal victimisation; all too often the use of the label 'victim' is underpinned by the assumption that it may only be applied to members of relatively powerless social groups, or that it describes a state of being which itself induces powerlessness. Though we have moved some way from the more or less explicit victim-blaming characteristic of von Hentig's (1948) view of victim as perpetrator and Wolfgang's (1958) concept of 'victim precipitation', there is some danger that we have moved so far in the other direction that victims are conceptualised as individuals who have no experience of crime as offenders, and/or as people who have little understanding of threat and harm other than being victims of random crime. Indeed, in much recent victimological literature, victims are characterised as helpless and vulnerable, and in need of advice so that they may avoid such misfortune in the future.

Such descriptions fail to tackle the complexity of relationships between 'offenders' and 'victims'. As far as the realities of the lives of some – especially young – males are concerned, such a dichotomy is hard to sustain. Young men, who according to crime surveys report the largest proportion of personal crime, are also the population which are most likely to be offenders. It is not the purpose of this chapter to explore this complexity in detail, rather to challenge victimologies that fail to examine the variety and puzzles of victimisation. More particularly, it will be argued that the victimisation of men, especially where the crime involves violence, reveals a significant gap in our current understanding of the impact of crime and, consequently, illustrates one of the limitations of extant victim services.

A BRIEF HISTORY OF VICTIMOLOGY

The term 'victimology' was first used in the late 1940s by Fredric Wertham (the author of *Seduction of the Innocent* (1955) which inspired the moral panic about horror comics in the 1950s in the UK) and the classic early studies in the genre appeared at about the same time. Beginning with von Hentig in the late 1940s and Marvin Wolfgang in the 1950s, early studies concentrated on the role of the victim in the aetiology of crime. At this point, criminologists were still searching for 'grand theories' that would explain crime, and victims of crime became, in part, another focus of that concern. For von Hentig and others, the specific focus was upon the role of the victim in the precipitation or perpetration of the crime.

It was not until the mid-1960s and the early 1970s, however, that victims 'attracted any serious public attention' (Pointing and Maguire 1988). The mid- to late 1960s saw the first murmurings of the nascent victims' movement and in its wake academic victimology, which was about to be radically transformed by the utilisation of large-scale survey techniques, moved its focus to the victim population rather than the individual (Fattah 1992). This gave rise to what one author has characterised as a 'lifestyle' approach to victimology or, alternatively, as 'conventional victimology' (Walklate 1989). In this approach, which is associated primarily with Hindelang *et al.* (1978) and Cohen and Felson (1979), it is argued that there is a link between routine daily activities and exposure to circumstances in which the risk of victimisation is high. Whilst this constituted a significant advance on the work of von Hentig, its dependence upon survey methodologies meant that such an approach failed (indeed was unable) to take account of those structural constraints which were not easily observable or measurable. Furthermore, in its concentration on the public domain and its avoidance of the private, it merely reinforced conventional views of victimisation and through its policy emphasis on individual lifestyle engaged in, at least implicit, victim-blaming once more.

The shortcomings of 'conventional' victimology were thrown into sharp relief, however, by the re-emergence of feminism and its impact on criminology generally. Feminists were critical of both the theory and methodology associated with the lifestyle approach, and they stressed the importance of the experience of victimisation. Focusing in particular on rape and domestic violence, a number of authors were able to illustrate the limitations of the social survey as a method of uncovering either the incidence of these forms of victimisation or the reality of the experience of victimisation. Central to their account was the issue of power for as Stanko, for example, has argued: 'unless policing and crime survey researchers lend credence to the concept and reality of gender stratification, violence against women will, on many levels, remain a hidden, but all too real part of women's lives' (1988: 46).

Crucially, feminism challenged not only the methodological basis of such work but also its implicit philosophy of knowledge. The claims to objectivity made by conventional victimologists were challenged, and suggestions that such survey-based work constituted 'science' were attacked for systematically excluding women's experiences and interests. From the feminist perspective,[1] *experience* constituted the epistemological basis of much feminist knowledge. The work of feminists, and particularly activists rather than academics was crucial to the transformation in understanding about the frequency and impact of rape, sexual assault and domestic violence. One simple but important historical lesson, therefore, is that certain forms of victimisation only become visible when they do, because of the campaigning work of representative groups. The victim categories that go with these forms of victimisation are not givens: not only would it be wrong to argue that they have always been visible to us, but also to suggest that they were there waiting to be uncovered. Certainly, attention has been drawn to certain forms of victimisation at specific points in history, but the victim categories that we use as a result are also historically specific. Specific forms of crime need to be understood within the cultural and historical context which gives them meaning.

Despite this far-reaching critique, much of criminology has managed to remain relatively impervious to feminist concerns and in a recent paper, Smart (1990a), concluded by suggesting that criminology had little to offer feminism. In recent years, however, there has emerged a victimological perspective – left realism – that claims to take the feminist critique seriously. It is worth looking in some detail at what left realism offers, if anything, by way of an alternative perspective, before moving on to consider the victimisation of men.

LEFT REALISM

Although the new realism is presented as a broad criminological enterprise (Matthews and Young 1992; Young and Matthews 1992), there are reasonable grounds for arguing that it is their 'victimology' that is the central plank of the perspective (Walklate 1992), and indeed Young has argued such 'realism necessitates an accurate victimology' (Young 1986: 23). Furthermore, in taking on board a feminist critique, this realist victimology was, we were told, going to put 'experience' centre-stage:

> Realism starts from problems as people experience them. It takes seriously the complaints of women with regard to the dangers of being in public places at night, it takes note of the fears of the elderly with regard to burglary, it acknowledges the widespread occurrence of domestic violence and racist attacks. It does not ignore the fears of the vulnerable nor recontextualise them out of existence by putting them into a perspective which abounds with abstractions such as the 'average citizen' bereft of class or gender.
>
> (Young 1986: 24)

Ironically, however, the preferred methodology of the new realists is based on large-scale, though locally focused, surveys, that are in many respects barely distinguishable from the tools used by the administrative criminologists that the realists are so critical of. Local crime surveys are defended on the basis not only of their geographical focus, but also their sampling procedures which are held to map better what is already known about patterns of victimisation (Jones *et al.* 1986 appendix 2; Young 1988: 169). This is a neat bit of footwork for it allows left realism to claim that it has taken the lessons of feminism on board whilst clinging to the tailcoats of a positivistic model of scientific discovery.

There are, however, a number of significant ways in which realism has failed in its attempt to 'take victimisation seriously' and, in the main, these are related to the difficulties that realism has in dealing with the variety and plurality which characterises victimisation in modern society. Indeed, Walklate suggests that realist victimology, like its administrative counterpart, focuses on crime as it is commonly understood and that therefore it 'neither tackles the question of victimisation by corporations or by implication the victimisation of children' (1992: 112). Crucially, she accuses realism of failing to incorporate fully an understanding of power relationships into its theoretical framework and therefore of being unable to help us understand how individuals actively resist their structural powerlessness. Once again, this is a shortcoming that it shares with the conventional victimology it has been at pains to distance itself from. We are surely left pondering whether realism and conventionalism are really so different.

Methodologically and ontologically then there are distinct parallels between realism and conventional victimology. However, it is the political underpinnings of the two positions that separates them most clearly. Administrative criminology in its eschewal of interest in aetiology and its association with social control theories clearly has an affinity with the political right, whereas realism is explicit in its espousal of vaguely 'left' politics. This comes out quite clearly in the agenda of realist victimology and, it will be argued, is central to its inability to take the complexity of victimisation seriously. The political agenda in realist victimology can be be seen clearly in the quote from Young earlier in which he sets out those areas of victimisation which realism is keen to take seriously: women, the elderly, victims of racist attacks, crimes against the least powerful. Few would wish to take exception to any of this, one assumes, except on the grounds that it is significantly incomplete. Uncomfortable though it may be, the reality of the world in which we live is that it is not just the 'least powerful' or even always the 'less powerful' who suffer criminal victimisation. Moreover, it is the articulation of the ways in which power is manifest in individual interactions, especially amongst those who have the benefits of structured privilege because they are men in a gender-stratified society. Men differ in economic flexibility, race, education, sexual orientation, and so forth, and men negotiate power and privilege amongst themselves as well as with women.

The central problem for realist victimology is that it is unable to wrench itself from a simple binary view of victims and offenders; a view which treats these categories as if they are not only mutually exclusive, but also characterised by uniform relations of power in which the victim is portrayed as 'weak, helpless, defenceless and unsuspecting' (Fattah 1992). The processes of criminal victimisation are not that simple, nor their politics that convenient. As Ruggiero has pointed out,

> some crimes confirm the existing distribution of power, but some do not. It is not enough for criminologists to assume the relations of dominance in victim–offender relations nor simply to present themselves as defenders of the weak. Their task is to uncover and explain the complex processes through which 'victims' and 'offenders' are reproduced.[2]
>
> (Ruggiero 1992: 129)

We suggest that this complexity also sheds light on how the notion of power is interpersonally negotiated, and how 'hegemonic masculinity', as conceptualised by Connell (1987), obscures our ability to deconstruct how power is managed between and amongst men.

As a consequence of this oversimplified view of the nature of victimisation, realism is unable to be realistic about the position of men. This stems from the desire of realists to remain steadfastly on the side of the underdog. Whilst not wishing to take issue with such political sympathies, we do wish to argue that the uncritical application of such sympathies to models of victimisation results in a unidimensional picture of social relations which divides the world into oppressors and oppressed. Thus, all men are oppressors unless they can be located in another oppressed group (elderly men perhaps, victims of racist or/and homophobic attacks certainly, male victims of child sexual abuse probably).

In the passage quoted earlier, Young talked of the importance of avoiding abstractions like 'average citizen' bereft of class or gender. The step forward made possible by this insight is only limited, however, if the theory of gender on which it is based is largely undifferentiated or even 'essentialist'. In a somewhat similar manner to their idealised view of the homogeneous working-class community (see the critical comments in Gilroy and Sim 1985), the realists continue to talk of men and women as if they too were largely homogeneous categories. However, as Scraton (1985) has noted, such assumptions about social cohesion are perhaps overly optimistic. Though, in this instance he is critical of their presentation of working-class community, his comments could just as easily be applied to their presentation of gender, for 'Just as it is probable that men from all classes see street violence as a "problem" for them, they would not see most actions of sexual harassment as a "problem" at all' (1985: 168).

One of the problems with realist victimology is that its underlying philosophy – 'that crime really is a problem for the working-class, ethnic minorities, for all the most vulnerable members of capitalist societies' (Young 1986:29) – is too simplistic to allow for a properly realistic understanding of the scope of victimisation. More particularly, it is unable to confront the reality in which men (and not just working-class men) not only victimise women, but also victimise each other, and that such victimisation may have a significant impact upon those who experience it. What, then, do we know about the impact of crime upon men?

MEN AS VICTIMS OF CRIME

The first point to be made is that there have been relatively few studies of male victims of crime. The bulk of early victimological literature focused on victims as a group largely undifferentiated by gender and, more recently, attention has been directed at uncovering and detailing the impact of violence by men against women (*inter alia* Dobash and Dobash 1979 and 1992). One of the results of this has, quite rightly, been to raise awareness of the frequency with which men *victimise*, especially within the 'home'. Adult men are rarely the *victims* in this context (although when they are, they are likely to meet with disbelief and disregard for their situation). Outside the home men are not only more likely to offend, but especially where 'public' violence is concerned, men – particularly young men – are most likely to seek police or medical assistance for personal crime, and report such incidents to crime researchers (Hough and Mayhew 1985, Shepherd 1990). However, little is known about men's experience of victimisation, even where violence is involved.

Much of this neglect is based upon a widely held but largely untested assumption that a central element of masculinity involves an unwillingness or talk about or admit 'weakness'. Thus, in the study of the fear of crime, of which gender is the most significant feature (LaGrange and Ferraro 1989), there is considerable discussion of the disparity between women's and men's reported levels of fear. In much of the literature, it is seemingly quite unproblematically assumed that men are reticent to disclose vulnerability (Maxfield 1984; Crawford *et al.* 1990), thus reinforcing the tendency to focus almost exclusively on women's experiences of physical and sexual assault.

A second but related point is that the evidence that is available, whilst indicating often major differences between men's and women's reactions to criminal victimisation, nevertheless indicates that a proportion of men are significantly affected by crime. Research by Maguire and Corbett (1987) on support schemes for victims of crime provides a good illustration of this point. Using data from the 1984 British Crime Survey, excluding vehicle theft and miscellaneous personal theft, a significantly higher proportion of female than male respondents reported themselves or their households being 'very much' affected, though the authors did continue to speculate 'whether this represents a "real" difference, or is caused by a greater reluctance among men to admit to being emotionally upset . . . is difficult to state with any certainty' (1987: 50). In one sense, of course, it is not the fact that there is a difference that is important. For the purposes of the argument here, the point to bear in mind is that this research, like other research of a similar nature (Shapland *et al.* 1985), shows that a proportion of men – albeit a proportion that is smaller than that of women – *do* admit to having been profoundly affected by crime.

Nevertheless, the differences between men's and women's reactions to crime ought not be allowed to obscure the fact that a considerable number of men *were* willing to admit to being severely emotionally affected by crime. Furthermore, in the case of assault or robbery, over half of all victims reported intense fear and 'shaking or shivering' and feeling 'dazed, confused or unreal', symptoms associated with shock as well as fear, were at high levels among . . . both sexes in the case of assault. This latter finding, together with the fact that there was no significant difference in these reactions by age in the case of male victims, helps to underline one of the key points to emerge from this exercise: *the effects of violent crime are severe for a high proportion of men, as well as for women*

(Maguire and Corbett 1987: 56)

A properly 'realist' victimology therefore, would have to confront the inescapable fact that men not only victimise women, but they also victimise each other, and in ways which may cause severe short-term and significant long-term trauma.

In a recent small-scale study of male victims of sexual assault, King (1992) explodes many of the myths about the impact of crime upon men. He was able to conclude that despite its limitations: 'the results of this study demonstrate that male sexual assault is a frightening, dehumanising event, leaving men who have been assaulted feeling debased and contaminated, their sense of autonomy and personal invulnerability shattered,' (King 1992: 8). There are a number of issues here which it is worth unpicking slightly. First, men are often extremely frightened by such events. They are, as such, emotional beings capable of feeling vulnerable, capable of expressing feelings and capable of asking for support. Second, in relation to the sexual assault of males, there is a further point that complicates the experience of victimisation, and that is the consequences that such an assault may have for the victim's view of himself as a man. Such attacks strike at the heart of stereotypical 'hegemonic masculinity' (Connell 1987) in which men are in control, are invulnerable and are heterosexual. Sexual assault potentially problematises such a view of masculinity, leading to a sense of loss of self. As Adler has argued:

Where the victim is male, any claim that he consented projects onto him a homosexual identity. Where the victim is homosexual, this can lead to considerable feelings of guilt, which tend to act as a deterrent to reporting. Where the victim is heterosexual, the very fear of being thought a homosexual may well stop him from reporting. Indeed, the reasons for not reporting for male victims are much the same as they are for female victims, and include shock, embarrassment, fear, self-blame, and a high degree of stigma.

(Adler 1992: 128)

Thus, King (1992) found that although there were many similarities between the reactions of male victims and those reported for women, 'the stigma for men may be even greater, however, in a society which expects its male members to be self-sufficient physically and psychologically' (1992: 10).[3]

There are significant parallels between the experience of sexual assault as described by men and women. This is not to suggest that the social context within which such assaults occur is the same for women and men – of course it is not – merely to say that the *experience* may be similar on other levels. Whilst men's sense of 'invulnerability' may be shattered by such events, this in itself may be a misreading. It is surely part of the same ideology of masculinity that presents men as uniformly powerful, controlling and non-emotional, which leads us to believe that men behave as if they *were* invulnerable. The available evidence suggests that at least some men feel vulnerable some of the time, though some of these are unlikely to admit feeling so. For at least some of the men in King's sample the experience of victimisation is more likely to have increased their sense of vulnerability rather than destroyed some sense of invulnerability. The most important lesson from this, however, is that we have 'discovered' a series of empirical questions: do men feel vulnerable? Which men? Under what circumstances? And so on.

We may also find clues to understanding some links for some men between experiences of victimisation as children and offending. For those sexually abused as young boys, the longer–term impact on their sexual identity/masculinity may have significant consequences for others as well as for the victim. There is considerable debate over the strength of the evidence in this regard (see Finkelhor 1986) though a recent review (Watkins and Bentovim 1992: 47) concluded that 'the sexual abuse of boys in childhood is an important contributory but not a necessary factor in the development of a perpetrator'. What does seem clear, however, is that sexual victimisation of boys at a young age – and the anger at the sense of powerlessness that this involves – frequently leads to them to attempt to reassert a controlling and powerful masculinity, often through hostile and aggressive behaviour (Rogers and Terry 1984). It would appear then that the dominant model of masculinity that we hold is a crucial mediating factor in the short- and longer-term outcomes for male victims of (sexual) assault.

Recent work by Stanko and Hobdell (1993) reinforces the point that the impact of assault (though in this study non-sexual assault) on men is an area that has for too long been neglected by criminologists. They conducted a study of thirty-three male victims of assault by other men, many of whom reported fear, phobias, disruption to sleep and social patterns, hypervigilence, aggressiveness, personality change and a considerably heightened sense of vulnerability. The authors suggest that masculinity is not only an important factor in helping make sense of the consequences of victimisation for these men, but that the ways in which offers of support were offered, together with the victim's ability to look for, or accept, help and support was also crucially affected by the ways they and others perceived them as 'men', within a context of what masculinity means more generally. This work raises many questions about how men cope with violence, how they order their lives as a result of violence, how criminal justice professionals and support organisations view male victims. In all of this there is the issue of whether male victims of crime require help and support and, if so, how it might be offered and what might help. One of the consequences of the centrality of the 'hegemonic' model of masculinity within both victimology and criminal justice, has been that the 'needs' of male victims of crime have remained largely unconsidered.

To an extent this position is reflected by the services that are provided for victims of crime. Although it is clear that men may be profoundly affected by crime, that some at least will be open to offers of help and support, relatively little thought has been given to providing services to this group of victims. This is not in any sense to suggest that the needs of men should be prioritised in some way or, indeed, that they should be singled out, but simply to point out that they should be recognised. Services which assume that men do not need help or will not accept help merely collude in the reproduction of an ideology which places the traits of 'strength', 'resilience' and 'emotional independence' at the centre of the dominant conception of masculinity. On the basis of the brief review above of research on the impact of assault on men it would be hard not to agree with Maguire and Corbett's conclusion in relation to Victim Support that: 'The findings strongly suggest that the low priority given by some schemes to young male victims of violence may be a mistaken policy' (1987: 56).

Finally, the neglect of masculinity also obscures other crimes against men: racist attacks, homophobic attacks, domestic violence between gay men (Island and Letellier 1991), men's experiences of attack by women (although it constitutes the smallest proportion of men's assault, an analysis focusing how power and safety are negotiated is essential). The small literature which addresses racist violence often neglects to articulate how being male is part of the way racist violence works. No doubt, many black and minority women and children are targets of such violence, but so too are adult and adolescent men. How do such men make sense of such violence within climates of racial hatred? So too, gay men confront homophobic violence (Herek and Berrill 1992). Thus, the frame of masculinity aids our understanding of men's reactions to crime and fear of crime as well. Maxfield (1984) for instance locates men's anxiety over crime as a concern for others, a concern which he characterises as 'altruistic' fear of crime. So too this frame contributes to a more holistic account of men's offending. What is now needed is some research to explore what impact victimisation has upon offenders' sense of themselves, and the harm they potentially do to others.

MASCULINITY, MALE VICTIMS AND THE SHORTCOMINGS OF VICTIMOLOGY

From this evidence we may speculate – as this is basically all that is possible given the paucity of empirical evidence – that all forms of (violent) victimisation may provide a threat to the well-being of some men in some circumstances. It is therefore, at the very least, an area of victimisation that needs to be taken seriously. All men will not experience or respond to violence in the same way or even in similar ways. Some, perhaps even the large majority, will remain largely unconcerned or lastingly affected by such experiences, whilst others may suffer long-term trauma not just as victims of crime, but as *male* victims of crime. Their experience will be directly mediated by their views of themselves as men, their socially located understanding of what men *are*, and the consequences of the experience may well be visible in a changed understanding of self.

Both conventional and left realist victimologies utilise a model of masculinity that is akin to what Connell (1987) has described as 'hegemonic masculinity', and therefore tend to avoid dealing with the issue of the victimisation of men. The promise by left realists to 'take victimisation seriously' is limited by its politics which has difficulty with any social relationships that do not fall neatly into dichotomic categories of 'oppressor' and 'oppressed'. The world in which we live is just not that simple or that comfortable. The amount of effort that has been put into studying victims of crime over the past twenty years should have convinced us by now that, at least where men are concerned, there is frequently no easy distinction between offender and victim. In order to think about the victimisation of men we have to confront some difficult political questions. Accepting that men also suffer as a result of criminal victimisation is not to deny that men continue to occupy an advantaged position in relation to women, or that women are 'unequal' victims of crime. However, what it requires us to do is to give up our essentialist models of gender which undifferentiatedly present women as victims and men as oppressors, and confront the social reality in which men not only routinely victimise women, but also victimise each other.

NOTES

1 What Harding (1986, 1987) has referred to as 'standpoint feminism'.
2 The use of this argument here should not in any sense be taken to imply some denial of the basic reality of the power structure within which violence against women and men takes place – the collective oppression of women by men.
3 As Stanko (1990) suggests:

> a 'real' man is a strong, heterosexual male protector, capable of taking care of himself and, if necessary, guarding his and others safety aggressively. He is the man who will stand up in a fight, but will not abuse his power by unnecessarily victimising others. And, according to the mythology of the 'real' man, he will do so fearlessly.
>
> (1990: 26–7)

Chapter 10

Masculinity, honour and confrontational homicide

Kenneth Polk

INTRODUCTION

While it is well established that males account for most homicide
offenders (Wolfgang 1958; Wallace 1986; Silverman and Kennedy
1987; Falk 1990; Johnson and Robinson 1992), perhaps less well
known is that slightly over half of all homicides are likely to be
male-on-male events, that is, involving men both as offenders and
victims. In a national study in Canada, homicides with both male
victims and male offenders accounted for 53 per cent of all
homicides (Silverman and Kennedy 1987), while an investigation
in New South Wales (Australia) reports a virtually identical 54 per
cent (Wallace 1986).

What factors account for these distinctively masculine homicides?
Unfortunately, the literature is scanty regarding such killings, despite
their relative frequency. Ever since the pioneering study of Wolfgang
(1958), analysis of the victim–offender relationship has been a central
feature of most homicide investigations. None of the major
investigations, however, has carried out an analysis of these
relationships for the specific group of male-on-male homicides.

Some rough clues can be found in the larger studies, however,
since these are likely to report relationship data by gender of
victims. Since close to 90 per cent of all offenders are male, it can
be presumed that the bulk of cases where males are victims will also
be cases where males are offenders, and then male victims can be
compared with female victims. Such analysis will show that females
are likely to be victimised by other family members (notably
husbands, but sometimes parents), whereas in contrast males are
much more likely to be victimised by either 'friends' or 'strangers'
(Wolfgang 1958: 207; Wallace 1986: 73).

This observation that homicides among males are more likely to fall outside of the family network in fact doesn't carry us very far in developing an understanding of what is going in these killings. For example, in Philadelphia (Wolfgang 1958: 207), almost two-thirds (64 per cent) of male homicide victims were killed by either friends, acquaintances, or strangers (in contrast to 21 per cent of female victims). While that information has traditionally featured strongly in discussions of homicide, it actually does not provide information about why friends kill, or why strangers kill, let alone why such killings should involve men more often than women. If a male kills a friend, he does not do so because the person is a friend, but because something has happened between them. Other factors are present which push an offender to do what would otherwise be unthinkable (taking of the life of someone close). Similarly, people are not killed because they are strangers, rather because something occurs which transforms the scene to the point where the taking of life of a person otherwise remote to the offender becomes a possibility.

Initially relationship data appear to be a bit richer when the focus shifts to the 'motive' (Wolfgang 1958; Falk 1990) or the 'circumstances' (Maxfield 1984) of the homicide. A potentially useful bit of information is found in Wolfgang's observation that a large proportion (41 per cent) of male homicide victims were killed as a result of a 'trivial' altercation. In his text Wolfgang speaks of the 'significance of a jostle, a slightly derogatory remark, or the appearance of a weapon in the hands of an adversary' going on to comment that:

A male is usually expected to defend the name and honor of his mother, the virtue of womanhood . . . his age, or his masculinity. Quick resort to physical combat as a measure of daring, courage, or defense of status appears to be a cultural expectation, especially for lower socio-economic class males of both races.

(Wolfgang 1958: 188–9)

When Wolfgang provides actual case examples of male-on-male homicide, these fit this formulation, including cases where a victim refused to pay a $2 bet in a card game, where a victim would not share his wine with his flophouse room-mate, or when a victim in the course of an argument referred to the offender as a 'Dago'.

Unfortunately, the matter becomes a bit confused when the data are treated quantitatively, since almost as many female offenders (28 per cent) as male offenders (38 per cent) in Wolfgang's study committed homicide because they were provoked by a 'trivial altercation' (Wolfgang 1958). Further, it is necessary to go beyond these terms, and perhaps follow the words of his text more closely, since it is obvious that in a strict sense people don't kill because of a trivial provocation. That is, there has to be something behind the apparently inconsequential event which generates the heated response which results in lethal violence.

One possibly helpful avenue of thought has been opened by Katz (1988) in a discussion of how humiliation and rage push individuals to the point where homicide becomes possible. Luckenbill (1977) has presented a view of homicide as proceeding through a set of stages, from an initial provocation to the ultimate killing. He urges that any view of homicide must be a dynamic one: 'homicide does not appear as a one-sided event with an unwitting victim assuming a passive, non-contributory role. Rather, murder is the outcome of a dynamic interchange between an offender, victim, and, in many cases, bystanders' (Luckenbill 1977: 185).

While perhaps providing a starting point in thinking through the processes involved in lethal encounters, neither Katz nor Luckenbill examine the critical masculine character of homicide. For ideas regarding masculinity and violence, a much richer source of information is to be found in the ideas of Daly and Wilson (1988). While much of their argument is concerned with the question of why it is that homicides in situations of sexual intimacy are more likely to involve males than females, they also recognise the role that masculine competition and honour play in male-on-male killings.

Drawing heavily upon the ideas of Daly and Wilson, the present research has been able to identify patterns within the general category of male-on-male homicides (Polk and Ranson 1991). A significant proportion of male-on-male killings occur during the course of other crime, as where the threat implicit in armed robbery becomes real, at the cost of the life of either the victim or offender in the robbery. A smaller proportion involve situations where males well at the boundaries of conventional life employ planned and intentional violence as a technique of conflict resolution.

The largest grouping of male-on-male killings, however, are a result of confrontations which begin as a contest over honour or reputation (Polk and Ranson 1991; following the usage first suggested by Daly and Wilson 1988). It is the purpose of the present discussion to discuss the structure of this form of homicide, and to identify the particular elements that make up this distinctive masculine scenario of violence.

THE DATA

The data for the present investigation, which is part of an on-going investigation of homicide (Polk and Ranson 1991), are drawn from the files of the Office of the Coroner of Victoria, Australia. These files contain a number of reports which are collected for the purpose of carrying out the coronial inquest, and include an initial police report of the incident, an autopsy report regarding the cause of death, a toxicology report if such is relevant, a police prosecutor's brief, and the report of the inquest itself. The most helpful of these documents is the prosecutor's brief, which typically contains lengthy witness statements as well as transcripts of interviews with defendants where these have been taken.

There were a total of 380 homicides reported in the years 1985–9. For each homicide a lengthy case history was prepared drawing upon the material in the coronial files. These case studies were then subjected to a qualitative analysis of the themes which characterised the relationship between the victim and the offender. These themes where then analysed, and yielded a number of distinctive scenarios of violence. Among these were the confrontational homicides, of which there were 84 cases (this scenario accounting for 22.1 per cent of all homicides).

CONTESTS OF HONOUR AND LETHAL VIOLENCE

Confrontational homicide has its source in the willingness of males, first, to lay down challenges to the honour of other males, and second, the masculine readiness to engage in physical violence in response to such challenges, as is made clear in our first case study:

> Gabe W. [age 32, soldier] boarded a train at Flinders Street Station after an evening of drinking with his friends (his blood alcohol level was subsequently established to be 0.224). When Gabe attempted to take a seat where Mike M. was sitting with his

feet spread across two seats, Mike ordered him in a clearly insulting manner to move on and find a seat elsewhere. Challenged, Gabe refused to move on, and attempted to force his way onto the seat. Mike leaped up and struck Gabe, and the two fought. Although Gabe received a number of blows, and was kneed in the face, he finally managed to pin Mike down.

Witnesses relate that at this point Gabe said: 'If you don't stop now, I'll break your neck.' Then, believing that Mike would stop, Gabe released him. Mike instead produced a knife, stabbing Gabe three times in the chest. One of the blows penetrated the heart. Gabe collapsed and died in the aisle.

(Case No. 4714–86)

This represents almost the ideal type of confrontational homicide. The incidents moved rapidly from initial exchange to the fatal wounding. It is not possible to know the nonverbal cues that preceded the violence. Once words were exchanged, the males quickly responded to the public challenge to their masculine reputation. There was no planning or premeditation regarding the death, since the parties could not have known even minutes before that a lethal encounter was about to ensue. Words lead quickly to a fight, the fight in turn escalated to the point where a deadly weapon was employed.

MASCULINITY, HONOUR AND WHEN WHAT APPEARS TRIVIAL BECOMES A LIFE-THREATENING MATTER

One further issue in this narrative is that the precipitating events appear exceptionally trivial when contrasted with the disastrous outcomes (Gabe's death and Mike's subsequent sentence to prison). These apparently minor triggering events are a common feature of the confrontational killings:

Late one Saturday night, Anthony N. (age 19, unemployed) was walking back towards their home after attending a local 'Octoberfest'. They had enjoyed a pleasant evening of drinking (Anthony's blood alcohol level was later established at 0.08). In a small park, they met up with another group, including Don B. (age 18, unemployed) and Peter. T. Before setting out, this second group had armed themselves with broken billiard cues and knives).

One of the young women in Anthony's group was part of the

triggering of the confrontation when she asked if she could ride Peter's bike. He replied: 'You can have a ride if I can ride you.' Insults and challenges began to flow back and forth between the groups. At one point, Anthony is recorded as having said to Don: 'You're a bit young to be going to Octoberfest, aren't you?' Don responded with: 'Don't call me a kid.'

The exchanges escalated into pushing and shoving. Anthony said: 'If you want to have a go, I'll have a go back.' Don then threw a punch at Anthony, and the fight was on. At first it was a general group scuffle, and at one point Anthony broke a beer stein (obtained at Octoberfest) over the head of a member of Don's group.

The main group conflict began to simmer down, but Anthony and Don sought each other out and continued their personal dispute. At first Don was armed with the broken pool cue, but Anthony was able to take it off of him. Peter then handed Don a knife. Witnesses agree that at this point, Anthony kept repeating to Don: 'I'll kill you, I'll kill you.' Don was able to come in close to Anthony, however, and slashed out with his knife, stabbing Anthony in the left thigh, right hand, and finally the left side of his chest. By now all eyes of the groups were on the two. They saw Anthony stagger, and he began to bleed profusely. The two groups broke off the fight, each going their separate ways.

One of Anthony's friends asked if he was feeling all right, to which he replied; 'I think I have been stabbed.' The friends helped him to a nearby house and called an ambulance, but Anthony died before medical help arrived.

(Case No. 3661–85)

As before, the initial set of precipitating events appear inconsequential to the outside observer. Daly and Wilson (1988) have warned, however, that care must be used in understanding the nature of these apparently trivial events:

The typical 'trivial altercation' homicide in America is an affair of honor with strong resemblances to the affairs of honor that have been described in other cultures. . . . The precipitating insult may appear petty, but it is usually a deliberate provocation (or is perceived to be), and hence constitutes a public challenge that cannot be shrugged off. It often takes the form of disparagement of the challenged party's 'manhood': his nerve, strength or savvy, or the virtue of his wife, girlfriend or female relatives.

(Daly and Wilson 1988: 69)

Such perceptions are actually consistent with Wolfgang's observations. After noting the apparently 'trivial' character in some of the disputes leading to homicide, Wolfgang (1958) went on to comment that it is the observers in the criminal justice system (rather than the social analysts) who, drawing upon middle- and upper-class values which have shaped legal norms, describe the disputes which lead to homicide as trivial in origin. For the working- or lower-class players in the homicide drama, the challenge to manhood is matter of consequence.

THE SETTING OF CONFRONTATIONAL VIOLENCE

Another characteristic of these events is that they occur in definitively public and leisure scenes. One of the most common of these leisure scenes of course is the pub:

Dennis [age 23, unemployed] and a group of three friends had been celebrating the birthday of one of the group when they stopped in the Doutta Galla Pub at 9.30 in the evening. Fred [age 31] was there drinking alone. The initial provocation for a fight was the challenging eye contact between Fred and one of Dennis's friends. The friend said: 'I don't like this arsehole Turk [Fred was born in Turkey] . . . he looks sleazy.' Fred then approached the friend and said: 'What are you staring at?' To which the friend replied: 'What are you on about?' Fred then claimed: 'You're staring at me,' to which the friend replied, 'Get out of here.' One of the other members of the group attempted to intervene at this point, and Fred told him: 'Fucking keep your head out of it.' In reply, the one who had attempted to intervene said: 'Well, fuckin' cop this,' and punched Fred in the head.

An all out bar room brawl developed. Fred produced a knife, and slashed his attacker across the stomach, and followed this by stabbing his opponent in the staring contest in the leg. Dennis and his friends, and other patrons in the bar armed themselves with billiard cues and surrounded Fred, who then sought shelter behind the bar. When Dennis reached over to pull him from behind the bar, Fred stabbed him in the chest.

One of Dennis's friends, known in the pub as 'Dogsbody', pummelled Fred several times over the head with a cue. Fred twisted around and was able to stab his attacker twice in the body. Patrons then started shouting: 'Let's kill him, he's stabbed Dogsbody, let's kill him!'

Fred attempted then to seek shelter in the pub office behind the bar, where the barman was counting the night's takings. Fred locked the door, and pleaded: 'Don't let them get me, they're going to kill me.' Several men kicked at the door until they were able to break it down. Fred then grabbed the barman, and held a knife to his throat, threatening to kill the barmen if the group approached any closer. Someone yelled 'The Turkish cunt has got him,' and the group started throwing bottles at Fred to make him release the barman. When the barman was able to break free, Fred was showered with an avalanche of bottles. The police entered at this point, and the fight subsided. Dennis was found, dead, on the floor (his blood alcohol was 0.309).

(Case No. 3631–87)

There is much in this that suggests a classic confrontation. The scene is a pub. There is a large social audience of other males who are witness to, and even participants in, the violence as it erupts. The initial provocations are what others might define as petty, including the mutual jousting with eye contact known as 'eyeing off'. Alcohol features in this event, not only in the sense that it has been consumed by the participants, but more importantly because it helps define the nature of the leisure scene where males relax among other males, some known and others unknown. In such scenes, the social audience plays a critical role in providing social supports for violence as an appropriate way of dealing with the challenge. It is not uncommon, as happened in this narrative, for members of the audience to do more than provide a backdrop for the violence, since they in fact may come to play an active role in the unfolding combat.

HONOUR AND THE PROTECTION OF WOMEN

There are numerous specific sources for the honour contest that flares to violence. One common theme is that men are quick to respond to insults directed at their female companions:

One weekend night, Tommy F. [age 29, unemployed] and his friend Charlie began their round of drinking first at the Crab Cooker restaurant, then gravitated to the Bowling Green Hotel where they remained, drinking for several hours. Another group came in much later in the evening, including Mike D. [age 26, assembly worker], Pete, and Rog, who was a boy friend of Jennie [a waitress at the pub].

At closing time, as Tommy and Charlie were leaving, they passed Rog and Jennie in the hallway. In passing, Tommy made a comment to Jennie which Rog took to be an insult. An argument developed between Rog and Tommy that led to a fight between them on the sidewalk outside. Tommy was punched to the ground, and the fight broke up with Tommy and Charlie withdrawing to their car which was parked nearby.

Shortly afterwards, Rog, Jennie, Mike and Pete came out of the hotel to head for home. Tommy and Charlie had waited for them, and the two once again approached and proceeded to confront and challenge Rog. When the other males joined in, Tommy pulled a knife and backed away to his car.

Mike and Pete gave chase to the car. Mike picked up a piece of timber, and began to hit the car repeatedly. Tommy suddenly leaped out of the car, and stabbed Mike with his knife. Badly hurt, Mike fell to the ground. Tommy kicked him several times in the head, then jumped back into the car and drove off. The knife had penetrated Mike's heart, he died before the ambulance arrived (his blood alcohol level was 0.05).

(Case No. 3264–86)

As in the previous account, the violence here emerges in a pub environment. Here the initial insult was directed at a woman, and the males felt compelled as a matter of honour to respond. One further interesting feature of this story is how quickly the social audience can move to centre stage in the evolving conflict. In this narrative, the ultimate victim of the homicide was peripheral to the initial flow of insults that initiated the violence, but became swept up in the events and the violence spilled outward to involve the wider group.

COLLECTIVE VIOLENCE

In many of these accounts, the violence is clearly collective in character. One form that this can assume is found in the following case:

> Colin [age 17] was a member of a loosely organised group known as 'Bogans', while Charles [age 19] was identified as a 'Headbanger'. Both were attending a disco in a local tennis centre, when a group of the Bogan males became involved in an argument with a group of girls who were hanging out with the Headbangers. After a brief exchange of taunts and insults, one of the girls punched Colin, who retaliated with a punch in return. Charles came over and attempted to pull the girl away. Colin called Charles a coward and a wimp, and began to throw punches at Charles. At this point, a general fight began between the two groups, involving 10–12 people. Charles then pulled out a knife, and stabbed Colin several times in the chest and abdomen. Colin died shortly after (his blood alcohol level was found to be 0.079).

> (Case No 1931–87)

In this account, the disco provides an open, public setting in which groups of males circulate, thereby opening up the possibility of conflict. Both groups involved in this account are distinctively working class, but set off from each other rather clearly in terms of clothing and hair styles. One of the factors in this narrative is the active role played by the female Headbanger, since it was her punching of the Bogan male that initiated the physical violence.

Given the group nature of the conflict found in these last accounts, a natural question which follows concerns the extent to which these findings indicate the presence of gang behaviour in Victoria. The media, certainly, have popularised the idea of gangs and gang violence in Melbourne. Melbourne newspapers have focused attention on the behaviour of groups such as the '3147 gang' (so-called because of the postal code of the neighbourhood), and one forensic specialist was quoted as being concerned that Victoria was 'heading towards becoming a state of warring gangs' (*Melbourne Herald-Sun*, 7.8. 1991: 2).

Assessing the issue of the degree to which there is a 'gang problem' in Victoria requires some clarity and agreement regarding the use of the term 'gang'. There is nothing new, obviously, about collective forms of trouble in Australia. Newspapers in Melbourne and Sydney complained of the 'larrikin' problem over a century ago, and somewhat before that there was the 'Kelly gang', so central now to Australian mythology of colonial life.

In the United States gangs and gang violence tend to be given a highly specific meaning. One concise definition offered in the US was:

> A youth gang is a self-formed association of peers, bound together by mutual interests, with identifiable leadership, well-developed lines of authority, and other organisational features, who act in concert to achieve a specific purpose or purposes which generally include the conduct of illegal activity and control over a particular territory, facility, or type of enterprise.
>
> (Miller 1980:121)

While there is not complete agreement among writers, it would seem that in the American scene the term 'gang' is likely to refer to a group that has a relatively high degree of organisation, with an explicit leadership structure, a defined territory which is part of the gang identity, and clear colours or other insignia which set them apart. Using these rough guide-lines, it would appear that such formalised gangs are rarely encountered in Australian communities. While for a short time after the appearance of the movie *Colors* there was a bit of faddish copying of American gang characteristics (including the wearing of colours), in the Melbourne environment there is little that resembles American street gangs. There are no groups who are formally organised, who maintain a clear sense of territory (including control of that territory), who consistently through time maintain a distinctive set of colours and clothing, and the groups rely on informal rather than formalised leadership.

At the same time, there are groupings of young people, especially originating in lower and underclass environments, whose collective behaviour is seen by the wider community as 'troublesome'. The groupings tend to be loosely organised, including their leadership structure. While they may emerge from a particular neighbourhood, their activities are spread over a reasonably wide geographical area. These informal groups may spend some time in their neighbourhoods, but it is also highly likely that they will be mobile, often flowing through the major spokes of the public transportation system (buses, trams and trains) into such readily available public spaces as train stations, shopping malls, pubs, parks or reserves, and, of course, the streets, laneways and sidewalks that make up the 'street' scene.

What seems characteristic of collective violence in Australia is that much of the conflict between groups seems to result from what can be seen as the 'social friction' that occurs as groups flow past each other in public space, often outside the neighbourhood of either group. Walmsley (1986) has observed a similar form of group movement, friction, and confrontations over honour in the UK:

> One troublespot in Newcastle was a small area of about four streets containing twelve pubs. Groups of young people moved from pub to pub during the evening and this led, towards closing time, to friction between groups suddenly arriving at a pub. . . . Such situations produce violent incidents whether inside or outside the pub. Again violence sometimes occurs when large numbers of people leave rival establishments (e.g., dance halls) at about the same time. Ramsay describes three violent late-night incidents at burger stalls. In each case 'individual worth and identity were at stake, in front of other bystanders, in an impersonal setting.' Provocative remarks were made, or something was seen by one party as provocative and the incidents escalated into violence.
>
> (Walmsley 1986: 17–18)

Such accounts are virtually identical with those described in the present case studies. It should be noted that the friction which occurs in the social space is probably highly concentrated in terms of the times when violence is likely to result. These open and public places are often occupied in the daylight and early evening hours by groups of other conventional citizens, whose separate claims to the space are likely to exert a dampening effect on violence. One is more likely to fight in front of an audience of masculine 'mates', and is inclined in other directions if the audience includes aunties, younger sisters, grandfathers, or strangers occupying disparate age and gender roles.

Where group identities exist in Victoria, such as 'Bogans', 'Headbangers', 'Wogs', or 'Skips', at least in the period being studied, these are loosely defined and derive more from general and widely spread lifestyles, rather than membership in territorial based gangs. As indicated in the accounts above, group identities can nourish collective violence in Victoria, as seen in the disco encounter between the Bogans and Headbangers. The nature of that collective violence, however, seems tied more to issues having to do with the uses of public spaces, rather than in protection of home territory.

VIOLENCE WHERE THE ACTION IS BROKEN

While in the homicide narratives up to this point the violence has proceeded rapidly and spontaneously from the initial insult or challenge to lethal violence, there is in some accounts a break in the interaction when one of the participants leaves to obtain a weapon:

> Mick F. [age 36, unemployed] started his drinking at the house of a friend late in the afternoon, and then the two of them moved off to their local, the Victoria Hotel. They continued drinking 'shout for shout' for some time (Mick's blood alcohol was later found to be 0.147).
>
> In the middle of the evening, the group was approached by Jimmy S. (age 53), another of the pub regulars. Jimmy, also feeling the effects of alcohol (some hours later, his blood alcohol was still found to be 0.197), upbraided Mick for some insulting comments he had made towards his 'missus' (observers commented that a trivial exchange had occurred between the two earlier in the day, or at least in their view the comments were trivial). There were mutual insults and challenges, and finally Mick hauled back and struck Jimmy, a short fight ensued, with Jimmy being rather badly beaten. Hurt as well as drunk, Jimmy needed help from bystanders to make his way out of the pub.
>
> Mick and his group settled back to their drinking, when they were interrupted by Jimmy's *de facto* wife, who proceeded to abuse Mick for his beating of Jimmy. Then, Jimmy himself re-entered the bar. Without a word he walked up to Mick, pulled out a knife, and stabbed him once in the chest. As before, Jimmy was set upon, this time by the friends of Mick. Jimmy was assisted out of the pub by his *de facto* spouse. Help was summoned for Mick, but the knife had penetrated his heart and he died before he could reach hospital.
>
> (Case No. 3778–85)

This is similar in many respects to the previous accounts of such violence. The action was played out in a pub. Insults directed at a woman companion provoked one of the males to initiate physical violence. In this particular narrative, the older male was publicly humiliated by the beating administered in front of both peers and his *de facto* wife. He then broke away from the scene to fetch a knife, and re-engaged the fight bringing it to a swift and deadly conclusion.

Another case of such a breaking of the action is of interest both because of the nature of the provoking incident, and because it provides an illustration of what Wolfgang (1958) termed 'victim premeditated' homicide:

Gregor B. [age 24, machine operator] and his friend Ned set out one evening for a pub crawl. After many drinks, and while they were at their third hotel, Gregor went to the toilet. When coming out of the toilet, Gregor became involved in an argument with a woman who, like him, had too much to drink (Gregor's blood alcohol level was found later to be 0.120). The nephew of the woman, Albert S. [age 18], intervened, shoving Gregor away. The two pushed at each other, arguing heatedly. The pub bouncer came over, and ordered Gregor to leave the pub.

When Ned came out, he found Gregor waiting in his car. Gregor was furious, explaining that he had been bashed up and 'called a "wog"' (Gregor was a recent migrant from Yugoslavia). Gregor then asked to be driven home so he could fetch his shot gun and bring it back in order to force his attackers to apologise. They went to Gregor's house to pick up the weapon. Gregor's wife pleaded with him to either stay home, or leave the gun behind, but he replied that this was '. . . something he simply had to do.'

Gregor and Ned returned to the pub just on closing time. As Albert and his group came out, Gregor threatened them with the shot gun, insisting that they all line up along the wall. They all stood quietly until Gregor turned to say a word to Ned, who was still in his car. At that moment Albert rushed Gregor, knocking him down and taking control of the gun.

Three of Albert's friends began to beat and kick Gregor. Albert ordered Ned out of the car, and when Ned refused, smashed one of the car windows. Ned sped off. Albert then added his bit to the beating of Gregor, hitting him with the butt of the shot gun. He then pointed the gun at Gregor, and fired a shot which hit him in the neck, killing him instantly.

When apprehended a few minutes later, Albert said: 'He was going to shoot me . . . I acted in self-defence. I know I acted rashly. Is the bloke all right, the bloke I shot? . . . I wanted to shoot the tires out . . . When I first got the gun, I tried to shoot it in the air but it wouldn't go off . . . I thought he wouldn't be hit . . . ' Circumstances suggest that Albert may not have intended to shoot when he did. Forensic tests revealed that the gun had a sensitive trigger. Further, Albert very nearly shot his own friends as well, one of them, in fact, receiving a burn mark on his jeans because he was close to the line of fire when Gregor was shot.

(Case No. 2069–86)

As in the previous account, one of the actors has broken off the action to search out a weapon, in this case a gun, to carry back to the scene, except here the male became a victim of his own weapon. We see as well in this account the role that ethnic slurs can play in the events which stir up males to the point where they take up violence.

ETHNICITY AND MASCULINE CONFLICT

Given the markedly multicultural environment of contemporary Australian cities, it is inevitable that, as in the previous case study, ethnic identities provide the spark for masculine confrontation:

V. [age 27, unemployed] was originally from Vietnam, but had lived in Melbourne for some time. He was planning to move to Queensland in a few days to accept a job offer. A group of his friends (all Vietnamese) decided to throw a party in his honour.

The group went along Racecourse Road to the local shops and pub to obtain the supplies for the party. While part of the group went into the Palace Hotel to buy beer, V. and a friend went across the road to buy some pizza. As they crossed the road, a battered green sedan pulled up with what the Vietnamese could only describe as 'western' males inside. These men alighted from their car, and started verbally to abuse the two Vietnamese, followed this with threats to use a chopping knife that one of the group produced. V. remained alone briefly while his friend went to summon help from their friends in the pub.

At the same time as the group of Vietnamese arrived on the scene, a further group of 'western' males poured out of the pub. A general mêlée developed, in which the Vietnamese group apparently threw beer bottles at their attackers in an attempt to defend themselves. Surrounded now by the original group augmented by those that had come from the pub, the outnumbered Vietnamese broke ranks and began to run to the safety of their flats further along Racecourse Road.

The green car followed in pursuit, grabbing and beating whatever stragglers they could reach. One of these was V., who was viciously beaten, including a severe blow to his head. Found shortly later unconscious in the street, V. was taken to Royal Melbourne Hospital where he died three days later of brain damage from the head injuries.

(Case No. 666–85)

This again shows how the frictional contact of persons moving through public space may result in masculine violence. In this account the violence occurs in the city streets, and the provoking incidents originate in ethnic conflict, here conflict between 'Old Australians' and the newly emerging Vietnamese community. In some instances, such clashes occur between ethnic groups:

As was his usual custom, Edgar L. [age 19] left his suburban home to go into the China Town section of the city in order to take Kung Fu lessons. He met his friend Keith L. in Little Bourke Street, where they played some of the machines in the 'Tunza Fun' amusement parlour for a few minutes, then went off to their Kung Fu lessons. Their class finished at 2.30 p.m., and the two first had coffee with friends, then returned to the Tunza Fun at about 3.30, and started playing the Kung Fu Master machine which was their particular favourite. Suddenly, 6 Vietnamese youths approached and started to strike both Edgar and his friend. Edgar then turned and challenged the group, saying (according to one witness): 'Come on, I'll do ya.' One of the Vietnamese group came in close, produced a knife, and stabbed Edgar once in the chest. The Vietnamese group then quickly slipped away. Edgar staggered outside, and collapsed on the sidewalk, where he died a few minutes later (the knife had penetrated his heart).

The police investigation was able to pull together only scanty details of this homicide. They were unable to identify or locate any of the six Vietnamese young people involved. One of Edgar's friends recalled seeing the Vietnamese group sitting outside a Little Bourke Street restaurant earlier in the afternoon, and commented that this group had previously caused trouble for Chinese young people in the street. Further, there was some provocation on Edgar's part, since earlier he and his friends had been yelling out anti-Vietnamese insults in Chinese as they had been walking down the street on their way back from their lessons.

(Case No. 1047–85)

Here the frictional movement of the two groups occurred in one of Melbourne's most popular laneways, the narrow street that contains some of the better-known restaurants in the city. In this incident, tensions between an older and more firmly established ethnic group (Chinese) and the more recent arrivals (Vietnamese) provided the background for the lethal violence.

A DEVIANT CASE: A CONFRONTATION INVOLVING WOMEN

While this analysis has proceeded with the presumption that confrontational homicides are definitively male behaviour, there is among these cases one in which the central actors were female:

Carol [age 31, single mother] was walking to the local supermarket near the council flats where she lived, when she became involved in an argument with Donna (age 21) and Tricia. The two women apparently felt that Carol had insulted them, and was responsible for graffiti alluding to their lesbian relationship. As the argument heated up, Donna suddenly punched Carol, grabbed her by the hair, and threw her on the ground. Since Carol had her six month old baby with her, she thought that a defensive response was called for, and she managed to break off the conflict and run with her child back to her own flat.

Carol then armed herself with a small wooden baton, and had two male friends drive her so that she could '. . . go down there to get them two bitches.' The men stood by the car while Carol went to the front door of Donna and Tricia's flat, calling out: 'Now, come on out and fight me.' Tricia came to the door, and alleged that Carol hit her across the face with the baton. Tricia then woke Donna who had been napping. Donna grabbed a knife and went outside. When she saw the weapon, Carol said: 'Hey, you don't have to use the knife.' Carol then backed off, and started running for the car. Donna followed, shouting 'I'm going to fuckin' kill you.' Donna lunged forward, and stabbed Carol in the chest. Carol's right pulmonary artery was cut, and she bled to death at the scene. It was later established that Donna had a long history of violence, and had previously stabbed Tricia during one of their domestic disputes.

(Case No. 4202–88)

There is much in common with other of the confrontations which have fatal outcomes. Insults are exchanged, a fight breaks out, the action breaks off and one of the parties leaves to fetch a weapon, and then returns to a scene where the final violence takes place. There was, as well, one further case where two women who had been close friends became embroiled in an argument over a male who had written to both of them while the two were in prison. Again, the argument flared up quickly and spontaneously from an initial set of insults to the final killing (Case No. 2174–87).

While these cases share much in common with the other confrontations we have observed, these two differ in that they involve women as the major participants. While women can draw upon the confrontational scenario in a scene of conflict, this is exceptionally rare, since well over 90 per cent of these events involve males. Despite these deviant cases, it can be concluded that confrontational violence is overwhelmingly and distinctively masculine in its makeup.

THE ISSUE OF CLASS, GENDER AND ECONOMIC MARGINALITY

It is the present contention that it is important to see confrontations as 'contests of honour' in which the maintenance of 'face' or reputation is a central matter. Further, these are seen as quintessential masculine matters. In looking for explanations, theorists such as Katz (1988), whose ideas are not grounded in gender, are not likely to be of much help. If we take Katz as providing a general view of homicide (as he proposes), then the great number of cases where the homicide falls well outside of events involving a spontaneous interplay of humiliation and rage (central to his description of 'typical homicide') raise fundamental questions about the adequacy of his view. His theory cannot encompass the many carefully premeditated homicides on the part of jealous husbands, the planned homicides of depressed males who kill their wives as part of their own suicide plan, the rationality of some homicides where males employ violence to resolve a long-term conflict with another male, or even the strange and complex motivations involved in neonaticide where in most cases the young women simply deny the birth. Even where the particular interaction between rage and humiliation might have some relevance, since something like this happens in some of the confrontational homicides, Katz's inadequate and flawed treatment of the gender elements of homicide requires us to look elsewhere for ideas regarding the nature of confrontational homicide.

Luckenbill's (1977) suggestion that homicide be examined as a 'situated transaction' fares only slightly better. Some of the confrontational homicides appear to correspond to the step-by-step movement from initial provocation to the ultimate killing laid down by Luckenbill. There are, unfortunately, two kinds of problems in this formulation. One is an empirical matter. Despite having a wealth of useful data in the records available to the present investigation, it is often not clear what the 'opening moves' of a homicide might have been. Quickly evolving scenes, such as those in the opening case studies (such as the fight on the train between Gabe and Mike), permit an observer to construct an account of the social dynamics as these moved through the various phases described by Luckenbill. Other homicides are more extended in time, and it is no longer possible to trace back to the opening move. Further, Luckenbill argues that his model applies to all homicides, when clearly such events as neonaticide or where depressed husbands intent on their own suicide kill their wives, fall outside his formulation.

Much more important, however, is the second matter. Luckenbill's argument is posed in gender neutral terms. While many of the confrontational homicides can be described as moving through the stages he specifies, Luckenbill offers no clues as to why it is highly likely that such confrontations are masculine. Neither Katz nor Luckenbill are likely to be of much theoretical relevance because neither addresses the question of why it is that males are likely to become involved in this pattern of violence.

Much more close to the mark are the ideas of Daly and Wilson (1988) who have argued that it is particularly males who become involved in violence around the issue of reputation:

A seemingly minor affront is not merely a 'stimulus' to action, isolated in time and space. It must be understood within a larger social context of reputations, face, relative social status, and enduring relationships. Men are known by their fellows as 'the sort who can be pushed around' or 'the sort that won't take any shit,' as people whose word means action and people who are full of hot air, as guys whose girlfriends you can chat up with impunity or guys you don't want to mess with. In most social milieus, a man's reputation depends in part upon the maintenance of a credible threat of violence.

(Daly and Wilson 1988: 128)

The theoretical account provided by Daly and Wilson is one of the few that recognises the diverse forms of masculine violence that make up contemporary homicide patterns. It is their argument that the general thread of masculinity that runs through homicide reflects forms of male aggressiveness that can be accounted for by evolutionary processes. While their formulation is helpful in moving us towards an understanding of the masculine character of violence, in its present form it needs some expansion to encompass the class elements of this form of homicide.

A possible line of argument which might help here has been advanced recently by the anthropologist Gilmore (1990). In reviewing data on masculinity across a number of cultures, Gilmore concluded that there were three essential features to masculinity: 'To be a man in most of the societies we have looked at, one must impregnate women, protect dependents from danger, and provision kith and kin' (1990: 223). In many societies, these 'male imperatives' involve risks, and masculinity can be both dangerous and competitive:

In fulfilling their obligations, men stand to lose – a hovering threat that separates them from women and boys. They stand to lose their reputations or their lives; yet their prescribed tasks must be done if the group is to survive and prosper.

(Gilmore 1990: 223)

At this level, the argument is consistent with that of Daly and Wilson. Can these ideas be expanded to include the underclass character of this violence as well? A possible line of reasoning is established in Gilmore's argument about the impact of differential social organisation on masculinity:

> The data show a strong connection between the social organization of production and the intensity of the male image. That is, manhood ideologies are adaptations to social environments, not simply autonomous mental projections or psychic fantasies writ large. The harsher the environment and the scarcer the resources, the more manhood is stressed as inspiration and goal.
>
> (Gilmore 1990: 224)

If Gilmore is correct, it would seem reasonable to argue by extension that the contemporary male who possesses economic advantages is able to provide the base for the procreative, provisioning and protective functions through his economic resources, and these same resources provide the underpinning for his competition with other males for a mate. In other words, physical prowess and aggression no longer become necessary for the economically advantaged male to assure his competence in reproduction, provision or protection.

For males at the bottom of the economic heap, however, the lack of access to economic resources has the consequence of rendering these issues, and therefore their sense of masculinity, as problematic. For such males, the expression and defence of their masculinity may come through violence. Messerschmidt, for one, has argued along these lines:

> Some marginalized males adapt to their economic and racial powerlessness by engaging in, and hoping to succeed at, competition for personal power with rivals of their own class, race and gender. For these marginalized males, the personal power struggle with other marginalized males becomes a mechanism for exhibiting and confirming masculinity. . . . The marginalized male expresses himself through a 'collective toughness, a masculine performance' observed and cheered by his 'buddies.' Members of the macho street culture have and maintain a strong sense of honor. As he must constantly prove his masculinity, an individual's reputation is always at stake.
>
> (Messerschmidt 1986: 70)

There are deeply rooted aspects of culture which place men in a competition with other men in terms of their reputation or honour. Assuming that Gilmore (1990) is correct in his assertion that the bases of masculine rivalry derive from competition regarding mating, provisioning and protecting, males who are well integrated into roles of economic success are able to ground their masculinity through methods other than physical confrontations and violence. For economically marginal males, however, physical toughness and violence become a major vehicle for the assertion of their masculinity and a way of defending themselves against what they see as challenges from other males.

It is the defence of honour that makes what might be considered a 'trivial' provocation for some to be the grounds for a confrontation which builds to homicide. Wolfgang was one of the early observers of the phenomenon of the apparent triviality of events which provoke some homicides:

> Despite diligent efforts to discern the exact and precise factors involved in an altercation or domestic quarrel, police officers are often unable to acquire information other than the fact that a trivial argument developed, or an insult was suffered by one or both of the parties.
>
> (Wolfgang 1958: 188)

It seems clear, however, that what is trivial to a firmly respectable observer may be quite central to the marginal actor's sense of masculinity. Daly and Wilson (1988) have argued along similar lines, that for some men it is important that they maintain their sense of honour, that they do not allow themselves to be 'pushed around', that they maintain a 'credible threat of violence' (Daly and Wilson 1988: 128).

SUMMING UP

Confrontational homicide involves behaviour which is essentially a contest of honour between males. In the initial stages of the encounter, what the participants in a confrontational killing intend is first to argue, then to fight. The argument which produces that fight is spontaneous, as are the events which follow. These conflicts typically occur in leisure scenes, especially scenes where males predominate. The venue is a public setting, taking place in and around pubs, in streets or laneways, in public parks or reserves, parties or barbecues, and in public transport settings such as bus stops, train stations, or even on the train or buses themselves. In most of such scenes, an active role is played by the social audience, particularly male peers. The social nature of these situations is reinforced by the role of alcohol, the use of which has been found to be a feature of a great majority of these homicides.

The lethal violence is not premeditated, at least at the starting point of the conflict. Some confrontation scenes move rapidly to the point where deadly violence is employed, as where the parties begin with a fist fight, then raise the stakes by pulling knives. Others are more complex, however, and may involve one of the parties leaving the immediate scene to return a short time later with a weapon. In some instances the conflict may become elaborated into a feud which simmers for weeks or months before the lethal violence results.

Through it all resound the joint themes of masculinity and lower social class position. Extreme violence in defence of honour is definitively masculine. But, not all males feel compelled to defend their reputation or status with such violence. Why it is that some males pursue violence to secure their reputation or status, while others avoid such challenges, is a major theoretical question which must guide further research.

Chapter 11

Masculinities, violence and communitarian control

John Braithwaite and Kathleen Daly [1]

Violence is gendered: it is a problem and consequence of masculinity. Contemporary state interventions to control violence are no less gendered: structures of response, from arrest through imprisonment, glorify tough cops, celebrate adversarial relations, and construct a virtuous 'protective' state by incarcerating or, in some countries, killing the 'bad guys'. What alternatives are possible in an apparently closed system, where masculinity and masculinist structures are both the cause and the putative cure of violence?

In this essay, we consider men's violence towards women and ways of responding to it. Recognising the failure of traditional justice system responses towards violent men, we outline a more promising approach, one compatible with the principles and visions of republican criminology (Braithwaite 1989; Braithwaite and Pettit 1990). This approach uses a community conference strategy adapted from the Maori culture in New Zealand as a key element in an overall regulatory ideal that repudiates exploitative masculinities (see Mugford and Mugford 1992). We elucidate the community conference, discuss its strengths, and address vexing questions about its efficacy in different contexts.

MULTIPLE MASCULINITIES AND NORMAL VIOLENCE

Multiple masculinities are implicated in the gendered patterning of violence. Men's violence towards men involves a masculinity of status competition and bravado among peers (Daly and Wilson 1988; Luckenbill 1977; Polk and Ranson 1991). Men's rape and assault of women reflects a masculinity of domination, control, humiliation, and degradation of women (Brownmiller 1975; Wilson 1978; MacKinnon 1987; Smith 1990; Alder 1991; Snider 1992). Other types of harmful conduct involve a shameless masculinity or a masculinity of unconnectedness and unconcern for others. When called to account for exploitative conduct, men's responses may be rage rather than guilt, or an amplification of non-caring identities such as 'badass' (Braithwaite 1991; Katz 1988; Miedzian 1991; Retzinger 1991). Some women may exhibit these masculine qualities, but their behaviour would likely be interpreted as pathology. They would derive little support for expressions of masculine violence from even the most marginal of subcultures.

For men, status competition through physical force, domination–humiliation of the less powerful, and knowing no shame have substantial cultural support. Few societies today contain a majoritarian masculinity that sets its face against violence. In general, women's and men's social movements have failed to nurture credible competing non-violent identities for heterosexual men.[2] When such identities are imagined or promoted, they are confined to men's potential to care for others in families, that is, to be loving or caring fathers, husbands, sons, or brothers. In fact, the caring masculine identities having some cultural support are more likely found within 'the family' than outside it. To suggest that masculine caring is featured in family life is expected and paradoxical. It is to be expected in light of the physical separation for men of 'work' and 'home' with the rise of capitalism (see Zaretsky 1976); historically, emotional life for men became centred on the home or the family 'as haven' (Lasch 1977). Yet, in the light of feminist research, it is paradoxical to associate masculine caring with family life. Evidence from the eighteenth and nineteenth centuries in Europe and the US shows that men exercised control over household members, including wives, children, servants, and slaves by physical force and violence, often with the support of the religious and secular law (Dobash and Dobash 1992: 267–9). Contemporary research indicates that women's experiences of physical and sexual violence are most likely to be within intimate relationships with men including fathers, husbands, boyfriends, and other men they know. Thus, while male identities in the family are a problem, the caring sides to those identities may be part of the solution.

FAILURES OF JUSTICE SYSTEM INTERVENTION

The failures of traditional justice system responses to men's violence against women can be summarised in three points.

Problem 1: Most men are not made accountable for acts of rape or violence against intimates. Women do not report the incidents (Dobash and Dobash 1979: 164–7; Estrich 1987: 13, 17; Temkin 1987: 10–12; Stanko 1985; Dutton 1988: 7; Smith 1989). There are also perceived evidentiary difficulties or police indifference leading to non-prosecution (Chappell and Singer 1977; Edwards 1989: 100–6, 172–3; Frohmann 1991; Hatty 1988; Temkin 1987: 12–15; Buzawa and Buzawa 1990: 58; Stith 1990; Zorza 1992: 71), plea bargaining, and acquittals (Kalven and Zeisel 1966: 249–54; Adler 1992: 121; Temkin 1987: 15).[3]

Problem 2: The men who are arrested and prosecuted for violence against women have likely got away with it before and may have entrenched patterns of raping and assaulting women. This follows from the evidence cited under Problem 1. When criminal conviction is a rare event for perpetrators, repeat offenders will often be hardened by the time of their first conviction. Because they are hardened offenders, rehabilitation programmes fail. They fail because they are attempted when a history of violence is so advanced; they fail because the prison that is seen as necessary for a hardened criminal is the least likely site for rehabilitation; and they fail because they occur in a context where a man is stigmatised as a fiend when he believes that he has been a normal (violent) male for many years.[4]

Problem 3: Women victimised by men's violence are re-victimised by engaging the criminal process. Complaints of intimate assault may not be taken seriously by the police or courts (Stanko 1982; Ferraro 1989; Stanko 1989). Rape survivors feel ashamed of coming forward and pursuing a complaint (Dobash and Dobash 1979: 164; Newby 1980: 115; Scutt 1983: 166; Stanko 1985: 72). The criminal process silences the victim. If the case goes to trial, the woman is denied the chance to tell her story in her own way. Rather, she becomes evidentiary fodder for a defence attorney. She is not allowed to tell the offender what she thinks of him, what he has done to her life. She has no opportunity to say what she thinks should happen to the man (Smart 1990b; Real Rape Law Coalition 1991), and there is no ceremony to clear her character (Smart 1989).

For rape, the reform literature tends to concentrate on evidentiary rules at trial. Some feminists have become disillusioned with the possibility of changing rape law and procedure; they urge that energies be focused on the bigger battles against patriarchal structures rather than dissipated on the minutiae of liberal legalism (Smart 1990b; Snider 1990, 1992). For domestic violence, debate has centred on the merits of the conciliation model and law enforcement model (Lerman 1984).

We acknowledge the limitations of liberal legalism as a reform agenda. Moreover, we think it important that a regulatory strategy not pitch law enforcement against communitarian forms of control. We suggest that justice system institutions can be reformed to give voice to women and to continue the struggle against men's domination of women. A radical shift of paradigm will be required: it will treat victims and offenders as citizens rather than as legal subjects, empower communities at the expense of judges, and confront exploitative masculinities with pro-feminist voices. It involves a shift from a liberal to a civic republican frame.

REPUBLICAN CRIMINOLOGY

Defended elsewhere (Braithwaite 1989, 1993a; Braithwaite and Pettit 1990), republican criminology contains the following elements and claims. Shaming is more important to crime control than punishment, and the most potent shaming is that which occurs within communities of concern. Shame has negative consequences for offenders and victims unless it is joined with a ritual termination of shame (reintegration ceremonies). The criminal process should empower communities of concern, and it should empower victims with voice and the ability to influence outcomes (Eijkman 1992). Communities of concern must negotiate social assurances that victims will be free from future predation and harm.

A reform strategy that embodies these principles, albeit in a tentative way, is the community conference. These conferences can become a key building block of a political strategy against exploitative masculinities.

THE COMMUNITY CONFERENCE STRATEGY

The idea of the community conference comes from New Zealand, where, since 1989, it has been the preferred approach in responding to juvenile crime. White New Zealanders (or *Pakeha*) adapted the idea of family group conferences from Maori culture, where it has been used for centuries in responding to sexual abuse and violence in families as well as for a variety of more minor offences. *Pakeha* have been more cautious about applying the Maori approach in response to family violence, partly because of the legitimate concern that power imbalances among family members can easily be reproduced in family conferences.

Let us describe the family group conference (FGC) approach in handling juvenile crime.[5] After an offence is detected by the state, a youth justice coordinator convenes a conference. Those invited are the offender (let us assume here a male),[6] the boy's family members (often extending to aunts, grandparents, cousins), other citizens who are key supports in the boy's life (perhaps a football coach he particularly respects), the police, the victim, victim supporters, and in some instances, a youth justice advocate.

These conferences can be viewed as citizenship ceremonies of reintegrative shaming (Braithwaite and Mugford 1993). The theory of the FGC is that discussion of the harm and distress caused to the victim and the offender's family will communicate shame to the offender. The assembling of people who care about and respect the offender fosters reintegration (or healing in Maori terms) of social relationships. In a successful conference, the offender is brought to experience remorse for the effects of the crime; to understand that he or she can count on the continuing support, love, and respect of family and friends; and to agree on a plan of action to prevent further harm. All conference participants are given the opportunity to explain how the offence affected them and to put forward proposals for the plan of action. The offender and his or her family members then propose a plan, which is discussed and modified until it is agreeable to all FGC participants, including the police.

Two features of the conference maximise its potential for reintegrative shaming. Giving voice to victims and victim supporters structures shaming into the process; and the presence of offender supporters structures reintegration into the process. These features are conducive to reintegrative shaming, though they do not guarantee it.

Those familiar with the uses of mediation in domestic assault cases, or in family law more generally (Lerman 1984; Fineman 1991; Rifkin 1989; Gagnon 1992), will immediately see the dangers in this approach. It empowers a family structure already characterised by deep imbalances of power between men and women, abusing adults and abused children. However, traditional Maori diagnoses of power imbalance, while not feminist, bear some resemblances to a Western feminist analysis. For example, in some Maori tribes an accused male abuser would have no right to speak at the conference. Any statements in his defence would have to be made through someone moved to speak on his behalf. Maori responses also challenge statist solutions to crime problems. Statist thinkers see a problem of power imbalance in the family and assume state personnel (such as social workers or police officers) are the best agents for correcting that imbalance. In Maori thinking, it is members of extended families who are in a better position to intervene against abuse of family power than the social workers or police officers. Communities of care and concern such as extended families are in a better position to exercise periodic surveillance of family violence or abuse, to talk with family members to ensure they are enjoying freedom from violence, to shame family members when abuse of power does occur, to enforce agreements such as not drinking alcohol, to negotiate understandings that an abused person has a safe haven nearby to stay (a kin member's or neighbour's house), and to negotiate the circumstances of the abuser's removal from the household until there is satisfactory assurance of violence-free family life.

Viable extended families do not exist for many abused individuals who live in Western societies. In New Zealand, the state at times has been impressively proactive on this score. If there is an aunt who has an especially loving relationship with the offender, but who lives hundreds of miles away, the state will pay for her to attend the conference. Occasionally, an agreement is reached in which an offender, who has run to the streets to escape an abusive household, can live with relatives in another community.

In 1991, a variation on the New Zealand conference strategy was implemented in Wagga Wagga (Australia), a city with a population of 60,000 a hundred kilometres west of the capital, Canberra. It has been introduced in other Australian jurisdictions, though taking variable forms.[7] One of the authors has observed the processing of twenty-three young people through conferences in Wagga Wagga and New Zealand during 1991–3; we shall draw from some of these conferences to illustrate its practice.

The genius of the Maori approach, as adapted in New Zealand

and Australia, is that it is a particularistic individual-centred communitarianism that can work in an urban setting. The strategy does not rely on fixed assumptions of where community will be found. It does not assume that there will be meaningful community in the geographical area surrounding an offender's home. Nor does it assume that members of a nuclear family will be a positive basis of care, though it always attempts to nurture caring in families. It does not assume that members of the extended family will be caring and effective problem-solvers. It does assume one thing: if a group who cares about both the offender and victim cannot be assembled, this means the conference coordinator is incompetent, not that these human beings are devoid of caring relationships.

The challenge for a conference coordinator is to find the people in an offender's life who really care about him or her, wherever they are. One example of the handling of a male teenager in Wagga Wagga illustrates this point. The boy had been thrown out of his home. The coordinator discovered that his community of concern was the football team where he enjoyed respect and affection. At the football club, the coordinator asked whether the parents of other team members would be prepared to take him in for a time. Several offered. The boy chose the one he liked best but then found he did not like living there; he moved on to another set of football team parents and seemed to be happy at the second try.

Another important feature is that the conference approach is geared to a multicultural society. Anglo-Saxon liberal legalism has crushed the communitarian justice of the Celtic peoples, the Maoris, Aboriginal Australians, native Americans, and Asian ethnic groups, with a unequivocal imperial system that sacrifices diversity in problem-solving strategies to belief in equal treatment under one standard strategy. The community conference, in contrast, empowers particular communities of citizens who care about particular people to come up with unique solutions in ways that seem culturally appropriate to those people and circumstances. Western liberal legalism does have a valuable role in plural problem-solving: constitutionalising it and providing citizens with guarantees that certain human rights cannot be breached in the name of cultural integrity. Hence, when conferences are established, advocates can ring alarm bells to engage court intervention when sanctions are imposed beyond the maximum allowed according to more universal state laws. There must be methods of reviewing decisions to ensure that offenders are not coerced into admitting guilt for offences they claim not to have committed. The New Zealand state has attended to these issues in its reform agenda (Office of the Commissioner for Children 1991; Ministerial Review Team 1992). What we might aspire to is a creative blend of empowered legal pluralism constrained by Western universalist legal principles.[8]

COMMUNITY CONFERENCES IN THE REGULATORY PYRAMID

How would the community conference be used in responding to men's violence against women? We shall consider men who assault intimates, an estimated 10 to 33 per cent of whom also rape them (Frieze and Browne 1989: 186–90). To do so, we first sketch how community conferences articulate with other forms of state intervention including powers to arrest and punish.

Republican criminology gives up on prison as the best way of responding to or containing men's violence towards women. It advocates minimalism in the use of imprisonment (Braithwaite and Pettit 1990), but it does not advocate abolitionism. Like Dobash and Dobash (1992: 210–12), we are wary of an abolitionist agenda of returning men's violence towards women to an ill-defined 'community', since power imbalances would reinforce patriarchal power. We are interested in the possibilities for communitarian institutions to empower victims 'to use the criminal justice process to negotiate their own security with suspects/spouses' (Fagan and Browne 1990: 190; see also Mugford and Mugford 1992). Both mandatory arrest and abolitionism deprive victims of the discretion necessary for such negotiation. Some feminist abolitionist proposals (e.g., Meima 1990) do contain an incipient conference strategy, but they do not allow for any accommodation of communitarian ideals with the option of imprisonment. If non-carceral approaches fail and if imprisonment of a violent man offers more protection of republican liberty than doing nothing, then the man should be imprisoned.

We envisage the regulatory ideal in the form of an enforcement pyramid (see Figure 11.1). The existence of imprisonment at the peak of the pyramid channels the regulatory action down to the base of the pyramid. Regulatory institutions can be designed such that state power enfeebles community control or, as in the pyramid

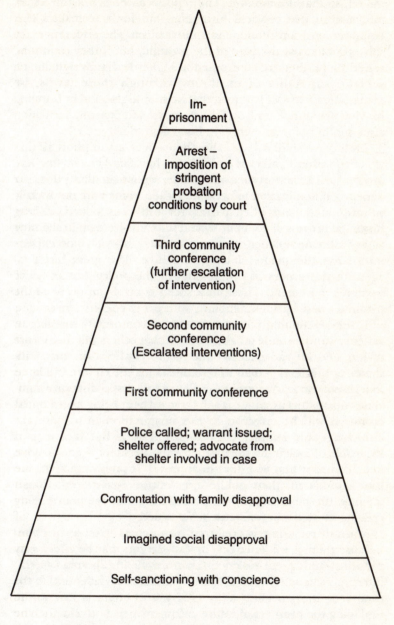

Figure 11.1 Domestic violence enforcement pyramid

model, so that it enables it. The republican does not call for an informalism that replaces formalism, but for a formalism that empowers and constitutionalises informalism. The preference is to solve problems at the base of the pyramid, but if they cannot be solved there, they are confronted at higher levels. By signalling a societal capability of escalating through these levels, we communicate to a violent man that he should respond by bringing his violence under control. Otherwise, he will face one escalation after another of intervention in his violent life.

At the pyramid's base, the theoretical assumption is that violence within families is least likely when family members have internalised an abhorrence of violence, when masculinity does not depend on domination to persuade, when women are not socially subordinated, and when caring for others is valued. A long historical process of community and state involvement in shaming acts of intimate violence can create a society in which most citizens internalise the shamefulness of violence. The great historical agent of this process is not families or the police, but an active women's movement. Thus, most social control can occur at the pyramid's base by self-sanctioning with pangs of conscience.

If self-sanctioning fails, the history of community shaming of violence can persuade an abusive man that others will disapprove of him and his violence. No one has to confront the man with shame at this level; a man who understands the culture will know that those who learn about his violence will gossip disapprovingly. When gossip hits its target, it will do so without being heard by the target; it will be effective in the imagination of a culturally knowledgeable subject (Braithwaite 1989). But if a man is incapable of imagining the disapproval others feel, then someone must confront him with that disapproval. If family members are too intimidated, then public intervention is required. Consequently, the next rung in the pyramid involves the police being called and a warrant for arrest being issued.

Warrant for arrest is preferred over actual arrest at this level because there is evidence that arrest warrants may be effective in reducing subsequent violence (Dunford 1990). Sherman (1992) interprets this as a 'sword of Damocles' effect. It is identical to the theory of the pyramid: automatic punitiveness is inferior to signalling the prospect of future enforcement, hence channelling the regulatory game towards cooperative problem-solving (for the underlying game theory, see Ayres and Braithwaite 1992:

Chapter 2). Issuing an arrest warrant, even if the man is present,[9] is the first intervention.[10] When the warrant is issued, the police may advise the woman to move to a shelter and seek the advice and support of a shelter advocate. The man has time to think about the 'sword of Damocles' that the warrant has put in place.[11]

The design, meaning, and results of the original Minneapolis police field experiment and subsequent replications continue to be debated (Sherman and Berk 1984; Lempert 1989; Sherman 1992; Dunford 1990; Lerman 1992; Bowman 1992; Frisch 1992). It is important to recall that the experiments randomly assigned different police 'treatments' in responding to domestic violence calls: arrest, separation, and mediation. The original Minneapolis study (Sherman and Berk 1984) revealed significant effects of arrest over separation in reducing subsequent violence. The accumulated evidence from recent research suggests a simple deterrence model of arrest is inaccurate. Sherman (1992) now rejects the pro-arrest conclusions drawn from his previous research. For a subset of violent men in four of the Minneapolis replications, those white and employed, he concludes that arrest seemed to have a shaming effect that reduced subsequent violence (see also Hopkins and McGregor 1991: 125–30; Williams and Hawkins 1989). But for another subset of men, those black (in three of the studies) and unemployed (in four), arrest seemed to promote rage or defiance rather than shame. For this group, arrest was another stigmatic encounter with the justice system, which increased the men's anger and violence. The stigmatic effect of arrest for the latter group was stronger than the positive shaming effect of arrest for the former; thus, across-the-board pro-arrest policies may cause more violence than they prevent. This is why we favour arrest warrants as the first state intervention; these would be followed by community conferences before moving up the enforcement pyramid to arrest.[12]

Although arrest may subsequently escalate an abuser's violence, at the time of the incident, taking a violent man into police custody may provide an abused woman a measure of safety. There can be ways to achieve such safety without arrest. While the man is issued a suspended warrant by one police officer, another could take the woman aside and suggest moving to a shelter until a community conference is convened.[13] Such a policy would mean shifting resources from police lock-ups under pro-arrest policies to community shelters. Although shelters are expensive, they are less costly to build and run than lock-ups. Another key benefit of encouraging shelters is that shelter staff are made available to abused women as caring advocates for community conferences.

The next rung of the pyramid is the conference. Several unsuccessful conferences might be held before warrants for arrest were acted upon, in the worst cases leading to prosecution and incarceration. Some may recoil at the thought of one conference failing, more violence, another failed conference, more violence still, being repeated in a number of cycles before the ultimate sanction of incarceration is invoked. But there can be considerable intervention into a violent man's life when moving from one failed conference to another. For example, there could be escalation from weekly reporting by all family members of any violent incidents to the man's aunt or brother-in-law (conference 1), to a relative or other supporter of the woman moving into the household (conference 2), to the man moving to a friend's household (conference 3).

There are many other possible ways to intervene. For example, agreement might be reached on a restructuring of the family's bank accounts so that the woman is economically empowered to walk out if she faces more violence. The conference might agree that the man move out for a month and participate in a pro-feminist counselling programme (for evidence on the effectiveness of such programmes, see Dutton *et al.* 1992; for violent men's reactions to such programmes, see Ptacek 1988; Warters 1993). When conference intervention escalates to taking away the man's home and handing it over to his wife, some will object that this amounts to a six-figure fine, higher than the fine any court would impose after due process. But if the man feels an injustice is being done, he can walk away from the conference, allow his warrant(s) to be activated and face any punishment a criminal court may impose. Agreement at a conference to hand over a house is therefore viewed as a consensual civil remedy to the breakdown of a violent relationship rather than as a criminal punishment.

Contrast our regulatory pyramid with what a pro-arrest or mandatory arrest policy yields: routine perfunctory criminal justice processing. One problem with contemporary police practices, noted in Sherman (1992), is that the police tend not to process any differently cases of domestic violence that are the first or the most recent in a repeated pattern of violence. Thus, if the incident is judged not to have caused significant physical injury to the victim, it will be treated similarly, whether it is the first or fifteenth time an incident has been reported. The idea behind the enforcement pyramid is that intervention is responsive to patterns of offending, where communities of care monitor those patterns with state back-up.

Men who repeatedly batter may ultimately have to be removed from their homes or imprisoned. But to repeat perfunctory arrests while waiting for the victim's luck to run out, waiting for the day when her arrival in the hospital emergency room or the morgue will justify locking him up, is a deplorable policy. Equally, locking up all assailants is unworkable: there are too many for our prisons to accommodate. A policy based on the enforcement pyramid is more practical and more decent.

COMMUNITY CONFERENCES AND THE PYRAMID AS A RESPONSE

We propose that a response to men's violence against women which places a heavy, though not exclusive, reliance on community conferences, can address some of the failures in justice system responses. Let us consider each of the three problems.

Problem 1: Most men are not made accountable for acts of rape or violence against intimates. Women do not report rape or intimate violence because they feel ashamed and responsible for the violence; they fear family disintegration, physical reprisal, and being degraded in the courtroom. Institutionalising community conferences provides a means of exposing men's violence without re-victimising women. It is a route of crime control that is not dependent solely on the courage or tenacity of victims. The proposal is unreservedly for net-widening, except it is nets of community rather than state control that are widened. It is important that a court processing option is kept in place; indeed, the community conference option can be managed in such a way as to increase rather than reduce the number of prosecuted rape cases. How could this be?

When a woman is concerned with one or more of the above consequences of a criminal trial, she will not continue with the case. But she may be persuaded by police to go with the more private, quicker and less traumatic option of a community conference. At the same time, the police pressure the man to cooperate with the conference, proposing that he may do better and get the matter handled more quickly than if it goes to trial. The conference can proceed without any admission of guilt on the man's part, and he has the right to stop the conference at any point, insisting on his right to have the matters in dispute argued in court. The conference proceeds on the woman's allegations; the man may choose 'not to deny' the allegations, though initially he may decline to admit guilt. If the conference goes well, it might conclude with the man's admitting guilt and agreeing to sanctions that are less than a court would have imposed, yet more than an absence of sanctions, had the complaint been withdrawn. The empirical experience of New Zealand and Australian conferences is that defendants are mostly willing to admit guilt to secure the gentler justice of the conference in preference to the uncertain consequences of a criminal trial. If the conference goes badly (e.g., the man refuses to admit his guilt and nothing is settled), the support the woman receives at the conference might embolden her to press charges.

The availability of a community conference option can encourage more women to come forward and to be supported in their victimisation. It can also encourage many women who do report offences, but who do not want to proceed with criminal prosecution, to do something to confront the offender with responsibility for his wrongdoing at a conference. Whether by community conference or trial, increasing numbers of men would be made accountable for their violence against women.

Problem 2: The men who are arrested and prosecuted for violence against women have likely got away with it any number of times before and may well have entrenched patterns of raping and assaulting women. When we consider the callousness of some men prosecuted for rape, we may question the plausibility of affecting them through reasoned dialogue and shaming. Equally, we may question the plausibility of deterring them through prison sentences. The objective should be to intervene earlier in these men's lives before they have reached a hardened state. Evidence suggests that abusive men were violent towards family members such as sisters, brothers and mothers when they were young (Straus and Gelles 1990).[14]

In the New Zealand and Wagga Wagga juvenile programmes, the aim is to communicate shame to male adolescents for their very earliest acts of violence. When community conferences become well established, forums are made available to families and concerned citizens for bringing violence and exploitation to light at early stages. The psychologists who dominated criminological thinking until the 1950s were strong advocates of early intervention, a position discredited by 1960s labelling theorists. On balance, we should be pleased that early intervention driven by psycho-therapeutic models was defeated.

Republican criminology incorporates the labelling theory critique by calling for a radically different justification for and modality of early intervention: community intervention. One patriarchal legacy of labelling theory is a squeamishness about shaming, a 'boys will be boys' approach to violent masculinity. We must distinguish between harmful and productive early intervention. We can and must be early interveners again: we can use the power of shaming to avert patterns of exploitation and degradation of women. This power will be sustained and amplified by a strong women's movement and pro-feminist men's groups.

A conference at Wagga Wagga illustrates the potential for early intervention. It concerned a teenage boy's assault of a teenage girl. Out of the dialogue among participants, it was revealed that the boy had assaulted other girls and had viciously assaulted his mother. Australia has a major problem of teenage boys assaulting their mothers, although one would not know this from media accounts or the scholarly literature, which focus on spouse abuse. While there has been a 'breaking of the silence' with spouse assault, this has not occurred for son–mother assault. In a patriarchal culture, it is mothers not sons who feel shame and responsibility for these assaults. Traditional courts and justice system responses offer little chance to break the silence of maternal shame and maternal protectiveness of sons from a punitive justice system. A problem-solving dialogue among people who care for both victim and offender, such as occurred at this Wagga Wagga conference, offers a way to break the silence and to confront a violent boy before his patterns become entrenched.

Another recent Wagga Wagga conference concerned the sexual assault of a 14-year-old girl in a swimming pool by a 14-year-old boy. The victim was most upset by the way the boy had been bragging to his mates, within the victim's hearing, that he had 'got one finger in her'. The victim was not only re-victimised by this humiliation, but was also labelled as a 'dobber' (a 'tattle-tale') by boys at her school after she reported the incident. Gossip among her classmates was that she 'deserved what she got'. Dialogue at the conference clarified that this was not the case. It also made it impossible for the offender's father to believe, as he had before the conference, that his son had been singled out unfairly for a bit of 'horseplay'. Participants at the conference affirmed her 'courage' for coming forward in the face of such social pressures. The offender not only apologised to the victim in a meaningful way, but undertook, together with five other classmates (one male, four female) who attended the conference, to spread the word among their peers that her conduct was blameless in every respect, while he took responsibility for his totally unacceptable conduct. In this conference, an exploitative masculinity of 14-year-old boys and an excusing 'boys will be boys' fatherly masculinity was confronted by six teenagers and the parents of the victim. Our hypothesis is that this is a better way to confront a misogynist culture than a criminal trial ten years later.

Problem 3: Women victimised by men's violence are re-victimised by engaging in the criminal process. One reason rape victims are re-victimised at trial is that criminal trials are transacted in the discourse of stigma.[15] Winning is the objective, and each side tries to win through maximum efforts to blacken the adversary's character. The rape trial is a ceremony that puts a highly trained practitioner at the defendant's disposal to deny responsibility, to deny injury, and to deny the victim (we draw from Sykes and Matza's 1957 'techniques of neutralisation' formulation here and below). The rape trial institutionalises incentives for a defendant to reinforce his denials, denials which he believed before the trial, and denials that may have encouraged the rape in the first place (see, e.g., Scully and Marolla 1984, 1985). Faced with prosecutorial vilification of his character, the trained competence to exaggerate evil, the transforming of a partially flawed person into a demon devoid of any redemptive potential, the defendant is ever more equipped to condemn his condemners. If he started the criminal trial in a mood of moral ambivalence towards the victim, he may end up holding the victim and prosecution in utter contempt. The discourse of stigma in rape trials reinforces misogynist masculinities (see also Bumiller 1990 on this point). Even if a man is convicted and imprisoned, he will be released eventually, perhaps a more deeply committed and angry misogynist.

When fact-finding processes are allowed to stigmatise, disputants slide into a vortex of stigma: stigmatisation is mutually reinforcing. More generally, as Lewis (1971), Scheff (1987), Scheff and Retzinger (1991), and Lansky (1984, 1987) find, when human institutions are designed to foster the by-passing or denial of shame, shame–rage spirals are likely. Justice system procedures promote such spirals.

The community conference is based on different principles. It is designed to minimise stigma. Participants are selected based on their capacity to provide maximum support to victims and offenders, not as in criminal trials, to exert maximum damage to the other side. The aim of community conferences is to reintegrate victim and offender, not to stigmatise.

Compared to the offender-centred criminal trial, community conferences, if managed well, are victim-centred. The victim can confront the offender in her own words in her own way with all the hurt she has suffered, and victim supporters add more. Offenders often admit there were effects they denied or had not realised. The aim of the process is to confront the many techniques of neutralisation offenders use. It is to engage in an unconstrained dialogue that leaves responsibility as a fact that is admitted, regretted rather than denied.

Victim reintegration can be accomplished by sub-ceremonies following the formal conference. For example, at a conference concerning two boys who had assaulted a boy and girl, the girl said she did not want the offenders to come around to her house to offer a more formal apology because she was still afraid of them. The coordinator asked the girl's family to stay, and in a post-conference session, the coordinator discussed what had been said, suggesting that the boys would not come after her or the other victim again. This session ended with the girl agreeing she was no longer afraid. Later, a minister at the girl's church confirmed that the victim reintegration session helped to allay fears and distrusts the girl harboured up until the conference.

In contrast to the rape trial, from which a victim can emerge more afraid, frustrated at not having any degree of control, and suffering more reputation damage than the offender, community conferences are designed to empower victims with voice and control. Victims and their supporters have the right to veto the plan of action proposed by offenders and their supporters.

Conferences typically conclude with an apology by the offender. This is important for relieving the victim of any taint of blame. The apology can be a much more powerful ceremony than punishment in affirming moral values that have been transgressed, as the contrast between American and Japanese culture attests (Braithwaite 1989; Tavuchis 1991). When an offender rejects any suggestion that the victim may have been at fault and openly condemns the wrongfulness of the act, the censure of crime is reinforced and the cultural support for techniques of neutralisation is eroded.

One wonders how the Clarence Thomas hearings might have gone if American political culture would have allowed Anita Hill's allegations of sexual harassment to be handled in a community conference format. Would it not have been better for women if Thomas could have admitted his abusing Hill and apologised for his acts without his being stigmatised and professionally destroyed (Daly 1992)? If after he apologised and stated his commitment to upholding anti-discrimination law, Thomas was then appointed to the court, one wonders whether we would have had a less misogynist US Supreme Court.[16]

When institutions trade in stigma and rule out apology-forgiveness sequences as outcomes, forces of exploitation are uncensured, reinforced, and legitimated. The community conference strategy attempts to break the shame–rage spiral, to intervene early in transgressors' lives, and to reintegrate rather than stigmatise victims and offenders.

QUESTIONS ABOUT THE CONFERENCE-PYRAMID ENFORCEMENT MODEL

We are advocating an alternative way of responding to men's violence against women. We are not tied to a standard ordering of the pyramid levels, only to the preference for a dynamic problem-solving model. Although our arguments are meant to be suggestively sketched, there are vexing questions about the conference strategy that should be addressed.

Question 1: Is this just another form of mediation with all of its attendant problems?

Traditional mediation has been criticised for failing to take violence seriously, lacking procedural accountability, 'bar[ring] abused women from access to courts for enforceable protection' (Lerman 1984: 72), neutralising conflict by individualising and privatising grievances (Abel 1982), and failing to deal with the unequal bargaining power of the parties. Balance of power questions will be addressed under Question 2.

Community conferencing is not like family counselling and traditional victim–offender mediation. The participation of other community members on the basis of special relationships of care[17] for victims and offenders has a transformative effect on the nature of the interaction and on the agreed action plans. David Moore's research on the Wagga Wagga process (private communication with the authors) concludes that 'more is better' with regard to participants beyond the nuclear family, so long as they are participants who have a relationship of genuine caring with one of the principals.

We agree that traditional mediation hands unaccountable power to mediation professionals whose 'assumptions about the nature and seriousness of family violence' (Lerman 1984: 72) should be open to public scrutiny. We agree that it is wrong to bar women from access to courts for enforceable protection. Accountability to the courts should be guaranteed for both sides. Victims, like defendants, should have the right to withdraw from a conference and insist on activating an arrest warrant. Accountability to courts is not the most important accountability, however. Accountability to those citizens who have concern for victims and offenders is the more deeply democratic form of accountability (Barber 1984; Dryzek 1990). The traditional justice process 'steals conflicts' from citizens (Christie 1977), keeping victims and offenders apart. The community conference requires victims and offenders to confront their conflict, without neutralising their emotions.

We agree that traditional mediation risks a limited, privatised justice. Scutt (1988: 516) argues that privatisation of justice is detrimental to the interests of the disadvantaged when it 'shuts off from public view the very nature of the inequality from which the individual and group suffer' (see also Allen 1985; Hatty 1985). In contrast to mediation, conferences are designed to encourage community dialogue on intimate violence.

Private justice does risk rendering 'the personal apolitical' in the traditional dyadic form of offender and victim, mediated by a professional. Traditional public justice hardly does better in grappling with domination: it silences communities of concern by the disempowering roles of legal professionals (Snider 1990). The important question is not whether private or public justice is the bigger failure in communicating censure. It is how to redesign both, and the dynamic interplay between them, so that incidents of violence become occasions for community debates about brutalising masculinities and inequalities spawning violence.

Question 2: Can we expect 'communities of concern' to be any less sexist or misogynist than traditional justice system responses or state intervention?

Some will think it naïve that communitarian dialogue can work in places like Australia, where one-fifth of survey respondents agree that it is acceptable under some circumstances for a man to hit his wife (Public Policy Research Centre 1988). It is not naïve precisely because four-fifths do not find such violence acceptable. The problem is that one-fifth are able to erect walls around the private space of the family to protect themselves from the disapproval of the four-fifths. Even if many of these four-fifths 'condemn wife beating, and yet at the same time actively support the type of marital relationship that encourages it' (Dobash and Dobash 1979: 179), at least their condemnation can be harnessed in conferences.

Voices in defence of exploitation and brutality will be heard in community conferences. But exploitation and brutality flourish more in secretive settings, when they go unchallenged and unnoticed (Hopkins and McGregor 1991: 127). When intimate violence is noticed and challenged, rationalisations sustained in secret settings are opened to dialogue. It would not be possible to have regulatory institutions where only feminist voices were heard and misogynist voices were completely silenced. However, dialogic institutions favour parties who are on the moral high ground, and feminists are clearly on the high ground. So we suspect that conferences can create spaces to advance struggles for feminist voices to be heard against those of misogynists.

As a flexible process of community empowerment, conferences permit more latitude for redressing power imbalances than the inflexible procedures of the court. Balance can be restored by the collective might of a victim's supporters (as in the case of the Wagga Wagga teenagers who supported their friend after she was sexually assaulted). It can be restored by powerful men, for example, a doctor, a brother, an uncle, a teacher, a neighbour, who subscribe to an anti-violent masculinity and who are more than a match for a domineering husband. Women can create institutions that give male allies a chance to show their mettle. Power imbalance can be most effectively restored by organised feminists who work as shelter advocates. Here, one strength of our proposal is that a shift in resources from police lock-ups to shelters can provide a base for feminist organisation. Improved criminal justice institutions are no substitute for a stronger women's movement as the keystone to controlling violence against women. In the meantime, we can design criminal justice institutions to enfranchise voices from the women's movement, coupled with those of abused women and caring men.

Conference coordinators need training to be effective in organising conferences that are responsive to men's violence against women. Training could include speakers from the women's movement and shelters, and role playing of conference scenarios subject to feminist interpretations. Coordinators can readily be required to hear feminist voices during in-service training, while it may take longer to require judges to do so.

Question 3: Do conferences work? Are participants satisfied?

Evaluation of conferences for juvenile cases in New Zealand (Maxwell and Morris 1993; Morris and Maxwell 1991) suggests 'there is much that is positive and novel about [this] system of youth justice' (Morris and Maxwell 1991: 88), including the diversion of most juveniles away from courts and institutions, involvement of families in decisions and taking responsibility and acknowledgment of differences in cultural groups. The authors cite these problems, however: professionals often took over the process; adolescent offenders often did not feel involved; and just half of victims said they were satisfied with the outcome. Levels of satisfaction with conference outcomes were substantially higher for offenders and family members (85 percent) than for victims (51 percent) (Maxwell and Morris 1993: 115–20). Victim dissatisfaction was explained by 'inadequate conference preparation . . . about what to expect . . . and unrealistic expectations [for] likely . . . outcomes, especially with respect to reparation' (Morris and Maxwell 1991: 86). More research is needed and more is under way. In particular, we need methodologically sound outcome evaluations (from both juvenile and adult samples) on whether violence falls following conferences more than it does following criminal trials.

We do not wish to hide implementation failures of conferences in New Zealand or Wagga Wagga or the difficulties of struggling against domination and stigma, nor would we suggest that conferences are a panacea even when perfectly implemented. We are suggesting that community conferences open an avenue for addressing the failures of contemporary justice processes which leave misogynist masculinities untouched by shame and victims scarred by blame.

CONCLUSIONS

Men's violence against women is a crime enabled by men's domination (Daly and Wilson 1988; Dobash and Dobash 1979; Evason 1982; Yllo and Straus 1990). Republican and feminist theory (Braithwaite 1991, 1993; Yllo and Bograd 1988; MacKinnon 1983) argue that a reduction in men's violence towards women will occur when gender inequality is reduced and when human social bonds are more caring. There are many ways of causing cracks in patriarchal structures that have barely been discussed here. Among the most central are transforming economic power, familial and sexual relations towards greater gender equity and strengthening the political power of the women's movement and pro-feminist elements in other liberation movements.

Contemporary criminal justice practices may do more to cement over cracks in patriarchal structures than prise them open. Current practices leave patriarchal masculinities untouched and victims more degraded and defeated; and to continue with more of the same policies may make things worse. This is not to deny a role for the criminalisation of violence and state intervention of the kind envisaged in the enforcement pyramid.

We have proposed an alternative way of thinking about responding to men's violence against women that is based on these ideas: (1) the threat of escalated state intervention (formalism) can empower more effective communitarian intervention (informalism); (2) ceremonies can centre on reintegrative shaming of offenders and reintegrative caring for victims; (3) communities of care can devise their own preventive strategies, and can be motivated to implement them by their affection and attachment to particular victims and offenders; and (4) dialogue can be sustained within communities of care about the rejection of violent masculinities and, more optimistically, about the search for non-violent masculinities. While non-exploitative masculinities have the potential to emerge in community conferences, their expression is largely foreclosed in courtrooms and prisons. The creation of institutions that require men to listen to women and open spaces for apology and dialogue might clear the way for a collective wisdom to emerge. That communal wisdom may re-define masculinities beyond the wit of our individual imaginings. Though it may not be possible to design criminal justice institutions that prevent violence, we can fashion institutions that generate less violence.

NOTES

1   Thanks to Susan Brennan for research assistance and to Lawrence Sherman and Iris Young for helpful comments on the paper.
2   Our remarks centre on expressions of hetero-masculinity. We note, for example, that men's caring and compassionate responses towards other men have been recently evidenced in response to AIDS. For an early review and critique of the 'men's studies' literature, see Carrigan *et al.* (1985), and more recently, Connell (1987).
3   Statistics for rape arrests and convictions are clearer than those for domestic assaults for several reasons. Domestic assaults are a sub-set of assaults, and researchers have focused more on police than court actions (see Ferraro and Boychuck 1992 for an exception). In the US, rates of reporting rape to the police vary by victim–offender relation (Williams 1984) and whether women viewed the incident as 'rape' (Estrich 1986: 1164–8). Rates of report vary from 7 to 30 per cent (for known and stranger, respectively, Russell 1984) to 50 per cent (National Crime Surveys). Some 20 to 32 per cent of arrests for rape lead to conviction; these percentages are similar to other violent offences and are not unique to rape (Estrich 1986: 1161–71).
4   The same facts cause not only the failure of rehabilitation, but the failure of deterrence and incapacitation as well. Deterrence fails in the face of these long histories of offending followed by non-conviction. Incapacitation fails for the string of victims prior to the first conviction, for the men in prison who are raped by those who have learnt to dominate the vulnerable and for the women who suffer post-release violence at the hands of men who emerge from the degradation of prison with a deepened hatred of women. Even under the toughest of incapacitative regimes in the Western world, for example the incarceration of men convicted of rape in the US, the incapacitation is very partial. In the US, 90 per cent of rape convictions lead to incarceration; of those receiving prison sentences, the average sentence length is twelve years (Bureau of Justice Statistics 1987: 8, 16). A man in prison from age 20 to age 32 can victimise a lot of women in his teens, forties and beyond.

5   For a more detailed description of New Zealand's youth justice system and the relationships among police, court, and FGC, see Maxwell and Morris (1993: Chapter 1).

6   Except when we discuss men's abuse of women, we shall not assume a generic 'he' for the offender or 'she' for victim.

7   The variety of modalities of implementation is dazzling in the states of New South Wales, South Australia, Western Australia, Victoria and the Australian Capital Territory. Some programmes are coordinated by the police, others by state welfare departments (as in New Zealand), others by the Juvenile Court, others by Aboriginal elders. Some are pre-court diversionary initiatives; others involve courts using conferences as an alternative to traditional sentencing. These programmes have varying success at empowering victims. At this point the Wagga Wagga model seems to stand out as a success story on victim participation and empowerment.

8   Republican theory requires unbreachable upper limits on any discretionary exercise of the power to punish. It is opposed to any constraining minimum levels of punishment, however (Braithwaite and Pettit 1990).

9   That is, the police for the moment choose to use their discretion not to activate the warrant, even in the presence of the alleged offender. This may require law reform to render the activation of warrants discretionary.

10 In the Charlotte replication (Hirschel *et al.* 1990), one condition was citation. This meant issuing a citation to the offender, usually in the presence of the victim, which the offender signed. The couple was advised of a court date, although the victim was not asked if she wished to go to court. Citation increased subsequent violence about as much as did arrest. Citation is more like arrest than the arrest warrant we propose because of its non-discretionary channelling of the case onto a courtroom track.

11 We recognise that for some men, an arrest warrant (like a restraining or protection order) will be merely viewed as a 'piece of paper' (Chaudhuri and Daly 1992), especially for men who have been arrested before. When this is true, the remedy is escalation up the pyramid. Note also a key difference between a criminal arrest warrant and a civil restraining order. The restraining order enables escalation to enforcement action in the face of further misconduct; the arrest warrant enables prosecution for the violence that has already occurred in addition to enforcement directed at the further misconduct.

12 Another relevant empirical finding that justifies a preference for the dialogue of the conference before any further escalation is from the Milwaukee experiment. Arrestees who said (in lock-up) that police had not taken the time to listen to their side of the story were 36 per cent more likely to be reported for assaulting the same victim over the next six months than those who said the police had listened to them (Bridgeforth 1990: 76; Sherman 1993).

13 Dobash and Dobash (1992: 203) point out that an important, but

'rarely noted' finding from the original Minneapolis experiment 'is that arrest was most effective when police officers established an alliance with the victim (in the eyes of the victim) where . . . she could threaten the offender more credibly in the future with a call to the police' (citing Berk and Sherman 1985).

14 While men's violence towards women may be learned and practised in families at an early age, we should not ignore the many developmental sites of masculine violence spawned outside familial contents. These include violent sports, the military and juvenile institutions.

15 Proof of a victim's 'non-consent' in rape trials places a higher burden on prosecutors than convictions for other violent crimes, however (MacKinnon 1983; Estrich 1986; Smart 1989).

16 Reactions to Daly's (1992) ideas were mixed. Most feminists found that an apology was insufficient; almost all believed that because the sexual harassment took place while Thomas was the head of the Equal Employment Opportunity Commission, this alone precluded him from being a Justice. Men, both pro-feminist and otherwise, were somewhat more receptive. Gender- and race-based divisions are essential to consider in these contexts (see, e.g., Morrison 1992; The Black Scholar 1992).

17 Unlike People's Courts in Cuba or China, where community engagement is based on stigmatisation and humiliation, the community conference is based on special relationships of care.

Chapter 12

Boys keep swinging
Masculinity and football culture in England

John Williams and Rogan Taylor

If you want to know a man,
if you find him excellent,
why you've got to have something to do together
    Williams Carlos Williams, 'A Voyage to Pagany'

INTRODUCTION

In this chapter we want to try to say something about the changing ways in which football in England works as a form of 'deep play'; 'a story people tell themselves about themselves' (Geertz 1972). More especially, we want to consider the extent to which shifts in football culture and styles of playing and presenting the game reflect, and have helped to reinforce, wider changes in the patterning of relationships, particularly among working-class men, as well as the nature and forms of expression of working-class masculine styles (Critcher 1991). In this sense, we take it as read that, 'if gender is cultural and social, then it is also historical. . . . There is no universal masculinity, but rather a varying masculine experience of each succeeding social epoch' (Tolson 1977: 13).

We will try to make our case by saying something about the game itself and, briefly, about its pre-war history in England (for accounts on football in Scotland, see Jarvie and Walker 1994). We, then, consider the changing post-war face of playing and spectating styles in the English game. We do this, firstly, through a reading of media accounts of the death, in February 1993, of Bobby Moore, the captain of the 1966 England World Cup-winning team, and, secondly, via some observations on recent academic and 'popular' debates about masculinity and spectator behaviour in English football.

IT'S A MAN'S WORLD . . .

Let us begin by making clear that in our view there is nothing intrinsic to football as a sport that excludes women from the enjoyment of watching, or indeed playing, the game (See Williams and Woodhouse 1991). As a visual spectacle which frequently includes high drama and intense emotional arousal it is, in principle, attractive to anyone disposed to attend such *divertissements*. Displays of exceptional skill, mental sharpness, physical strength and courage, played out within the context of a struggle for supremacy between powerful opposing forces are the very stuff of communal 'entertainment' in human societies. Indeed, such spectacles often have their ancient roots in demonstrations of power and endurance designed to illustrate the performer's intimacy with religious or spiritual forces (Taylor 1985).

Nonetheless, football – like many other sports, in England at least – is invariably described and largely understood to be 'a man's game'. Hornby (1992: 22), for example, recalls the 'simply incalculable' cultural capital bestowed upon English schoolboys by a knowledge and enjoyment of football. Masculinity, for Tolson, becomes gradually institutionalised in young boys as an explicit system of taboos, recognition of status and a complex boyhood culture of mutual challenge communicated via a 'masculine language which prescribes certain topics (sports, machines, competitions) and certain ways of speaking (jokes, banter and bravado)' (1977: 32). In many accounts, sport is reduced to a kind of subtle and ubiquitous male language; a bond between husbands. Wives have their own world of neighbours and relatives. Women run the family; men have their Saturday sport (Holt 1989: 178). British media discourses on sport condense the oppositions of expert/novice and male/female, with the implicit assumption being one of male expertise and female ignorance. Four fifths of all television sports programmes contain no women's sport. (Whannel 1992: 89). Women attending or expressing an interest in sports such as football invite censure or constraint both from men (Woodhouse 1991; Williams and Woodhouse 1991; Rowlings 1992) and from women (Davies 1992: 174). As Whannel argues, 'There is a close fit between sport and masculinity; each is a part of the other, so that prowess in sport seems to be, and is seen as, the completion of a young boy's masculinity' (1992: 126). For girls and women, by way of contrast, to be interested or successful especially in 'masculine' sports is to fail as a woman because in certain symbolic ways they 'become' men (Willis 1982).

However, it is clear that the extent and form of the gendering of sports such as football is, of course, culturally prescribed. In some Scandinavian countries, for example, female players outnumber their male counterparts (Williams and Woodhouse 1991). In the USA, 'soccer' is a major college sport for young women and for mixed-sex play among younger people. Women in Italy watch – and play – football in large numbers and are members of the fanatical 'Ultras' fan groups. (Bromberger 1990). As the game's popularity grows in Africa, so too, does the enthusiasm of its female fans who, grouped together, took an active part in the music making, singing and dancing that invariably accompanied matches during the 1992 African Nations Championships in Senegal (Taylor 1992a). This occasion seemed to be available to the whole community, with a wide range of people present, their numbers limited only (though substantially) by their inability to reach the stadium or buy a ticket. Support for the English national team at home and abroad is, of course, by contrast, heavily and prohibitively masculinised, chauvinistic and aggressive (Williams *et al.* 1989; Williams and Goldberg 1990).

MAKING SPORTING HISTORIES

We have dealt elsewhere with something of the experience girls had of sport in Victorian England (Williams and Woodhouse 1991). The Victorian public school, however, was the forcing house of a new kind of English masculinity which focused on the physical and moral characteristics of the loyal, brave and active man – the natural counterpart to the spiritual, sensitive and vulnerable woman; the ideal partners for the new standards of psychological and social normality based around the nuclear family and the new emerging forms of sexual division of labour (Weeks 1981, 38–40). Sport was the fulcrum of this newly 'civilised' masculinity, promoting, as it did, the cohesiveness of the team effort and the sanctity of 'fair play' in creative tension with the ideology of competition. As Holt (1989: 97) points out, work and sport were mutually reinforcing: man does, woman is;

or, in the words of John Berger 'men act and women appear' (1972: 47).

Organised sport – if not the fair play ethic of the public schools – came to have a central place in the new world of urban male working-class industrial culture. Charitable and religious bodies, promoting the muscular Christianity of the public schools and the temperance of social reformers, played their part in the spread of team games, especially football, but the clubs, pubs and factory associations of working men were much more significant in their effects (Holt 1989: 150). The professional game developed espec- ially vigorously in the industrial towns and cities of Lancashire, the Midlands and Scotland. The new professional clubs revealed a special power in creating bonds of territory, identity and solidarity – new forms of 'neighbourhood nationalism' (Cohen 1988: 33) – amongst the working-class men who, mainly, supported them. 'The match', for those who remember older, rural forms of sport helped to fill the vacuum left by the passing of the often violent and disorderly festivals and traditions which were difficult to import into city life. Despite the violence, drinking and gambling which seemed to be regular occurrences around the staging of early professional football matches, especially those between local rivals (Dunning *et al.* 1988), women clearly did attend and, at particular clubs, in some numbers (Mason 1980: 152). In the main, however, organised football provided a rite of passage for males – a bridge – between the world of working-class juvenile street gangs and street play and the associated struggles over 'who rules the streets' (Cohen 1976) and the tutelage and informal social controls provided by an adult male world of work and leisure in which,

> 'boys learned how to drink and tell jokes as well as the language of physical aggression. . . . Football clubs were only a part of the wider process of male socialisation which took place in the workplace, the pub and the world of hobbies.
>
> (Holt 1988: 73)

New football grounds sprung up at an astonishing rate in the early years of the new century. In contrast to the opposition to new grounds today, so powerful and popular was the new professional football and so prestigious to a local municipality was the siting of a new ground that clubs were able to monopolise some of the prime open land which might otherwise have remained or become private property. As Simon Inglis points out:

A football ground was in many ways as much part of a
burgeoning corporation as a public library, town hall and law
courts, and was certainly used by more people. Furthermore, a
football ground was often the only place in a town outsiders
would visit.

(Inglis 1983: 12)

The civic pride invested in clubs and their stadia, was cemented, in
the main, by highly localised forms of funding and control (Clarke
1992). This helped, at the match, to regulate and contain survivals
of the 'rough' behavioural ethic within a social structure
increasingly characterised by the virtues of self restraint and
respectability and by the sorts of 'spiritual' provision – 'free'
municipal baths; libraries; playing fields; museums and art
galleries – which local capital regarded as its propitious and
bounden duty to provide so as to sustain moral and social cohesion
(Richards 1990).

The precise forms of this cohesion for working-class men – its
heavy localism, solidarity and defensive conformity; its focus on
hardness and maleness rather than more formal and institutionalised 'middle class' notions of toughness and manliness –
helped to shape, and was reflected in, football playing styles. If
aggression is the universal currency of working-class male relationships and, 'aggression is the basis of "style", of feeling physical, of
showing feelings and protecting oneself . . . a kind of performance'
(Tolson 1977: 43), then local symbolic representatives of
working-class masculinity – the traditional/located professional
footballer, prior to the lifting of the maximum wage – seemed
tailor-made to the task (Critcher 1991). As Wagg (1984: 62–3)
argues, the ideology of playing football before the war was that
players were in a tough sport and should be prepared to play it
hard to win. Few would have suggested that 'robust tactics' were an
inevitable part of professionalism; it was more part of their gender
than their jobs. Anyone who shrank from this required standard
placed ominous question marks against his masculinity. Stan
Cullis, a celebrated 'hard man' from the pre-war era, later recalled
his interview in 1934 by Major Buckley, the reputable disciplin-
arian manager of Wolverhampton Wanderers. It provides an
interesting window into playing styles, generational relationships
and manager–player relations of the time.

He [Buckley] looked me up and down as I imagine a bloodstock owner would look at a racehorse. He said, 'Stand up.' He tapped me on the chest. . . . He said, 'Are you frightened?' I said, 'Of what?' He said, 'Of getting hurt?' I said, 'No.' That was all he said to me. He had some words with my father, which I couldn't hear, and I was a professional footballer.

(Quoted in Hopcraft 1968: 25)

Football playing styles also mirrored wider working-class male solidarities, perhaps especially those forged in, and associated with, the industrial heartlands of Britain. There was no room here for 'fancy dans' or indeed, for the deviousness and dishonesty associated more in the minds of the chauvinist English with the 'feminised' foreign traditions of playing the game. (The FA refused to join FIFA on a permanent basis until after the Second World War or to play in the World Cup until 1950.) However, the fair play ethic of the public schools and 'limits of decent partisanship' were only for those who could afford it; the English football pro was expected to deal with 'trouble' in ways which demonstrated traditional working-class masculine ideals of self sufficiency and straight-forwardness. Recalling his own, brief, playing career in the 1950s, Derek Dooley a 'hard' English centre forward, typically said of pro players of the late 1960s, 'I think players should accept a bit of boot. Nowadays, a bloke gets knocked and he turns around and he's got someone around the throat. In the old days he'd just say, "Right, I'll get him next time!"' (Quoted in Hopcraft 1968: 56). Working men who were, in the main, the bulk of the football audience, wanted from their players, generally, what they expected from their male friends at work in the pub and on the street.

Football was a celebration of intensely male values; 'grit' was the great virtue in the north especially, but there was also sticking at the task, persisting and never letting your mates down even if you were injured or dropping with tiredness. Football was a saga in which skill and cunning were valued, but, hardness, stamina, courage and loyalty were even more important.

(Holt 1989: 173)

SOMETHING'S HAPPENING HERE . . .

In general terms, the standards and style of masculinity displayed by the 'workers' on the pitch were mirrored in and reinforced those celebrated by working men on the terraces during the long run period of the increasing 'respectablisation' of the game (Dunning *et al.* 1988). Spectator culture, especially in the cheap areas, was harsh, frequently crude, but was generally controlled. In Scotland, the story was made more complex by the violent sectarianism which continued to be expressed at football, primarily via support for the major Glasgow clubs (See Murray 1984). The first decade after the Second World War produced, in England, groaning grounds, record crowds, a minimal police presence and, by modern standards, exemplary levels of self policing and internal discipline on what were packed and often ill-equipped terraces. There was no segregation, little violence and, miraculously, but one serious spectator tragedy, at Bolton in 1946 (Williams 1991: 163–5).

The role and place of female fans in post-war football culture, remained largely subordinate and submerged (see Williams and Woodhouse 1991). Before the war, 'Ladies committees' sometimes drew thanks from clubs for their fundraising efforts (Fishwick 1989: 44). In 1948, the 'Ladies section' at Torquay United raised £1000, bought a house with the money and gave it to the club for the use of incoming players (*Sports Weekly* 21.8.1948: 15). Women were poorly represented in supporters' groups and, perhaps not surprisingly, 'women's issues' in relation to football very rarely broke the surface of public debate about the game and its fans. When the subject of women's toilets at grounds was raised at the 1961 AGM of the National Federation of Football Supporters' Clubs, for example, the Chairman cut short any debate claiming it was 'not a pleasant matter' (NFFSC AGM Minutes 1961, see Taylor 1992b). Large sections of some league grounds remained without toilet facilities and, therefore, effectively off-limits to women at least into the late 1980s. Indicative, too of the conservative Federation's attitude towards women fans was its running from 1955 onwards of a National Football Queen competition. The competition was unsuccessfully opposed by female fans from Tottenham but, in 1960, the retiring Federation Secretary, Leslie Davis, urged football husbands, 'If you are a proud possessor of a wife who will ultimately become the Football Queen, you will be on velvet from that day until you die' (NFFSC AGM Minutes 1960, see Taylor 1992b).

A major shift in styles of football support and in the masculine codes which were prominent and celebrated at football and elsewhere began to occur slowly, but overtly, in the mid-1950s. The greater cultural, social and financial independence of working-class male youth encouraged regularised away travel in numbers and significant segregation by age inside and en route to grounds, really, for the first time. Football 'special' trains began to suffer substantial and regular damage. Disorderly young fans, and especially the youth 'ends' which began to become established over the next decade drawing their distinctive identities from aspects of the expanding teenage leisure industry, attracted mushrooming media coverage and public censure. The new leisure markets; the spread of car and TV ownership; the privatisation of consumption; anxieties about the new youth hooliganism; and the slowly growing power of women – these all chipped away at the 'organic' links which had ritually tied 'respectable' working-class men to their local clubs. As wages rose for top players, their links with 'ordinary' fans also gave way to the attractions and increasing demands of celebrity culture (See Wagg 1984). These conditions, and the myth-making associated with the deaths of the 'Busby Babes' in an air crash at Munich in 1958 contributed towards making Manchester United the first English club to attract effective and active non-local football support. Fifteen years later, the club's nationally drawn hooligan following temporarily eclipsed all competitors too.

A key, symbolic moment in the generation of public concern about the growing hooligan problem was the staging of the World Cup Finals in England in 1966 under the full and intrusive glare of the world's media. As it turned out, the Finals passed without major spectator unrest. It was the last time for twenty-five years that a major football championship involving England in Europe would do so (see Williams and Goldberg 1990; Ward 1989; Williams and Goldberg 1991; Buford 1991; Williams 1992). After thirty years of routinised, sometimes calamitous, fan disorder, it has finally been decided that England will be ready to stage a major football championship.

Arguably, the central English icon from these last hooligan-free Finals was the England captain, Bobby Moore. In character and style Moore captures some of the key shifts in the playing and lifestyles of top footballers in the early post-maximum-wage era. His recent, early death has also provided considerable scope for the British media to play off images of Moore against more recent developments in the game and in British society more generally. He stands, in these accounts, as a symbol of more 'innocent' and successful times and of lost opportunities. We want to use the coverage of Moore's death to try better to focus on changes in the game and its audience over the past thirty years.

THE DEATH OF A GOLDEN ENGLISHMAN

The death of England World Cup winning captain, Bobby Moore, from cancer at the age of 51 on 24 February 1993 was widely interpreted and reported by the British news media as symbolic of the passing, not just of an era of past sporting success, but also of a particular kind of masculine sporting identity and even of the corruscating decline of Britain itself. Contrasting Moore with Arsenal's Tony Adams, the man who occasionally wears Moore's England shirt and who had recently suffered both a stay in prison and injury from a serious nightclub 'fall', the *Daily Mail* (3.3.1993) commented, 'Bobby Moore's sad and premature death, coming at such a turbulent time, has become a symbol of the decline of the entire country.'

Moore's untimely death undoubtedly caused less soul mining in, say, Scotland than it did south of the border, and the loss of 'England's' hero, a gentle giant, a great Englishman, provided opportunities for claims that, 'Sport . . . has become one of the few areas where an uncomplicated celebration of Englishness is possible' (*Independent* 23.2.1993). Nevertheless, in sport, as in other social and cultural domains, constructions of collective identity serve to sustain relations of dominance in British society, in gender, class and national terms and for English sports commentators at least, English and British identities are frequently presumed to be identical (Blain *et al.* 1993).

But, why was Moore's death seen to carry such gravely symbolic weight? For one thing, football is supposed, along with parliamentary democracy, to have been England's gift to the world, and as Britain declined economically and shed its empire, so for the popular press the England football team has increasingly been seen as a metaphor for the nation itself (Wagg 1991: 222). For another, the game continues, even in the post-Thatcher 1990s, passionately and obstinately to reach aspects of the human social condition and its relation to locality and place which cannot be fulfilled in private life or in ritualised public consumption (Taylor 1991: 6). In fact, 'one of the mysteries about football is the depth of the need it seems to fill' (see Lanchester 1989).

The timing of his passing was obviously crucial, too. His death occurred only weeks after the killing of two-year-old James Bulger in Bootle on Merseyside and during a period of widespread public unease about the alleged 'lawlessness' spreading among juveniles on threadbare council estates around the country, about 'an age of moral nullity and barbarism, where cruelty and abuse and even murder are classed by some among us as forms of self satisfaction' (*Sunday Telegraph*, 28.2.1993). It was used as an occasion for a rallying cry for wider moral reconstitution by, among others, Labour MP, Frank Field, who asserted that, 'Britain has lost, in Bobby Moore, a symbol of all that is good in life, and the murder of James Bulger has registered a growing presence of evil'. Field called for children to be taught the 'Bobby Moore morality' to counter the 'armies of louts' who today, 'spit and swear their way through life' (*Sunday Express*, 28.2.1993). Never slow to appropriate popular national heroes, the *Sun* later wondered at how, during a minute's silence for Moore at a West Ham match, 'In an age of disrespect, even the yobs stay silent for our Bobby' (1.3.1993).

Also, Moore, from Barking in Essex, was still a relatively young man when he died. Press photographs of the player in his prime recall an untroubled and dominating figure – a man and a symbol from an age yet to be consigned to the history books. Many of today's fans remember seeing Moore play: the 1966 World Cup Final was the first to be captured on a colour print. Moore, therefore, while in his attitudes and values a product of the 1950s, was profoundly a modern footballer of the post-ration book era of social reconstruction after the war; an era when 'the cloth cap and the wooden rattle had gone for good', and when new patterns of working-class cultural consumption had re-ordered footballing loyalties in ways which by the early 1960s had made 'going to the match', as Richard Williams put it, 'as much a part of a smart Saturday as buying a new Ben Sherman button-down or checking out the latest Otis Redding single' (*Independent on Sunday*, 28.2.1993).

According to this view, Moore epitomised a new kind of working-class male cultural hero – part prosperous business executive; part consummate and controlled athlete (a wise innocent, criticised in the north for his southern lack of traditional 'hardness', and once even presented with a handbag by a Scottish fan at Hampden Park); and part media celebrity, equally at ease among the cocktails and comedians as he was imperiously organising the nation's last line of football defence. In fact, of course, Moore was never quite a popular footballing hero on the terraces. His apparent aloofness and style meant he lacked the 'die for the club' qualities prized by many young male fans. He would never threaten to 'chin' opposing 'hard cases', no matter how hard his followers might have wished it (Hobbs 1993). Nor did Moore have the dangerous and irreverent skill of the celebrated forwards.

However, as Janet Daley points out, what is noteworthy about images of Moore and his colleagues in the 1966 World Cup squad is that: 'By today's standards, they look scarcely working class at all. Well-groomed and utterly respectable, they seemed more like the products of a semi-detached suburban existence than a backstreet urban one' (*The Times* 26.2.1993). The image presented here is one of a society, a sport and of a class, confident in itself and its sense of future purpose; its members bound on the upwardly mobile option and set to banish, apparently for all time, the brutishness of older codes and of deprivation and class division. Moore's death, as one broadsheet put it recently, 'is a reminder of a time when pessimism seemed to have been uninvented' (*Independent on Sunday*, 28.2.1993).

Ironically, of course, far from resolving class tensions the new commercialism which was growing in and around the game, served only to feed into wider structural uncertainties, particularly in England in the 1970s and 1980s, about class, gender and place identities. These new developments helped to re-order and intensify more traditional forms of, sometimes violent, football support (Dunning *et al.* 1988). Hargreaves (1986: 106) points to the way in which the ideological role of modern sports, perhaps especially football, is to preserve and restate 'conservative' ideals of masculinity and class against the backcloth of a socio-historical context – the dislocating effects of home centredness and consumerism – which have effectively displaced notions of what it is to be male and working class. In this sense, according to Critcher (1991: 83) modern football and its style may be seen as an index of cultural uncertainty. Taylor (1987) argues that the recent violence by English fans abroad is the product of an upwardly mobile and 'detached' fraction of the 'Thatcherised' working class which has a certain residual solidarity born of neighbourhood and gender, but it is generally individualistic, chauvinistic and racist. Jeremy

Seabrook claims that the widespread hooliganism at football in the 1970s and 1980s – the real brutishness in post-war British football spectator culture – should be read as an example of the sorts of 'surrogate and distorted solidarities' which have taken the place of older working-class masculine forms; a form of 'sublimated memory of forfeited identity' (*Guardian* 3.6.1985). In a connected vein, Buford (1991: 264–5) describes recent hooligan forms as 'a more exaggerated, ornate version of an ancient style, more extreme because now without substance. . . . It is only style. . . . It is lad culture without mystery, so deadened that it uses violence to wake itself up'. Seabrook continues:

> What is clear is that the identity of the manufacturing centres of Britain, the function to which they owe their very existence, has been severely eroded in the past few decades. And, the passionate feelings which have crystallised around football teams in these places are in large part the most conspicuous popular reaction against the injured sense of place. They represent a symbolic resistance against the disgracing of the regional and the local, against the delayed industrial function whereby each district was identified with the making or production of tangible, necessary things.
>
> (*Guardian* 3.6.1985)

In the 1980s, as secure employment and the establishment of identity through work and connected networks became more uncertain, so 'style' – a 'community of taste' – became of increasing significance (Hebdige 1992: 355). The celebrated football 'casuals', for example, in their appropriation of the signs of 'quality' and 'distinction' signalled their refusal to be excluded from the 'good life' or from the new 'sophisticated' hooligan rivalries. Casual fashions euphemised joblessness or irregular employment by converting 'casual' work in the hidden economy into a comfortable and affluent 'casual' style. They swapped the leisure of enforced idleness for a life of leisure and for the class-conspicuous hierarchies of violence and conspicuous consumption (Frith 1990: 179; Hobbs and Robins 1991: 566). More prosaically, perhaps, Hornby (1992: 54) convincingly describes the contradictory attractions of hooligan cultures and styles to 'non-hooligan' fans, producing, as it does, fear and bluster in almost equal measure and, for a fatherless 15-year-old, 'a quick way to fill a previously empty trolley in the masculinity supermarket' (Hornby 1992: 80).

APPROPRIATING MYTHS

As with all mythologised views of some heroic 'golden age', closer inspection inevitably reveals a rather more equivocal picture of the life and times of a lost England football captain. For example, 1966 remains in the mind not only for World Cup success but also for public sector pay freezes, the Krays, the tragedy of Aberfan and for the Moors murders. Press commentaries of the time talked of a nation which had 'lost its pride and confidence'; a nation in which 'envy and mass bribery are the currency of domestic politics' (quoted in *Sunday Telegraph* 28.2.1993). Nor was footballing success simply a question, nicely gendered, of, 'clean, white shirts, family loyalties and the kind of behaviour which would not put your mother to shame' (*The Times* 26.2.1993). Hooliganism was already beginning to cloud football's still outwardly sunny horizon (Dunning *et al.* 1988: 157–64).

On the pitch, attitudes were hardening, too. During the opening matches of the World Cup itself, Nobby Stiles, the carrier of rather longer-standing and more deep-rooted masculine values in the British game, which now seemed to be becoming more openly instrumental in their use, illegally 'disposed' of the French forward, Simon. The patrician Corinthians of the Football Association (See Tomlinson 1991) wanted Stiles withdrawn from the rest of the tournament. The manager, the cautious and pragmatic exponent of the 'new professionalism', Alf Ramsey, would have none of it. Stiles would be needed to battle it out against Argentina; the Latins were simply 'animals' according to his manager.

Moore himself was also not quite the club loyalist and 'perfect professional' he became in later accounts. In the highly understated and deeply masculine discourses of the changing room and sports desk, Moore 'liked a drink', and his club manager had once threatened him with banishment after the breaking of curfew on the night before an important FA Cup tie. Moore also tried, strenuously, to leave his local club, West Ham, and was denied by uncompromising management rather than, as recounted later, by any overriding sense of local attachment and loyalty (see Keating 1993). By the 1990s, of course, top players moved almost at will and to wherever the best offers came.

After his playing career was over, and following failures in football management and business, Moore casually sold the mantle of 'ex-England World Cup winning captain' to the back page of the 'tits and football' *Sunday Sport*, owned by porn entrepreneur, David Sullivan. The *Sport*, an ugly parody even of the British tabloid press of the late 1980s, is, nevertheless, a vehicle which nicely encapsulates the news values in tabloid discourses about sport and also the ways in which sports' cultures have been and remain, rooted in masculine values and patriarchal exclusiveness (Williams and Woodhouse 1991: 85–8; Whannel 1992: 31). But there are also harsher textures revealed here which underpin the modern relationship between sport and male discourses about women. Aggressively sexist banter and chants, for example, are now commonplace among young male fans. Women fans attending matches must prepare for harassment and sometimes worse (Williams 1987; Woodhouse 1991). Young men – 'pulling machines' – aggressively out 'on the hunt' in city nightclubs, predictably use the lexicon of football to describe their easy and mechanical success with seaside female 'talent' – 'like the Football League season, picking up points, week in week out'-and the greater challenges of provincial nightlife locations – 'Tonight's like the FA Cup: 90 minutes of do or die' (*Independent* 11.12.1992). Today's 'male talk' about sexual conquests is often, tellingly, about the orgasmic sense of victory associated with 'scoring'. More seriously, despite the crudity and harshness of terrace culture in the 1950s and early 1960s it is difficult, indeed, to imagine then the response of football fans at Leeds United in 1979 to a police appeal for help in the so-called Yorkshire Ripper case:

> He became known as the Yorkshire Ripper. . . . A hoaxer, who called himself 'Jack', sent a tape to the police. The police had it played on the loud speakers of Leeds' football stadium hoping it would jog someone's memory, but the Leeds fans drowned out the voice with chants of, 'Eleven–Nil'. Eleven was the number of known (female) victims. Nil was the police score.
>
> (Ward Jouve 1986: 31)

Chanting Leeds fans were also reported to have jeered the police and to have sung, 'You'll never catch the Ripper' (*Daily Mirror* 14.10.1979).

As sports editor, of the *Sunday Sport*, Moore presided over headlines such as 'Hang 'em up by the Balls', which followed a particularly miserable England performance (one among many) in the late 1980s. He later opened a pub, fittingly called, in 1980s tabloid bar room speak, 'Mooros'. Particularly these later aspects of the Bobby Moore parable, which are largely absent from the accounts of the 'East End boy who became a shining example to the world of sport' (*Daily Telegraph* 25.2.1993), do help to mark rather more clearly wider shifts in masculine sporting styles and in discourses about masculinity and sport over the past three decades.

BACK TO THE FUTURE?

Moore's death came at an inauspicious time for English sport. The nation's cricketers, savaged in the British press for their bedraggled appearance and 'unprofessional' approach to test cricket, had returned from India and Sri Lanka well beaten by hosts displaying an unreconstructed post-colonial lack of grace. The slouching, unshaven England captain, Gooch, a new 'Essex man', was easily contrasted with Moore, 'the conquering golden boy', who had displayed, 'high and self-imposed standards, not only of performance but also of comportment' (*Daily Express* 25.2.1993). A number of press accounts had stressed Moore's near-narcissistic, almost military, concern with tidiness and presentation on and off the field; an approach likely to find much favour with the elites of the FA. In India, by way of contrast, England press conferences had been conducted with participants in shorts and sporting three-day growths of beard. Form, here, was, apparently, a sure indicator for the content of sporting performance. Most telling of all, of course, around this time was the prescient demise of the fictional comic strip character, Roy of the Rovers – as opposed to Moore's 'real life' version – allegedly forced out of the comics' market by the space-age violence and destructiveness of new heroes, and the success among the young of computer games. According to the strip's artist, Barry Mitchel, 'Roy's gone because he just doesn't reflect the times' (*Guardian* 15.3.1993).

As Roland Barthes (1972) has observed, 'Pictures . . . are more imperative than writing, they impose meaning at one stroke, without analysing or diluting it.' For English football, the image in the public consciousness, annually repeated, is of Cup winning captains receiving their trophy from the Royal Box. These occasions and images are part of a constructed national sporting calender. They contribute to the production of the imaginary coherence of national identity by articulating two de-politicised elements of national culture – sport and the monarchy (Whannel 1992: 20). They are part of the ritual expressions of a corporate national life (Cardiff and Scannel 1982). The moment Moore picks up the World Cup from the Queen has, perhaps, been reshown more than them all. It is an image which is simply deconstructed to illustrate the deference and respect of the supposedly 'permissive' 1960s against the excess and irreverence of the cash-soaked 1990s. Nick Hornby, for example, contrasts Moore's calm, silent and uncomplicated collection of the trophy in 1966 – an endlessly repeatable, and repeated, emblematic moment – with Mark Wright's disposable, alehouse exaltation of, 'You fuckin' beauty!', when turning to the camera to show the FA Cup on the same steps in 1992 (*Sunday Times* 28.2.1993). Other commentators, contrasting the moment with later football fare, describe Moore, 'lifting the World Cup one-handed above his head, clutching his medal in the other. No tears, no sticking out tongue, no clenched fist, just a proud, broad smile' (*Sun* 25.2.1993).

Wider contrasts are also drawn between other male sporting heroes taken from the respective decades – the venerable, respected and sportsmanlike heroes of an England now lost: Cooper, Charlton and Cowdrey from the 1960s, men whose identities were contained by their sports; and the gimcrack celebrities and wealthy opportunists of the 1990s: Eubank ('Ambition?: to make money'), Gascoigne (inevitably) and the disgraced Gooch (*Sunday Telegraph* 28.2.1993). These articulations through sport of the representations and transformations of masculinity and national identity also have an important 'racial' dimension. In terms of cultural identity, neither blackness nor Britishness is a fixed, stable element (Gilroy 1987). This mourned and ordered sporting world of the 1960s constructs 'the nation', and its heroic and 'organic' past, along very clear and uncomplicated lines. There are no black faces behind Moore, waiting to meet the Queen; there are few, if any, British black faces in the Wembley crowd. Throughout the late 1970s and 1980s, of course, black England players struggled against an active core of racist support for the national football team. John Barnes and others still struggle (see Williams *et al.* 1989; Williams 1992; Hill 1989).

BYE BYE BOBBY, HELLO GAZZA

These sorts of accounts rest, finally, on comparisons between the

media-contoured and necessarily vulnerable 'superstars' of
football's fully 'deregulated' and globalised era, and the days when
Moore's FA Cup Final colleagues of 1964 still included a
traditional/located player on the right wing who owned a part
share in a local butcher's shop (Critcher 1991; Hobbs 1993).
Commenting on Moore's performance in the Royal Box in 1966,
Russell Davies observes 'Now that we accept as a fact of life that
possessors of great footballing talent may range from snarling,
belching superstars to cocaine-trading renegades, that picture
looks a quaint relic of the days of chivalrous mutual respect'
(*Sunday Telegraph* 28.3.1993).

References like these to the hyperreal lifestyles of today's
football megastars (notably, here, Gascoigne and the Argentinian,
Maradona) sit uncomfortably alongside the great Brazilian Pele's
valediction for Moore who was, 'the fairest, the best and the most
honourable of his opponents' (*Guardian*, 25.2.1993). Gary Linekar
stands out today in similar, unstained, mode. But, in accounts
which map out the new football masculinities in England it is
currently, of course, the talented and troubled Gascoigne who is
the key. His chauvinistic tears at the World Cup Finals in Italy in
1990 – captioned for T-shirt sales with 'There'll always be an
England' – made 'Gazza', in the Barthesian sense, a myth (see
Whannel 1992: 148). Now wealthily, if uncomfortably, displaced to
play his football in Italy, it is Gazza who, in the anomic global
studio which hosts his waking hours, sneers and burps at the
media. Arguably, he personifies abroad images less of English
players than he does of young English male spectators; of 'the
lads'. It is Gazza who, unreflectively and apparently unforgivably,
wears, 'kiss-me-quick hats, bongo drum underpants, sticks his
tongue out, belches at camera lenses and, no doubt, lifts his leg up
at lamposts' (*Daily Express* 26.2.1993). It is Gascoigne too who
stumbles into pub brawls, screams 'unrepeatable' expletives down
public telephones to girlfriends (Davies 1990) and who responds
to TV requests for a message for the friendly Norwegians with a
cheery, and 'lad-like', 'Fuck off'.

English warriors, like the ageing Bryan Robson – 'It is war . . .
you could put him in any trench and know he'd be first over the
top' (Bobby Robson quoted in Davies 1990: 89) – or current
captain, Stuart Pearce – fiercely uncomplicated, teak tough and
with a 'patriotic' disregard for foreigners, 'Psycho' to his followers
– symbolise aspects of the older 'call-to-war' bunker mentality still

demanded by England managers, players and spectators even in an age when top stars are cossetted and manicured (see Downham and Worthington 1992). According to this view, matches can still be won through displays of national pride and intimidation in the players' tunnel, and, so say the fans, by the same on the terraces. English football support, especially abroad, here becomes a metaphor for just one more successful military campaign, stoked and abetted by a virulently xenophobic tabloid press. As one Englishman commented before the 1990 World Cup Finals, 'We won two world wars and it goes to your head a bit. We are not going to take anything from anybody now. We will just give them a good hiding' (*Sunday Times* 18.3.1990).

But it is Gazza's wilfully inarticulate and 'patriotic', 'couldn't give a fuckness', which best comes close to aspects of the new football masculinities; to the buzz, the *frisson*, the grounded aesthetics of risk which test young male identities at football today and which enable the unexpected, the situations in which anything can happen, to be created (Willis 1990: 102). At football, especially away from home and especially abroad, it is release from domestic constraint, and into comradely 'anonymity', the endless drinking and the possibilities it provides for loss of control, which defeats boredom and which seems to open up symbolic and real opportunities not available in normal life. Here, especially, are the best opportunities for adventure; for displaying and facing the dangerous and contradictory forces of violence; for exhibiting the values and identities which also concern, 'a desperate kind of honour, a strange respect for the space around dignity and a mad courage which confronts banality with real, live drama' (Willis 1990: 109). At football abroad in the 1990s, ill-educated and courageous young Englishmen in flimsy shorts and T-shirts, drawn from anonymous towns and suburbs and incapable of any meaningful contact with local cultures, are still aggressively on the prowl. Fortified by drink and the knowledge that they are English – and together – they guilelessly attack the best armed and most violent police forces on the continent. Most of them also fully expect to 'win' these confrontations.

THEY THINK IT'S ALL OVER: REFLECTIONS ON RECENT DEVELOPMENTS

One does not have to adopt the moral rhetoric of the political

Right, which runs through much of the reporting of Moore's death and of hooliganism, or to subscribe to some 'socialist utopian' view of the game in which, 'people play for the place where they were born and have no desire to earn a professional's crust' (Lee 1992: 117), to recognise that recent shifts in the manner in which English football is supported, funded, played and played back to its public, particularly by the tabloids, reflect wider cultural and economic changes in British society which mark key differences in the life and times of 'our Bobby' and the mercurial 'Gazza'. They reflect, among other things, the recent rise in social and economic policies which favour a 'self absorbed social individualism' and the subsequent decline in the sorts of 'organic' community ties which traditionally both defined and ordered links between football clubs and their supporters. Such trends and their consequences have, interestingly, recently been pilloried even in right wing accounts of the rise of the 'new' masculinities in Britain (Richards 1990).

However, that the recent disorderly behaviour of Englishmen and youths at football is echoed by similar examples in other less 'newsworthy' contexts – routinely, in city centres; on 'drinking' holidays abroad; at other licensed and unlicensed sporting and social events, etc., etc. – and by the behaviour of Englishmen drawn from a wide variety of social class backgrounds (see *Observer* 9.10.1988; *Independent* 2.1.1993), points, in this context, to the relatively independent importance of patriarchy and the construction of gender identities across the whole social formation and, more specifically, to the 'troubled and pressing condition of traditional British masculinity' (I. Taylor 1991: 102).

Perhaps this more pervasive concern is the most sympathetic way to read recent academic accounts of the hooligan phenomenon, which stress the 'ordinariness' of those involved and the 'symbolic significance' of football violence. But, surely, such accounts underplay the level of 'public irritation' (sic) caused by the real disturbances which young men seem to find so attractive at football and elsewhere? (Armstrong and Harris 1991: 434–51). Other approaches, arguably similarly misconceived, seem to suggest that the construction of hooliganism as a serious social problem is the product of some simple police conspiracy (Armstrong *et al.* 1991), while others still, using the forbidding and opaque discourses of the postmodernists, allegedly to provide a 'bottom-up' account of the phenomenon, seem to marginalise almost completely questions of gender relations and gender identity (Giullianotti 1993).

Since the Hillsborough disaster in 1989, the coverage of which disrupted prevailing stereotypes of 'fans as hooligans', substituting discourses focused through a sense of 'family' and 'belonging' (Brunt 1989: 23), hooligan rivalries at football have had a rather lower profile than has been recently the case. The programme of 'modernisation' of material conditions and human relations in the game invoked by the liberal and progressive Taylor Report (1990) has been modified, but largely supported, by the present government. Broadly progressive new cultural movements – the 'alternative' supporters' organisations, the fanzines and the new football/music crossovers – have also contributed to a slowly changing spectator climate, though it is important not to overstate the extent to which such developments are able to address the structural crises in the game or have displaced traditional and prevailing ideologies about gender and football (see Moorhouse 1994). Perimeter fencing has now disappeared from most major football venues in England and there are modest signs of improving relations between the police and football spectators as increased levels of stewarding becomes the norm (see Middleham 1993).

Debates about the replacement of terracing by seating – arguably a key metaphor for change in football's 'new future' – continue to provoke opposition from spectators – and not just from young male fans (see Woodhouse 1991). Such opposition, with some reason, cites increased cost of admission and the plans of the game's administrators to convert the game into a television-controlled, 'integrated leisure package' for middle-class 'family' consumers as key points of contention (see 'The Final Whistle', *Time Out* 29.4.1992 – 6.5.1992: 12–13) It laments the loss of the strongly masculine 'atmosphere' and camaraderie of the terraces, though, arguably, it recalls in these accounts an earlier, mythologised and idealised terrace culture and in doing so risks an association with the 'inert, reactionary nostalgia' of some of the game's administrators which has been a traditional barrier to much needed modernisation and change (see Taylor 1991: 14; Hornby 1992: 220). The reshaping of the game, whatever its form, will necessarily involve changes which reflect the shifting contours of class and gender identities in Britain, and the changing priorities of a society – and a sport – slowly emerging into a future which is likely to be both sustained, and blighted, by its past.

Chapter 13

Masculinities and white-collar crime

Michael Levi [1]

FROSBY:
My lovely city sadly changes.
Sic transit gloria! Glory passes!
Any wonder I'm deranged,
Surrounded by the criminal classes.

GRIMES:
You've been coining it for years.
All you fuckwits in the City.
It just don't look quite so pretty,
All the cunning little jobs,
When you see them done by yobs.

Churchill (1987: 88)

GENDER AND WHITE-COLLAR CRIME

One problem confronting those who would seek to connect white-collar crime to any phenomenon is that 'white-collar crime' is used to cover an enormous diversity of behaviours, from violation of worker protection legislation through insider trading and the looting of pension funds to credit card fraud and embezzlement by bank cashiers (Geis 1992; Levi 1987: xviii–xix). Even the term 'City fraud' is too all-inclusive, covering acts as different as enhancing the prestige of the merchant bank by misleading the market about the level of take-up of a share flotation it sponsored on the one hand and, on the other, the alleged theft of millions from pensioners, bankers or shareholders for direct personal financial benefit at the expense of employers or creditors.[2] While not neglecting the dimensions of class and status, this article has been influenced by Shapiro (1990), who argues that we ought to focus on the essential characteristic of trust violation rather than on the socioeconomic characteristics of offenders. However, 'trust violation' can place behaviours such as cheque and credit card fraud squarely in the frame, and since so many more people commit such acts than, for example, defraud pension funds, the result is to make the set of white-collar criminals much more like other property offenders and much less like 'the powerful' than many authors such as Sutherland (1983) intended.

The relationship between gender and white-collar crime has preoccupied even fewer criminologists than has white-collar crime itself. Unsurprisingly, perhaps, gender remained undiscussed in the classic early aetiological texts of Sutherland (1983) and Cressey (1953). Despite the fact that Pollak's (1950) 'theory' that women are as criminal as men but just more deceitful and manipulative might have cued us into thinking about the relationship between gender and white-collar crime, there was little empirical or theoretical interest in white-collar crime (and, *a fortiori*, in gender and crime) during the 1950s and 1960s, and it was only when women started writing about 'liberation' and criminality that female participation in fraud came to be discussed. (For some early attention to fraud, see Simon 1977.) Even today, gender is a marginal issue in white-collar crime, appearing only in statistical tables of offenders in a recent textbook by Croall (1992), while Hagan's (1988) collection of essays turns to examine power and gender only after chapters on white-collar crime have been completed.

Convicted offender statistics indicate the usual major gender gap in white-collar crime, but the ratio is not as high in favour of males as it is for most other property crimes.[3] This is because the considerable gender differences among those committing 'serious fraud' – which are discussed later – are masked by the large number of 'minor' frauds which are agglomerated within the category of 'other frauds' in the English criminal statistics and which are far more commonly committed by women than are serious fraud or non-fraud crimes; likewise in the Uniform Crime Reports and Offender-Based Transaction Statistics in the US, where credit card frauds (and other inter-state frauds) are federal offences. Consequently, it is not surprising that the male:female ratio is less than 2:1 in both state and federal courts in America (Daly 1989), though Weisburd *et al.* (1991: 70) found that men constituted 82.5 per cent of their sample of Federal white-collar criminals (compared with 68.6 per cent of Federal 'common criminals' and 48.6 per cent of males in the general population at the time of their research, in the late 1970s). In England and Wales, in 1990, the male:female ratio for those convicted at all courts was 3:1 for thefts by employees (mainly till thefts from shops); 9:1 for theft from the mail; and 4:1 for frauds generally. Though the ratio is much higher for the seldom-prosecuted bankruptcy frauds and frauds by company directors, interestingly, neither the major fraud prosecution bodies in England nor the US Department of Justice keep any statistics on the gender of those they prosecute.

Few women have attained senior positions, particularly not chief executive or finance director positions – there have been no female bank directors in the UK – and so it is not surprising that out of over 200 persons prosecuted since the Serious Fraud Office, which deals with the major cases in the UK, was established in 1988, there are only fifteen women, all of them as alleged very junior partners. As for fraud and other 'misconduct' by professionals, from 1989–June 1993, the Institute of Chartered Accountants in England and Wales has excluded or suspended 445 men and no women, while 110 men and no women have been banned because they are bankrupt: 14 per cent of all members are women. The Law Society does not keep aggregate data on disciplined members by gender, but officials state impressionistically that given their general numbers, women are no more fraud-prone than men.

Despite the fact that female personal assistants and secretaries may come to know about prospective bids – not least because senior executives (who are generally male) are reluctant to type documents themselves or dial direct! – only one female has been charged with insider trading in Britain to date, and none have been charged in the major US cases. In the one British case, the woman was the sister of a stockbroker and was alleged to have leaked details to him while she was working as a secretary at the Office of Fair Trading: the charges were dismissed. It should come as little surprise that my review of police cases in one force area indicates the predominance among female fraud of low-level clerical fraud in financial services, which involves many women and which, for both women and men, is the modal 'white-collar occupation'. (This is true of Federal offenders in the US: see Daly 1989.) The modality issue is a function of the fact that most jobs

are low status, though the sex ratios may be affected by auto-
mation: sources in the financial services industry state that the
proportion of women in middle and senior management is higher
in the US than in the UK, though some UK institutions include
greater representation for women at these levels as part of their
corporate plans. Work in progress suggests that the fact that
gender is specified on many (but not all) cheques and credit cards
creates particularised criminal opportunities for women and men,
which may increase as photographs on cards become more
common (Levi and Pithouse, forthcoming).

One of the few women in America to have been convicted of
serious fraud was Leona ('paying taxes is for the little people')
Hemsley, and her wealth was acquired via her husband; likewise
Imelda Marcos, widow of the Philippines President, who was
acquitted of charges partly because the jury could not be certain
that she, rather than her husband, was responsible.

In areas of corporate crime(or, since few of them involve criminal
conviction, 'misconduct'), such as the manufacture of harmful
automobiles or pharmaceutical products, women likewise feature
very seldom, whether as senior executives or as the managers of the
sub-units who are set goals to produce goods cheaply or find a new
profitable product which complies with safety standards.[4] The latter
is crucial, as crime is often an unintended, though insufficiently cared
about (by the corporation) method of achieving ruthlessly set sales or
cost targets. In England and Wales during 1991, sixty-six men and
eight women were prosecuted at Crown Court, while 893 men and 79
women were prosecuted at Magistrates' Court for Trades
Descriptions Act offences; twelve men and one woman were
prosecuted at Crown Court, and 428 men and twenty women were
prosecuted at Magistrates' Court for Health and Safety at Work
offences; and 196 men and thirty-three women were prosecuted for
adulteration of food. Though these prosecutions of individuals rather
than companies normally reflect the small size of the businesses, one
cannot deduce whether the gender distribution is due to gendered
occupational variations or to differential propensities to offend.
(Croall 1992, observes that most prosecutees are small business
people who are surviving on the margins.)

Importantly, there seems no reason to suspect that (a) the
reporting, recording, or prosecution data are systematically
distorted so as to produce an artificially low rate of female business
crime, nor (b) (*pace* Box 1983) that 'control' factors, such as the

rise in the numbers of female police, have generated variations over time which did not reflect changes in female and male involvement in fraud. (In reality, largely because of bias in general CID recruitment, there have always been very few female fraud squad or security officials with a fraud brief.)

My research has yielded examples where women have not been prosecuted because their involvement was seen as marginal: but as far as I could deduce, their involvement in the fraud actually was marginal, so this is neither paternalism nor 'double-punishment'. Most serious frauds are multiple-defendant cases in which prosecutors are urged only to take the core offenders to court (Levi 1993), and prosecutions generally reflect this. The only Serious Fraud Office case in which a woman was alleged by investigators to have been the principal offender resulted in the prosecution and imprisonment of her. Her daughter and daughter's lover were acquitted. A convicted male lawyer who was 'under her spell' was the principal prosecution witness. In none of the national and international headlined cases – Guinness, Blue Arrow, Bank of Credit & Commerce International, Maxwell, and Polly Peck – was there any remotely plausible case for prosecuting women. (In an alleged conspiracy to manipulate the market's perception of the success of the rights issue of Blue Arrow shares, a female Compliance Officer was charged, but after the convictions of four men in the first trial were quashed, her case was not proceeded with. On the basis of my interviews and reading of the case papers, her defence would have been a very strong one and essentially, she was accused of having failed to stop the men's scheme. She was certainly the most marginal of the defendants.)

Explaining the gender–crime connection

How has the relationship between gender and white-collar crime been theorised? Braithwaite's absorbing review essay on crimes of the middle classes (1993b: 223) asserts that

> Crime can be motivated by (a) a desire for goods for use; (b) a fear of losing goods for use; (c) a desire for goods for exchange; and (d) a fear of losing goods for exchange. My proposition is that (a) and (b) are more relevant to motivating the crimes of poor people; (c) and (d) are more relevant to motivating the crimes of wealthy people and organisations.

Although – whether in white-collar or violent crime – it is illuminating to focus upon fear of (symbolic and material) loss as well as the more conventional criminological orientation of prospect of gain, having surplus to what one can use is almost a necessary condition for the label 'wealthy'. 'Use-value' is a more elastic concept than Braithwaite implies: the desire to retain one's fleet of Rolls Royces, Lear jets and helicopters *for use* may motivate many white-collar crimes. One can only drive one 'Roller' at a time, but the others in the garage are not for (literal) exchange, but a sort of fetishism of commodities for use (e.g., transporting 'popsies' on weekend jaunts) and for display on *Lifestyles of the Rich and Famous.*

An alternative commonplace way of expressing the principle is that white-collar crimes are committed out of greed, not need. Without getting too heavily into a neo-Freudian debate about whether unbounded materialism is a substitute for sexual happiness and/or emotional fulfilment (*vide* 'Rosebud' in the movie *Citizen Kane*), a subjective concept of relative deprivation ought to force us to take serious account of the felt needs of people with high incomes, though social policy studies (e.g., Townsend 1979) of poverty which espouse such subjectivist definitions of poverty nevertheless tend to stop when they reach the top of the lowest income quartile. Marginal utility of income may fall as income rises (Braithwaite 1992; Wheeler 1992), but the perceived sufficiency of disposable income is affected by what are deemed in their reference group to be 'necessities', as well as by 'addictions' to drugs, gambling, etcetera. Their absolute income levels may vary considerably, but high levels of personal indebtedness are a common feature of male white-collar offenders compared with 'garden variety' offenders and with citizens generally. Cressey (1953) found that embezzlers had generally lived well beyond their means for some time before deciding to embezzle (or, as they saw it, to 'borrow').

Cressey argued that embezzlers went through four phases: they had an unshareable financial problem; they realised that embezzlement would solve the problem; they had the technical ability to commit the offence; and they developed a rationalisation for the act. However, later research modified this, Nettler (1974) and Benson (1985) observing that a taste for high living was salient for males, and Zeitz (1981) observing that support of families and/or maintaining a relationship with husband/lover was the principal motivation for women who embezzle. None of Zietz's women rationalised their debts as 'just borrowing': rather they had what she described (1981: 58) as a 'Joan of Arc quality . . . a willingness to be burned at the stake'.[5] Nevertheless, insofar as the non-shareable problem is an important component of embezzlement – as it is for *some* fraudsters – one could construe this as an effect of men becoming trapped into a conception of masculinity which denies them the possibility of opening up emotionally. Furthermore, if there are gendered differences in the propensity to become seriously indebted – whether as a result of involvement in gambling and narcotics subcultures, or of obsessional shopping (for goods for use, or for corporations for use or exchange) – then the proportion of females and males 'at risk' of developing 'non-shareable problems' will be different.

The other major aetiological strand that has addressed white-collar crime and gender is 'blocked opportunity' theory. The general conclusion from the modest empirical attention paid in Britain is that women turn to petty fraud – principally to social security fraud and to cheque and credit card fraud – because of their economic marginalisation (Box 1983; Carlen *et al.*. 1985). However, outside 'Human Relations' departments which exercise traditional 'female' skills of 'working with people', there are so few women in senior posts where there is an opportunity to defraud that this obviously acts as a structural constraint upon female involvement in high-value 'insider' fraud. Traditionally, this under-representation in high finance posts has also been true for males of lower working-class origin, whatever their colour: the social class distribution of 'white-collar criminality' depends partly upon what sorts of acts one wishes to include in this category (Shapiro 1990). But white-collar criminals are significantly more likely to be white, middle-aged, and employed compared with convicted offenders generally, even though the broad sweep of Federal laws means that in the US, a surprisingly high percentage are unemployed (Daly 1989).

At least in principle, dishonesty is an equal opportunity skill, as one may note from the semi-authorised biography of Wall Street dealmaker Jeff 'Mad Dog' Beck: 'Like his mother, too, Jeff early on began to apply his intelligence primarily to the manipulation of other people's thoughts and emotions' (Bianco 1991: 38). However, in culture stereotypes, it may be possible to draw a distinction between greater trust by the predominantly male businesspeople and potential investors in the *integrity* of women (as evidenced by women's greater risk aversion and lower conviction rate), and less trust in women's financial *competence* ('high finance is a man's business'). The theme of the film *House of Games* is illustrative: a rather unimaginative and honest female psychotherapist is fooled and corrupted by male confidence tricksters, and ends up as a killer who has been liberated from her inhibitions and has come to terms with the 'hidden dishonesty' in her 'nature'. Senior merchant bankers to whom I have spoken refer frequently to themes such as 'the City is a place for men, not for boys', and the distinction they are making receives legal support in the differentiation in the Financial Services Act 1986 between 'professional investors' – who need or deserve less regulation – and the others, often characterised by politicians and market professionals in a patronisingly sexist way as 'Aunt Agathas'.

WHITE-COLLAR CRIME AND MASCULINITIES

The connection between 'manliness' and white-collar crime is not as self-evident as is the connection between it and violent crime, where despite the presence of many 'Jekyll and Hyde' middle-class persons who reserve their violence for behind closed family doors, offenders (and victims) are disproportionately working class and people of colour. (For a recent overview of violent crime data and theories, see Levi 1994.) Industrial sociologists have carried out few studies of elite occupations in general, and financial services in particular. This is partly because of a 'sociology of the underdog' approach but partly because of the class background and income of almost all sociologists: as I pointed out (Levi 1981: Appendix A), 'fraudsters did not 'hang out' in any place I could afford to go to'. The absence of such upperworld ethnographies or even surveys makes separating the culture(s) of business crime from the culture(s) of business deeply problematical. For if we take seriously Veblen's observation (1967: 237) that 'the ideal pecuniary man is like the ideal delinquent in his unscrupulous conversion of goods and persons to his own ends, and in a callous disregard of (i.e. freedom from) the feelings of others or remoter effects of his actions', it is hard to see how the cultural values of a *criminal* capitalist can differ greatly from a *law-abiding* one, at least in terms of constructs such as an obsession with power and control (Hagan 1988). Evidence about offence diversity among delinquents has tended to negate conventional assumptions which separate the causes of crime for gain from crimes of violence, and those white-collar crimes that involve wrecking competition can be viewed as but one of many crimes of aggression committed by men which do not directly involve control over women. As may be noted from many business texts and biographies of takeover battles, the metaphors of war and intense social competition are deeply embedded in the core values of deregulated capitalism. These are transmitted via the peer culture, and reinforced by highly competitive business school training for those who are not self-taught entrepreneurs, and the even more aggressive 'university of life' for those who are self-taught. Survival in a competitive local or global market becomes an overriding value or 'technique of neutralisation' which can justify white-collar law-breaking. That aspect of masculinity which emphasises individual striving and achievement may account for breaking the rules, while the other aspect which stresses group loyalty and support may account for covering up the misconduct.

Nevertheless, though the family relationships of such economic Vikings may be patriarchal in form, the role of the affectionate and stable 'family man' is culturally available, or is even required in some socially conservative and religious circles. Seeming trustworthy and socially respectable – especially in selling and in deal-making roles which involve repeat relationships – is an important economic as well as social attribute for both legitimate and illegitimate businesspeople.

At the lower end of the 'white-collar crime' spectrum, Mars (1982) shows how workplace crime is related to group values and identities, and though he does not dwell on the gendered dimensions of this, the modal form of the tightly knit 'buddy-buddy' social and work group is clearly masculine. At the upper end of the spectrum, it is possible to point to the long, undomesticated hours and to the dislocatory travel patterns of both top executives and professionals as being part of a (conventionally) masculine culture which stresses preparedness to sacrifice personal leisure and family goals both to meet the objectives of the firm and for unbounded prestige and money. Social networks based around family background and attendance at elite schools, universities, and membership of (sometimes all-male) clubs reinforce the 'male hut' ambience, and the maleness has not been inhibited by the 'new money' financial entrepreneurs of the 1980s and 1990s.

Clarke (1986) and Whimster (1992) make the plausible but untested assumption that prior to the 1980s, elite social regulation of a small number of people in the City served to prevent far more malpractice than was possible after its 'democratisation' before and following its deregulatory 'Big Bang' in 1986, as contrasted with the possibility that they simply repressed scandal more effectively in 'the good old days'. The rise of the 'yuppie' was a key phenomenon of the 1980s, and many expanding investment banking firms recruited young people in their twenties or thirties who were driven over-achievers, some of whom resented what they regarded as the hypocritical ethical constraints of Old Money, as well as the non-profit yielding efforts of their in-house compliance officers and self-regulatory organisations to get them to stick to the rules. The 'greed is good' credo popularly associated with *arbitrageur* Ivan Boesky before his fall from grace and imprisonment freed young City folk from the dead weight of honour-seeking corporate respectability (real or imaged) to which their elders were (in the contemptuous perception of these super-capitalist 'Red Guards') enslaved. As the Boesky figure, Gordon Gekko, puts it in the film *Wall Street*:

'The new law of evolution in corporate America seems to be the survival of the unfittest. Well in my book you either do it right or you get eliminated. . . . The point, ladies and gentlemen, is that greed, for lack of a better word, is good. Greed is right.'

Leitmotifs in general business deal-making of 'screwing the opposition' serve to conjure up images of rape (by fraud rather than by force) or at best 'heavy seduction', though there is often an underlying cosy reality of mutual trading between status players. Underpinning many corporate fiefdoms are networks of personal trading relationships of mutual trust and favour-granting (making, *inter alia*, the existence of price-fixing cartels among that appropriately gendered group the 'good old boys' extremely difficult to prove). The particular style in which status is manifested varies widely: though the upper reaches of the 'new money' craved social respectability and acceptance, and sought to attain them by charitable involvements, others, like lower class 'badasses' (Katz 1988) just demanded respect from their peers. The top players in finance capitalism were characterised by the boundless energy and egoism (in Durkheimian terms) to become and remain Masters of the Universe, as satirised by Tom Wolfe

(1987) in *Bonfire of the Vanities*. Their fear of downward mobility – in status and money – helped to keep them motivated, lawfully or otherwise. Accompanying this are images of unregulated power to do what one wishes. Von Hoffman (1993: xii) describes Malcolm Forbes, the son of the founder of *Forbes Magazine*, in the following way:

> The multitudes knew Malcolm, the happy spender, drifting about the sky, leaning over the side of the gondola under a hot air balloon . . . they knew him as the sunny days millionaire ripping through the sky in his gold jet named *Capitalist Tool*. . . . *He was the platinum-plated Good Time Charlie vrooming over hill and dale on his chromium Hog with the purple-eyed Movie Queen seated behind him. . . . As time went on, conditions changed, life got harder: Hefner didn't make sense anymore. Who has time for three days of sex with five people? While holding down two jobs?*

If we focus on fraud, and in particular on high-status fraudsters, then what we are generally left with is a portrait of the domineering chief executive who surrounds himself with lackeys – nearly all of them male (with all the attendant underlying images of castration) – who either do not question his orders or are junior conspirators. In business, women are background, are pure domesticity or sexual/image-generating playthings (the latter, on occasions, by using their family name or money to bring their menfolk into the Establishment, in some Darwinian integration of Old Money with New Ambition). Women's occupational roles seldom enter into it except as obedient secretaries who, under instruction or out of loyalty, may sometimes destroy notebooks or diaries or other paperwork crucial to the prosecution.[6] After charge, the wives are generally there to meet the usual 'Stand By Your Man' stereotypes: examples include top fashion model Cristina de Lorean – who divorced her husband directly after his acquittal – and the glamorous wives of Gerald Ronson and Anthony Parnes who, despite their husbands' imprisonment following the first Guinness trial, stayed with them. (Women also feature sometimes as disgruntled mistress whistleblowers on their partners.)

Despite the 'survival pressures' generated by the globalisation of production and financial intermediation, business culture is not the same everywhere, nor are its forms in any one country constant over time. One hypothesis worth exploring is that in countries involved in civil or external wars, an attitude of corner-cutting and risk-taking may become culturally embedded and, once introjected, may be difficult to eliminate. (Though recent American managerial thinking argues that *macho* styles may harm organisational development, which requires more 'feminine' listening and cooperating.) Another issue of analytic significance is that – seeking to avoid tautology – those white-collar offenders who are not part of an alternative criminal subculture of 'con artists' (Levi 1981) both have and covet current social respectability, and those operating in an organisational setting evade responsibility by appealing to the necessity of obedience to corporate objectives and/or of supporting their families. (If arrested or convicted, they sometimes counter-claim that they are victims of political persecution, thereby seeking to *enhance* their heroic image. Examples include former car-maker John De Lorean, Guinness Chairman Ernest Saunders, and Polly Peck Chairman Asil Nadir.)

There may be male (or ungendered) subcultures which set high standards to which members conform: that success drives are marked by puritanism rather than simple rapaciousness may be one reason why levels of serious fraud (recorded and as generally perceived) are lower in the flourishing financial services sector in Edinburgh than they are in London. In the absence of such peer group constraints, however, the underlying personality attribute of the successful organisational climber is one of 'blind ambition': the appropriate title of former White House Counsel's book about Watergate (Dean 1976). The ambition – like that of the professional thieves discussed by Sutherland (1937) – is to be recognised as a major force by one's peers, but for senior business executives it is also (and largely unlike professional thieves) to make it in the league tables of the most seriously rich. Highly rated white-collar 'criminals' such as Mike Milken and Robert Maxwell were 'deal addicts', but so too are many businesspeople for whom there is no plausible evidence of criminality. 'Crime', like influence-buying, is just one way of 'getting the job done', of expressing 'entitlement', though some people may get an extra (and reinforcing) 'high' from *criminal* risk-taking. White-collar crime research has evaded the role of individual personality, perhaps assuming that because the unalloyed pursuit of profit by whatever means was so rational a part of the capitalist system, such questions were irrelevant. But just as a focus upon the culture of masculinity overpredicts levels of violence against women, so too does one on the *macho* business culture appear to overpredict levels of business crime.[7] Do many businesspeople (of whatever gender) refrain from crime simply because large bureaucracies have been socialised into conformity and risk-aversion (Braithwaite 1993b; von Hoffman 1993)? And/or do those white-collar criminals who are not stealing for use possess 'risk-taking personalities', which could be unevenly distributed by gender?

If, as Weber argued, the future-sacrifice orientation as well as other features of Protestantism (at least as compared with Catholicism, if not with Judaism) was relevant to the success of capitalism, part of this orientation was the relative lack of self-indulgence. By contrast, von Hoffman (1993: 104) gives the following description of the former Chief Executive Officer (CEO) of (now defunct) bankers E.F. Hutton:

> Whatever he may have wanted to hear about at dinner with his popsies, it was next to impossible to discuss anything with this casebook Mad Ludwig in his office because of the two Catalina macaws flying around the room on their three-foot-long wings, screaming 'Shit, shit, shit!' at his visitors when his two feathered meances weren't taking a bite out of their legs. . . . 'I've never seen the man sober', a banker of the Street remarked when another business acquaintance mentioned at the time if Fomon [the CEO] 'had as much interest in his company as he did in his libido or his own bank account, all three would be in better shape today'. The CEO ethos being what it is, Mad Ludwig with his macaws kept his job for seventeen years.

Likewise, the personal style of corporate raider Victor Posner as described by Bianco (1991: 364) is equally unappetising:

> Visiting Posner was like walking into an English-language Fellini film. A short man, Posner sat atop a thronelike platform chair surrounded by bodyguards with guns jammed holsterless into their belts. He was liable to lose his temper at any moment. Among the bodyguards' duties was emptying elevators of old ladies and other menacing characters before Posner entered. They were also quick with a coffee cup. Posner was so insistent on drinking his coffee hot that he would drink a cup and then snap his fingers. The cup was taken away and replaced by a fresh one, repeatedly.

Clearly, these people are written about partly *because* of their eccentricities and/or because of the fame of their companies. Others are neglected because they are too dull: as one white-collar defendant in a famous alleged crime committed 'for the company' rather than for personal benefit observed to me: 'The media tried their best to dig up some sensational stuff on my lifestyle, but even the tabloids had to admit I was just too boring to write about.' Whereas some accountants and solicitors get into fraud because of their taste for gambling, sex or drink/drugs, many do so simply because they cannot accept that their firms are no longer making money and/or because they cannot face the inability to maintain a comfortable lifestyle following their anticipated bankruptcy: this is far from being 'aggressive masculinity', though it might be argued that this is a typically masculine notion of 'entitlement' which pervades explanations of violence against women.

Messerschmidt (1986: 119) observes:

> The corporate executive's masculinity, then, is centred around a struggle for success, reward, and recognition in the corporation and community. . . . This image of work, rooted materially in the corporate executive's gender/class position . . . helps to create the conditions for corporate crime. Devotion to achievement and success . . . brings about the 'need' to engage in such crime.

To place Robert Maxwell in the same category as Cressey's embezzlers with their non-shareable problems might strike some as ludicrous: Maxwell's principal non-shareable problem was the continued concealment of his alleged embezzlement of £400 million of his pensioners' money. (The criminal trials may or may not illuminate the extent to which others shared his knowledge of his problem.) Former *Daily Mirror* Foreign Editor Nick Davies (1992: 4) – who had a personal grievance – observes:

> He did behave like a dictator whenever he had his employees around him; he did treat them in any way he wished; he did seem to derive pleasure, perhaps sadistic pleasure, from seeing people squirm before him. But more than that, Maxwell liked others to see him performing; he seemed to enjoy ridiculing and bullying his employees, particularly in front of other members of staff.

This is the mentality of those stripped of human dignity – as Maxwell allegedly was in childhood – inflicting their own humiliation upon others. The 'badasses' discussed by Katz (1988) vent their 'righteous rage' in violence, whether in the home or on the street, or both; others – people like Maxwell – do so in a more controlled form, at least when it suits them. There are echoes of the Kray and Richardson London gangs of the 1960s in Davies' portrait of 'the man' at work (1992: 14):[8]

> Maxwell would want to know who was on every line before making the decision to talk to them. Most of the time his insatiable need to know everything at all times made him speak to everyone who called. It didn't matter a jot to him how long they might be left holding on, waiting for the great man to complete another call before answering those patiently waiting. If he didn't want to talk to them he would either wave his hand dismissively or say brusquely, 'Tell them to fuck off.'

Thus is greatness manifested! Later, Davies describes further the style of operation which Maxwell used to keep staff subservient, which revolved around the early morning meetings with senior executives in which he kept them all waiting:

> Then Maxwell would come in and sit down, pick up the typed agenda, look at it and put it on one side. Everyone would have their relative files to go with the agenda. . . . Invariably, however, he would pick on something entirely different, something not on the agenda, some minor, trivial little point. He always seemed to do that. . . . so he could torture someone, attack someone, make someone at the table feel incompetent.
>
> (Davies 1992: 14)

One could hardly look for a better portrait of impaired masculinity, using the production of psychological stress rather than physical violence as its instrument. Much of his life was spent creating an impression, using wealth to display power. There is a further important issue. Much of the focus in the literature on masculinities has been on male oppression of women (at home and at work) and of gays and other groups with 'deviant' sexual orientations (Hearn and Morgan 1990). Yet in white-collar crime and, in a slightly different way, in business competition generally, most of the competition is inter-male, and it is male-run corporations and investors who are the primary direct *victims*. In some cases, being defrauded does indeed produce a crisis in the victim's self-concept as a 'competent male [businessman or investor]', but particularly in an organisational setting, it is often regarded in a more routine way – though perhaps not entirely *sans* masculine cultural baggage – as the price of doing business. As one banker put it to me:

> One must of course *try* to minimise the chance of loss, but banking is a risk business. If you don't take risks you will never make any serious money (except by insider dealing, obviously). If one makes a judgment call and it turns out bad, one has to take it like a man and accept it.

Indeed, these themes of 'victim precipitation' and 'risk must accompany reward' are important sub-texts in discussions about compensation for victims of fraud and/or what accountants are pleased to call 'irregularities', whether acknowledged crimes such as Barlow Clowes or more legally uncertain cases such as Lloyd's of London syndicates (see Levi and Pithouse 1992 and forthcoming, for more detailed review of the patterns and impact of fraud victimisation).

CONCLUSION

Morgan (1992: 97) observes that

> Workplaces set limits for the range of masculinities that might be legitimately deployed. . . . many workplaces will have little scope for the exercise of brawn . . . although there may be some attempt to search out their moral equivalents. Workplaces may, further, give positive endorsement for certain characteristics with strong masculinity connotations: group loyalty or aggressiveness for example.

Adherents of 'control theory' may have noted that the constraint factor that has been omitted to date is deterrence. Braithwaite (1989) has written evocatively about the superior regulatory power of shame, in particular reintegrative shaming, compared with retributive punishment. This varies not only between societies but typically by gender also. Braithwaite suggests that women are more likely to feel guilty or ashamed than men when they contemplate crime or after they have committed it. However, shame levels depend significantly upon the reference group values of those who contemplate crime: the narrower the reference group and the more tolerant it is of particular forms of crime in particular circumstances, the less that shame will operate. Thus Japan, which regulates street and household crime very effectively, has an almost unrivalled appetite for financing political parties (principally, the Liberal Democratic Party) out of 'donations' from those who wish to be awarded government building contracts or issue their shares on the stock market. Although many political leaders – all of them male – have been forced to resign when exposed, they remain powerful behind the scenes thereafter. The explanation for crime then shifts to how particular 'rationalisations' develop, to the visibility of the crimes to others inside and outside the reference group (and the time lags involved in this visibility), and to cultural transmission theories of how tolerance and/or stigma are perpetuated.

We have seen a number of ways in which those committing frauds and corporate crimes involving health and safety have developed an attitude set and rationalisations conducive to both the onset and continuation of a white-collar criminal career. Their concept of entitlement is much less often called to account than in the lower class spheres where police normally do battle. This partly accounts for the outrage some of them experience when previously unknown or tolerated practices land them in criminal courts. Most convicted fraudsters – whether outsiders or insiders – are far from the high-status image popularised in the media and movies. As regards the more notorious cases, some of the male offenders may be 'lounge lizard' types, with a very relaxed lifestyle. However, from my observation and from media and biographical accounts, many of them are 'driven' characters for whom, in the words of Gordon Gekko in *Wall Street*, 'lunch is for wimps' and everything is subordinated to the objectives of attaining peer-group respect, of controlling others and avoiding being controlled by them. It may be also that despite the apparent gender-neutrality of 'deceitfulness' that is at the core of fraud, men are prone to adopt an 'aggressive' rather than 'compliant' style of manipulativeness. It may be no accident that mega-salespeople in financial services attract the *sobriquet* 'Big Swinging Dick': I know of no women who have been awarded that honorary title!

Crimes and other social harms committed in an organisational setting, which aim to further the interests of the company or other grouping (such as political party), may often display the characteristics of 'the banality of evil', and must be analysed in terms of macro–micro theoretical frameworks (Vaughan 1992) which look at general and peer group cultural values, including obedience to authority. Fraud is less clearly located in enhancing the purposes of legitimate social institutions, though many of what I have described as 'slippery-slope frauds', i.e. trading whilst insolvent (Levi 1981) are committed because of the status insecurity and 'fear of falling' consequent upon the closure of their otherwise legitimate businesses. Some white-collar convicts and unconvicted executives have hectic 'fun' along the way, but although – in the words of Mr Justice Henry summarising the prosecution case in the first Guinness trial (Levi 1991) – their rewards are 'too big to be honest', serious criminal money is seldom made by the idle, absentee *rentier* playboy or capitalist. Not least because one has to appear 'upfront' before so many people who can identify one subsequently, ripping off the public in a big or 'manly' way requires a great deal of emotional 'bottle' and serious dedication to the psychopathic qualities of learned care-lessness.

NOTES

1 The author thanks David Morgan, John Richardson and the editors for comments on an earlier draft.
2 The former may entail a different attitude set from the latter, since it is more readily rationalisable as 'victimless' and more 'altruistic', not being for immediate personal gain.
3 Inasmuch as a higher chance of conviction and imprisonment could be said to be 'favouring' them!
4 Except at the very abstract level of confounding some people's faith that the market will provide a safe and humane solution to consumer demand, this does not fit with the Shapiro approach – see the introductory paragraph – but it is central to corporate culture issues.
5 Daly (1989) found that women were much more likely than men to say that they did it only for their family, though men too often made this claim. But these responses may partly reflect gendered differences in learned 'appropriate accounts'.
6 Examples include Oliver North's secretary (in 'Contragate'), Ernest Saunders' secretary (in Guinness, in relation to which specific charge Saunders was acquitted), and the Rossminster tax avoidance scandal in the 1980s which, partly because a vital diary was destroyed, was never prosecuted.
7 However, the problems in generating reliable and valid indices of any forms of business crime are far greater than the task of uncovering violent crime.
8 As in evaluating witnesses in white-collar and other prosecutions (Levi

1993b), one must always treat with caution *ex post facto* accounts of 'what happened' which inculpate others and wholly exculpate authors! See Levi (1981: Appendix A) for a general discussion of the problems of validity in offender accounts.

References

Abel, R. (ed.) (1982) *The Politics of Informal Justice*, New York: Academic Press.

Adler, Z. (1992) 'Male victims of sexual assault – legal issues' in Mezey, G.C. and King, M.B. (eds) *Male Victims of Sexual Assault*, Oxford: Oxford University Press.

Alder, C. (1991) 'Explaining violence: socioeconomics and masculinity', in Chappell, D., Grabosky, P. and Strang, H. (eds) *Australian Violence: Contemporary Perspectives*, Canberra: Australian Institute of Criminology.

Allen, J. (1985) 'Desperately seeking solutions: changing battered women's options since 1880', in Hatty, S.E. (ed.) National Conference on Domestic Violence, vol. 1, Canberra: Australian Institute of Criminology.

Amir, M. (1971) *Patterns in Forcible Rape*, Chicago: University of Chicago Press.

Anderson, E. (1989) 'Sex codes and family life among poor inner-city youths' in Wilson, J. (ed.) *The Ghetto Underclass: Social Science Perspectives. The Annals of the American Academy of Political and Social Science*, Newbury Park, CA: Sage.

Anderson, R., Brown, J. and Campbell, E. *et al.* (1993) *Aspects of Sex Discrimination in the Police Service in England and Wales*, London: Home Office.

Anderson, S., Kinsey, R., Loader, I. and Smith, C. (1990) *Cautionary Tales: A Study of Young People and Crime in Edinburgh*, Edinburgh: Centre for Criminology.

Arce, C. (1981) 'A reconsideration of Chicano culture and identity', *Daedalus* 110(2): 177–92.

Armstrong, G. and Harris, R. (1991) 'Football hooligans: theory and evidence', *Sociological Review* 39(3): 427–58.

Armstrong, G., Hobbs, D. and Maguire, M. (1991), 'The professional foul: covert policing in Britain: the case of soccer', paper given at the Law and Society Annual Meeting, Amsterdam, June 1991.

Ayres, I. and Braithwaite, J.(1992) *Responsive Regulation: Transcending the Deregulation Debate*, New York: Oxford University Press.

Baldwin, J. (1963) *The Fire Next Time*, New York: Dial Press.

Barber, B. (1984) *Strong Democracy: Participatory Politics for a New Age*, Berkeley: University of California Press.

Barrett, M. 1991 *The Politics of Truth: From Marx to Foucault*, Cambridge: Polity Press.

Barry, K. (1979) *Female Sexual Slavery*, New York: Avon Books.

Barthes, R. (1972) *Mythologies*, London: Paladin.

Bauman, Z. (1987) *Legislators and Interpreters*, Oxford: Polity Press.

Bauman, Z. (1992) *Intimations of Modernity*, London: Routledge.

Beirne, P. and Messerschmidt, J.W. (1991) *Criminology*, San Diego, CA: Harcourt Brace Jovanovich.

Benson, M. (1985) 'Denying the guilty mind: accounting for involvement in white-collar crime', *Criminology* 23: 583–607.

Berger, J. (1972) *Ways of Seeing*, Harmondsworth: Penguin.

Berk, R.A. and Sherman, L.W. (1985) 'Data collection strategies in the Minneapolis Domestic Assault Experiment' in Burstein, L., Freeman, H.E. and Rossi, P.H. (eds) *Collecting Evaluation Data: Problems and Solutions*, Newbury Park CA: Sage.

Bhat, A., Carr-Hill, R., and Ohri, S. (1988) *Britain's Black Population* 2nd edn, Aldershot, England: Gower.

Bianco, A. (1991) *Mad Dog: The Rise and Fall of Jeff Beck and Wall Street*, London: Pan.

The Black Scholar (ed.) (1992) *Court of Appeal: The Black Community Speaks Out on the Racial and Sexual Politics of Thomas vs. Hill*, New York: Ballatine Books.

Blain, N., Boyle, R. and O'Donnell, H. (1993) 'Battling along the boundaries: Scottish identity-marking in sports journalism' in Jarvie, G. and Walker, G. (eds) *Ninety Minute Patriots? Scottish Sport in the Making of the Nation*, Leicester: Leicester University Press.

Bland, L. (1984) 'The case of the Yorkshire Ripper: mad, bad, beast, or male?' in Gordon, P. and Scraton, P. (eds) *Causes for Concern*, London: Penguin.

Bowles, S. and Gintis, H. (1976) *Schooling in Capitalist America*. New York: Basic Books.

Bowling, B. (1993) 'Racial harassment and the process of victimisation: Conceptual and methodological implications for the local crime survey', *British Journal of Criminology* 33(2): 231–50.

Bowman, C. (1992) 'The Arrest Experiments: A feminist critique' *Journal of Criminal Law and Criminology* 83: 201–8.

Box, S. (1983) *Crime Power and Mystification* London:Tavistock.

Box-Grainger, J. (1982) 'RAP – a new strategy?' *The Abolitionist* 12, 14–21

Boyle, J. (1992) [1977] *A Sense of Freedom*, Edinburgh: Canongate Press.

Boyle, J. (1984) *The Pain of Confinement*, Edinburgh: Canongate Press.

Braithwaite, J. (1984) *Crime and the Pharmaceutical Industry*, London: Routledge & Kegan Paul.

Braithwaite, J. (1989) *Crime, Shame and Reintegration*, Sydney: Cambridge University Press.

Braithwaite, J. (1991) 'Poverty, power, white-collar crime and the paradoxes of criminological theory', *Australian and New Zealand Journal of Criminology* 24: 40–58.

Braithwaite, J. (1992) 'Poverty, power, and white-collar crime: Sutherland and the paradoxes of criminological theory', in Schlegel, K. and Weisburd, D. (eds) *White-collar Crime Reconsidered*, Boston: Northeastern University Press.

Braithwaite, J. (1993a) 'Inequality and republican criminology' in Hagan, J. and Petersen, R. (eds) *Inequality and Crime*, Palo Alto: Stanford University Press.

Braithwaite, J. (1993b) 'Crime and the average American', *Law and Society Review*, 27(1): 215–31.

Braithwaite, J. (1993c) 'Transnational regulation of the pharmaceutical industry', *Annals of the American Academy of Political and Social Science*, January, 12–30.

Braithwaite, J. and Mugford, S. (1993) 'Conditions of successful reintegration ceremonies: dealing with juvenile offenders', *British Journal of Criminology*, in press.

Braithwaite, J. and Pettit, P. (1990) *Not Just Desserts: A Republican Theory of Criminal Justice*, Oxford: Oxford University Press.

Brewer, J. (1991) 'Hercules, Hippolyte and the Amazons – or policewomen in the Royal Ulster Constabulary', *British Journal of Sociology* 42(2): 231–47.

Bridgeforth, C.A. (1990) *Predicting Domestic Violence from Post-arrest Suspect Interviews*, MA thesis, Institute of Criminal Justice and Criminology, University of Maryland.

Brittan, A. (1989) *Masculinity and Power*, Oxford: Blackwell.

Brod, H. (1987) 'Introduction: themes and theses of men's studies' in Brod, H. (ed.) *The Making of Masculinities: The New Men's Studies* Boston: Allen & Unwin.

Bromberger, C. (1990) 'Allez L'om! Forza Juve!: the passion for football in Marseille and Turin', Unit for Law and Popular Culture Working Paper: New Metropolitan University of Manchester.

Brown, C. (1965) *Manchild in the Promised Land*, New York: Macmillian.

Brown, J. and Campbell, E. (1992) 'Less than equal', *Policing* 74: 324–33.

Brownmiller, S. (1975) *Against Our Will: Men, Women and Rape*, New York: Simon & Schuster.

Brunswick, A.F. (1988) 'Young black males and substance use' in Gibbs, J.T. (ed.) *Young, Black and Male in America: An Endangered Species*, Westport, CT: Auburn House Publishing Company.

Brunt, R. (1989) 'Raising one voice', *Marxism Today*, September 1989: 22–25.

Buford, B. (1991) *Among the Thugs*, London: Secker and Warburg.

Bumiller, Kristin (1990) 'Fallen angels: the representation of violence against women in legal culture', *International Journal of the Sociology of Law* 18: 125–42.

Burgess, A.W. (1985) *Rape and Sexual Assault: a Research Handbook*, New York: Garland.

Bureau of Justice Statistics, US Department of Justice (1987) 'Sentencing outcomes in 28 felony courts 1987', NCJ-105743, Washington, DC.

Buzawa, E. and Buzawa, C. (1990) *Domestic Violence*, Newbury Park, California: Sage.

Cain, M. (1990) 'Towards transgression: new directions in feminist criminology', *International Journal of the Sociology of Law*, 18(1): 1–18.

Cameron, D. and Frazer, E. (1987) *The Lust to Kill: A Feminist Investigation of Sexual Murder*, Cambridge: Polity Press.

Campbell, A. (1984) *The Girls in the Gang*, Cambridge, MA: Basil Blackwell.

Campbell, A. (1990) 'Female participation in gangs' in Huff, C. Ronald (ed.) *Gangs in America*, Newbury Park, CA: Sage.

Campbell, C. (1976) 'Perspectives of violence' in Tutt, N. (ed.) *Violence*, London: HMSO.

Campbell, J. (1986) *Gate Fever*, London: Weidenfeld and Nicolson.

Cardiff, D. and Scannel, P. (1982) 'Serving the nation: Public service broadcasting before the War', in Waites, B., Bennett, T. and Martin, G. (eds) *Popular Culture: Past and Present*, London: Croom Helm.

Carlen, P. (1985) *Women's Imprisonment: A Study in Social Control*, London: Routledge.

Carlen, P., Hicks, J. O'Dwyer, J. Christina, D. and Tchaikovsky, C. (1985) *Criminal Women*, Cambridge: Polity Press.

Carrell, C. and Laing, J. (eds) (1982) *The Special Unit Barlinnie Prison*, Glasgow: Third Eye Centre.

Carrigan, T., Connell, R.W. and Lee, J. (1985) 'Toward a new theory of Masculinity', *Theory and Society* 14: 551–604.

Cazenave, N.A. (1981) 'Black men in America: the quest for manhood', in H.P. McAdoo (ed.) *Black families*, Beverly Hills: Sage Publications.

Centre for Police Studies (1989) *The Effect of the Sex Discrimination Act on the Scottish Police Service*, Strathclyde: University of Strathclyde

Centers for Disease Control (1992) *Homicide surveillance, 1979–1988*, Atlanta, GA: US Department of Health and Human Services, Public Health Service.

Chambliss, W.J. (1973) 'The Saints and the Roughnecks', *Society* 11 (1): 24–31.

Chappell, D. and Singer, S. (1977) 'Rape in New York City: A study of material in the police files and its meaning' in Chappell, D., Geis, R. and Geis, G. (eds) *Forcible Rape: The Crime, the Victim and the Offender*, New York: Columbia University Press.

Chaudhuri, M. and Daly, K. (1992) 'Do restraining orders help? Battered women's experience with male violence and legal process' in Buzawa, E.S. and Buzawa, C.G. (eds) *Domestic Violence: The Changing Criminal Justice Response*, Westport, CT: Auburn House.

Chesney-Lind, M. and Sheldon, R.G. (1992) *Girls, Delinquency and Juvenile Justice*, Pacific Grove, CA: Brooks/Cole.

Chibnall, S. (1977) *Law and Order News*, London: Tavistock.

Children's Defense Fund (1991) *A Children's Defense Budget*, Washington, DC: author.

Chodorow, N.J. (1978) *The Reproduction of Mothering: Psychoanalysis and the Sociology of Gender*, Berkeley: University of California Press.

Chodorow, N.J. (1989) *Feminism and Psychoanalytic Theory*, London: Yale University Press.

Christie, Nils (1977) 'Conflict as Property', *British Journal of Criminology* 17: 1–26.

Churchill, C. (1987) *Serious Money*, (play script), London: Methuen.

Clarke, A. (1992), 'Figuring a brighter future' in Dunning, E. and Rojek C. (eds) *Sport and Leisure in the Civilising Process*, London: Macmillan.

Clarke, M. (1986) *Regulating the City*, Milton Keynes: OUP.

Cleaver, E. (1968) *Soul on Ice*, New York: Dell Publishing Company.

Cloward, R.A., and L.E. Ohlin (1960) *Delinquency and Opportunity*, New York: Free Press.

Coffey, S., Brown, J. and Savage, S. (1992) 'Policewomen's career aspirations', *Police Studies* 15(1): 13–19.

Cohen, Albert. (1955) *Delinquent Boys: The Culture of the Gang*, New York: Free Press.

Cohen, L. and Felson, M. (1979) 'Social change and crime rate trends: a routine activity approach', *American Sociological Review* 44: 588–608.

Cohen, P. (1971) 'Policing the working class city' in Fine, B., Kinsey, R. Lea, J., Pociotto, S., and Young, J. (eds) *Capitalism and the Rule of Law* London: Hutchinson.

Cohen, P. (1972) 'Sub-cultural conflict and working class community', *Working Papers in Cultural Studies* 2, Birmingham: Centre for Contemporary Cultural Studies.

Cohen, P. (1976) 'Working class youth cultures in East London', in Hall, S. and Jefferson, T. (eds) *Resistance Through Rituals*, London: Hutchinson.

Cohen, P. (1986) *Rethinking the Youth Question*. Working Paper 3. London: Post 16 Education Centre in association with Youth and Policy.

Cohen, P. (1988) 'The perversions of inheritance', in Cohen, P. and Bains, H.S. (eds), *Multi-racist Britain*, Macmillan, London: 9–118.

Comstock, G. D. (1991) *Violence against Lesbians and Gay Men*, New York: Columbia University Press.

Connell, R.W. (1987) *Gender and Power: Society, the Person and Sexual Politics*, Cambridge: Polity Press.

Connell, R.W. (1989) 'Cool guys, swots and wimps: the interplay of masculinity and education', *Oxford Review of Education* 15 (3): 291–303.

Connell, R.W. (1991) 'Live fast and die young: the construction of masculinity among young working-class men on the margin of the labour market', *Australian and New Zealand Journal of Sociology* 27 (2): 141–71.

Cookson, P. W. and Persell, C.H. (1985) *Preparing for Power*, New York: Basic Books.

Corrigan, P. (1979) *Schooling the Smash Street Kids*, London: Macmillan.

Cousins, M. (1980) '"Mens rea": a note on sexual differences, criminology and the law' in Carlen, P. and Collison, M. (eds) *Radical Issues in Criminology*, Oxford: Martin Robertson.

Crawford, A., Jones, T., Woodhouse, T. and Young, J. (1990) *Second Islington Crime Survey*, Middlesex Polytechnic: Centre for Criminology.

Cressey, D. (1953) *Other People's Money*, New York: Free Press.

Critcher, C. (1991) 'Putting on the style: aspects of recent English football', in Williams, J. and Wagg, S. (eds) *British Football and Social Change*, Leicester University Press: Leicester.

Croall, H. (1992) *White-Collar Crime*, Milton Keynes: Open University Press.

Cross, W.E. (1978) 'The Thomas and Cross models of psychological nigresence: A literature review', *Journal of Black Psychology* 4: 13–31.

Cross, W.E. (1991) *Shades of Black*, Philadelphia: Temple University Press.

Cruse, D. and Rubin, J. (1973) 'Police behaviour: Part I', *Journal of Psychiatry and Law* 1.

Dalton, M. (1959) *Men Who Manage*, New York: Wiley.

Daly, K. (1989) 'Gender and varieties of white-collar crime', *Criminology* 27: 769–94.

Daly, K. (1992) 'What would have been justice? Remarks to plenary on sexual harassment in the Thomas Hearings', Law and Society Association Annual Meeting, unpublished.

Daly, M. and Wilson, M. (1988) *Homicide*, New York: Aldine de Gruyter.

Davies, N. (1992) *Maxwell: the Inside Story*, London: Pan.

Davies, P. (1990) *All Played Out*, London: Heinemann.

Davies, T. (1992) 'Why can't a woman be more like a fan?' in D. Bull (ed.) *We'll Support You Evermore*, London: Duckworth.

Davis, J.A. (1976) 'Blacks, crime, and American culture', *Annals of the American Association of Political and Social Science* 423: 89–98.

Dean, J. (1976) *Blind Ambition*, New York: Simon & Schuster.

Defleur, M. and Westie, F. (1958) 'Verbal attitudes and overt acts', *American Sociological Review*, 23: 667–73.

Dembo, R. (1988) 'Delinquency among Black male youth' in Gibbs, J.T. (ed.) *Young, Black and Male in America: An Endangered Species*, Westport, CT: Auburn House Publishing Company.

Dews, P. (1984) 'Power and subjectivity in Foucault', *New Left Review* 144: 72–95.

Dobash R.E. and Dobash R.P. (1979) *Violence Against Wives: A Case Against Patriarchy*, New York: Free Press.

Dobash, R.E. and Dobash, R.P. (1992) *Women, Violence and Social Change*, London: Routledge.

Dobash, R.P., Dobash, R.E., and Gutteridge, S. (1986) *The Imprisonemnt of Women*, Oxford: Blackwell.

Downes, D. and Rock, P. (1982) *Understanding Deviance*, Oxford: Oxford University Press.

Downham, C. and Worthington, C. (1992) 'Wake up England', TV Documentary for Channel 4, 29.10.1992.

Drake, St. C. and Cayton, H. (1945) *Black Metropolis: A Study of Negro Life in a Northern City*, New York: Harcourt Brace.

Dryzek, J. (1990) *Discursive Democracy*, Cambridge: Cambridge University Press.

Dumond, R. (1992) 'The sexual assault of male inmates in incarcerated settings', *International Journal of the Sociology of Law* 20: 135–57.

Dunford, F. (1990) 'System-initiated warrants for suspects of misdemeanor domestic assault: A pilot study', *Justice Quarterly* 7: 631–53.

Dunning, E. Murphy, P. and Williams, J. (1988) *The Roots of Football Hooliganism*, London: Routledge.

Dutton, D. (1988) *The Domestic Assault of Women: Psychological and Criminal Justice Perspectives*, Boston: Allyn and Bacon.

Dutton, D.G., Hart, S.D., Kennedy, L.W. and Williams, K.R. (1992) 'Arrest and the reduction of repeat wife assault' in Buzawa, E.S. and Buzawa, C.G. (eds) *Domestic Violence: The Changing Criminal Justice Response*, Westport CT: Auburn House.

Eaton, M. (1993) *Women After Prison*, Milton Keynes: Open University Press

Edwards, A.R. (1975) 'The prison' in J. McKinley (ed.) *Processing People*, London: Holt, Rinehart and Winston.

Edwards, S. (1989) *Policing Domestic Violence: Women, the Law and the State*, Newbury Park, California: Sage.

Edwards, T. (1990) 'Beyond sex and gender: masculinity, homosexuality and social theory' in Hearn, J. and Morgan, D. (eds) *Men, Masculinites and Social Theory*, London: Unwin Hyman.

Eijkman, H. (1992) 'Police, victims and democracy: rewriting the priorities,' in Moir, P. and Eijkman, H. (eds) *Policing Australia: Old Issues, New Perspectives*, Melbourne: Macmillan.

Elliott, D.S. and Voss, H.L. (1974) *Delinquency and Dropout*, Lexington, MA: Lexington Books.

Ellison, R. (1947) *Invisible man*, New York: Vantage Books.

Elstain, J.B. (1981) *Public Man, Private Woman*, Princeton, New Jersey: Princeton University Press.

Equal Opportunities Commission (1990) *Managing to Make Progress*, London: Metropolitan Police.

Erickson, R.V., Baranek, P.M. and Chan, J.B.L. (1991) *Representing Order*, Milton Keynes: Open University Press.

Erikson, E. (1959) 'Identity and the life cycle', *Psychological Issues* 1(1): 1–171.

Erikson, E. (1964) Memorandum on identity and the Negro youth, *Journal of Social Issues* 20: 29–42.

Erikson, E. (1968) *Identity: Youth in crisis*, New York: Norton.

Estrich, S. (1987) *Real Rape*, Cambridge, Massachusetts: Harvard University Press.

Estrich, Susan (1986) 'Rape', *The Yale Law Journal* 95: 1087–184.

Evason, E. (1982) *Hidden Violence*, Belfast: Farset Press.

Fagan, J. and Browne, A. (1990) 'Violence towards intimates and spouses', report commissioned by the Panel on the Understanding and Control of Violent Behavior, National Research Council, National Academy of Sciences, Washington, DC.

Falk, G. (1990) *Murder: An Analysis of its Forms, Conditions, and Causes*, London: McFarland & Company.

Farley, R., and Allen, W.R. (1989) *The Color Line and the Quality of Life in America*, New York: Oxford University Press.

Fattah, E.A. (1992) *Towards a Critical Victimology*, London: Macmillan.

Ferraro, K.J. (1989) 'Policing woman battering', *Social Problems* 36: 61–74.

Ferraro, K.J. and Boychuk, T. (1992) 'The court's response to interpersonal violence: a comparison of intimate and nonintimate assault' in Buzawa, E.S. and Buzawa, C.G. (eds), *Domestic Violence: The Changing Criminal Justice Response*, Westport CT: Auburn House.

Fielding, N. and Fielding, J. (1992) 'A comparative minority: female recruits to a British constabulary force', *Policing and Society* 2, 205–18.

Fineman, M, (1991) *The Illusion of Equality: The Rhetoric and Reality of Divorce Reform*, University of Chicago Press, Chicago.

Fingerhut, L.A., Ingram, D.D., and Feldman, J.J. (1992) 'Firearm homicide among black teenage males in metropolitan counties', *Journal of the American Medical Association* 267: 3054–8.

Finkelhor, D. (ed.) (1986) *A Sourcebook on Child Sexual Abuse*, Beverley Hills: Sage.

Finkelhor, D., and Yllo, K. (1985) *License to Rape. Sexual Abuse of Wives*, New York: Free Press.

Fishman, Laura T. (1988) 'The vice queens: an ethnographic study of black female gang behavior', paper presented at the annual meetings of the American Society of Criminology.

Fishwick, N. (1989) *English Football and Society, 1910–1950*, Manchester: Manchester University Press.

Flax, J. (1990) *Thinking Fragments: Psychoanalysis, Feminism and Postmodernism in the Contemporary West*, Oxford: University of California Press.

Franklin, A. J. (1982) 'Therapeutic interventions with urban black adolescents', in Jones, E.E. and Korchin, S.J. (eds) *Minority Mental Health*, New York: Praeger.

Franklin, C. W. (1986) 'Conceptual and logical issues in theory and research related to black masculinity', *Western Journal of Black Studies* 10(4): 161–88.

Frazier, E. F. (1949) *The Negro in the United States*, New York: Macmillan.

Freeman, R.B., and Holzer, H. (1986) *The Black Youth Employment Crisis*, Chicago: University of Chicago Press.

Frieze, I.H. and Browne, A. (1989) 'Violence in marriage' in Ohlin, L. and Tonry, M. (eds) *Family Violence*, Chicago: The University of Chicago Press.

Frisch, L.A. (1992) 'Research that succeeds, policies that fail', *Journal of Criminal Law and Criminology* 83: 209–16.

Frith, S. (1990) 'Frankie said, but what did they mean?', in Tomlinson, A. (ed.) *Consumption, Identity and Style*, London: Routledge.

Frohmann, L. (1991) 'Discrediting victims' allegations of Sexual Assault: prosecutorial accounts of case rejections', *Social Problems* 38: 213–26.

Frosh, S. (1987) *The Politics of Psychoanalysis: An Introduction to Freudian and Post-Freudian Theory*, London: Macmillan.

Frosh, S. (1991) *Identity Crisis: Modernity, Psychoanalysis and the Self*, London: Macmillan.

Gagnon, A.G. (1992) 'Ending mandatory divorce mediation for battered women', *Harvard Women's Law Journal* 15: 272–94.

Gardener, C.B. (1990) 'Safe conduct: Women, crime and self in public places', *Social Problems* 37(4): 311–28.

Gardener, C.B. (1993) 'Gay baiting: The verbal harassment of gay men in public places' paper presented to the International Conference: The Public Sphere in Free Market Societies, University of Salford.

Gebhard, P.H., Gagnon, J.H., Pomeroy, W.B., and Christenson, C.V. (1965) *Sex Offenders: An Analysis of Types*, New York: Harper & Row.

Geertz, C. (1972) 'Deep play: notes on a Balinese Cockfight' *Daedalus* 101, winter.

Geis, G. D. (1992) 'White-collar crime: what is it?' in Schlegel, K. and Weisburd, D. (eds) *White Collar Crime Reconsidered*, Boston, Mass: Northeastern University Publications.

Gelles, R.J. (1987) *Family violence*, Beverly Hills, CA: Sage.

Gelsthorpe, L. and Morris, A. (1990) 'Introduction: transforming and transgressing criminology' in Gelsthorpe, L. and Morris, A. (eds) *Feminist Perspectives in Criminology*, Milton Keynes: Open University Press.

Gibbs, J.T. (1974) 'Patterns of adaptation among black students at a predominantly white university', *American Journal of Orthopsychiatry*, 44(5): 728–40.

Gibbs, J.T. (1975) 'Use of mental health services by black students at a predominantly white university: a three-year study', *Journal of Orthopsychiatry* 44(3): 430–45.

Gibbs, J.T. (ed.) (1988) *Young, Black and Male in America: An Endangered Species*, Westport, CT: Auburn House Publishing Company.

Gibbs, J.T. (1992) 'The Janus face of despair: homicide and suicide in young black males' in National Urban League, *The second emancipation*, New York: The National Urban League.

Gibbs, J.T. (1993) 'British, black, and blue', *Focus*, April, 3–5, Publication of the Joint Center for Political and Economic Studies, Washington, DC.

Gibbs, J.T. and Hines, A. M. (1992) 'Negotiating ethnic identity: issues for black–white biracial adolescents' in Root, M.P. (ed.) *Racially Mixed People in America*, Newbury Park, CA: Sage.

Giddens, A. (1981) *A Contemporary Critique of Historical Materialism*, London: Macmillan.

Giddens, A. (1991) *Modernity and Self-Identity: Self and Society in the Late Modern Age*, Cambridge: Polity Press.

Giddens, A. (1992) *The Transformation of Intimacy: Sexuality, Love and Eroticism in Modern Societies*, Cambridge: Polity.

Gilbert, N. (1991) 'The phantom epidemic of sexual assault', *The Public Interest* 193: spring: 54–65.

Gilmore, T.C. (1990) *Manhood in the Making*, New Haven: Yale University Press.

Gilroy, P. (1987) *Ain't No Black in the Union Jack*, London: Hutchinson.

Gilroy, P. and Sim, J. (1985) 'Law, order and the state of the left', *Capital and Class*, spring.

Giullianotti, R. (1993) 'Keep it in the family: an outline of Hibs soccer casuals' social ontology', unpublished paper, University of Aberdeen.

Glasgow, D. (1980) *The Black Underclass*, San Francisco: Jossey-Bass.

Godenzi, A. (1989) *Bieder, brutal. Frauen und Maenner sprechen ueber sexuelle Gewalt*, Zuerich: Unionsverlag.

Godenzi, A. (1993) *Gewalt im sozialen Nahraum*, Basel: Helbing & Lichtenhahn.

Goffman, E. (1963) *Stigma*, Englewood Cliffs, NJ: Prentice-Hall.

Goode, W. (1971) 'Force and violence in the family', *Journal of Marriage and the Family* 33: 624–36.

Gordon, M. and Riger, S. (1988) *The Female Fear*, New York: Free Press.

Gordon, V. (1980) *The Self-concept of Black Americans*, Lanham, MD: University Press of America.

Grade, M. (1989) *Working Group on the Fear of Crime*, London: HMSO.

Graef, R. (1990) 'What's gone wrong with the police?', *Independent on Sunday* 18.3.90.

Gramsci, A. (1971) *Selections from the Prison Notebooks*, London: Lawrence & Wishart.

Gray, L. (1986) 'Predicting interpersonal conflict between men and women: The case of black men', *American Behavioral Scientist* 29(5): 635–46.

Green, P. (1990) *The Enemy Within*, Milton Keynes: Open University Press.

Greenberg, David F. (1977) 'Delinquency and the age structure of society', *Contemporary Crises* 1(2): 189–224.

Grier, W.H., and Cobbs, P.M. (1968) *Black rage*, New York: Bantam Books.

Groth, A.N., and Birnbaum, H.J. (1979) *Men Who Rape: The Psychology of the Offender*, New York: Plenum Press.

Groth, A.N., Burgess, A.W., and Holmstrom, L.L. (1977) 'Rape: power, anger, and sexuality', *American Journal of Psychiatry* 134: 1239–43.

Grubin, D. and Gunn, J. (1991) *The Imprisoned Rapist and Rape*, unpublished report to the Home Office, Department of Forensic Psychiatry: Institute of Psychiatry.

Hagan, J. (1988) *Structural Criminology*, Cambridge: Polity Press.

Haley, A. and Malcolm, X (1964) *The Autobiography of Malcolm X*, New York: Grove Ross.

Halford, A. (1987) 'Until the twelfth of never', *Police Review*, October: 2019.

Hannerz, U. (1969) *Soulside: Inquiries into ghetto culture and community*, New York: Columbia University Press.

Harding, S. (ed.) (1986) *The Science Question in Feminism*, Milton Keynes: Open University Press.

Harding, S. (ed.) (1987) *Feminism and Methodology*, Milton Keynes: Open University Press.

Hargreaves, J. (1986) *Sport, Power and Culture*, Cambridge: Polity Press.

Harris, M.G. (1988) *Cholas: Latino Girls and Gangs*, New York: AMS.

Harry, Joseph. (1992) 'Conceptualizing anti-gay violence' in Herek, G. H. and Berril, K.T. (eds) *Hate Crimes*, Newbury Park, CA: Sage.

Hatty, S. (1985) 'On the reproduction of misogyny: the therapeutic management of violence against women' in Hatty, S.E. (ed.) *National Conference on Domestic Violence*, vol. 1, Canberra: Australian Institute of Criminology.

Hatty, S.E. (1988) 'Male violence and the police: an Australian experience', working paper, School of Social Work, University of New South Wales, Sydney.

Hawkins, D.F. and Jones, N. (1989) 'Black adolescents in the criminal justice system' in Jones, R. L. (ed.), *Black Adolescents*, Berkeley, CA: Cobb and Henry Publishers.

Hearn, J. and Morgan, D. (eds) (1990) *Men, Masculinities, and Social Theory*, London: Unwin Hyman.

Hebdige, D. (1992) 'Digging for Britain: an excavation in seven parts', in Strinati, D. and Wagg, S. (eds) *Come on Down: Popular Culture in Post-war Britain*, London: Routledge.

Heidensohn, F. (1985) *Women and Crime*, London: Macmillan.
Heidensohn, F. (1989) *Women in Policing in the USA*, London: Police Foundation.
Heidensohn, F. (1992) *Women in Control*, Oxford: Oxford University Press.
Henriques, J., Hollway, W., Urwin, C., Venn, C., and Walkerdine, V. (1984) *Changing the Subject: Psychology, Social Regulation and Subjectivity*, London: Methuen.
Herek, G. (1986) 'On heterosexual masculinity', *American Behavioral Scientist* 29(5): 563–77.
Herek, G., and Berrill, K. (1992) *Hate Crimes*, Beverly Hills, CA: Sage.
Hesse, B., Rai, D.K., Bennett, C. and McGilchrist, P. (1992) *Beneath the Surface: Racial Harassment*, Aldershot: Avebury.
Heward, Christine (1988) *Making a Man of Him*, London: Routledge.
Hill, D. (1989) *Out of His Skin*, London: Faber.
The Hillsborough Stadium Disaster (15 April 1989) (1990) Inquiry by Rt Hon. Lord Justice Taylor, Final Report, Cm 962, HMSO, London.
Hindelang, M.J. (1978) 'Race and involvement in common law personal crimes', *American Sociological Review* 43: 93–109.
Hindelang, M.J., Gottfredson, M.R. and Garofalo, J. (1978) *Victims of Personal Crime: An Empirical Foundation for a Theory of Personal Victimisation*, Cambridge, Mass: Ballinger.
Hirschel, J.D., Hutchinson. I.W. III, Dean, C., Kelley, J.J. and Pesackis, C.E. (1990) Charlotte Spouse Assault Replication Project: Final Report, National Institute of Justice, Washington, DC.
Hirschi, T. (1969) *Causes of Delinquency*, Berkeley, CA: University of California Press.
Hobbs, D. (1988) *Doing the Business*, Oxford: Clarendon Press.
Hobbs, D. (1991a) 'A piece of business: the moral economy of detective work in the East End of London', *British Journal of Sociology* 42(4).
Hobbs, D. (1991b) 'Business as a master metaphor: working class entrepreneurship and business-like policing' in Burrows, R. (ed.) *Deciphering the Enterprise Culture*, London: Routledge.
Hobbs, D. (1993), 'Obituary for Bobby Moore', *Independent*, 26.2.1993.
Hobbs, D. (forthcoming) *Mutant Enterprise*, Oxford: Oxford University Press.
Hobbs, D. and Robins, D. (1991) 'The Boy Done Good', *Sociological Review* 39(3).
Holdaway, S. (1989) 'Discovering structure: studies of the British police occupational culture' in Weatheritt, M. (ed.) *Police Research: Some Future Prospects*, Aldershot: Avebury.
Hollway, W. (1983) 'Heterosexual sex: power and desire for the other' in Cartledge, S. and Ryan, J. (eds) *Sex and Love: New Thoughts on Old Contradictions*, London: The Women's Press.
Hollway, W. (1989) *Subjectivity and Method in Psychology: Gender, Meaning and Science*, London: Sage.
Holt, R. (1988) 'Football and the urban way of life in Nineteenth Century Britain' in Morgan, J.A. (ed.) *Pleasure, Profit and Proselytism*, London: Cass.

Holt, R. (1989) *Sport and the British*, Oxford: Oxford University Press.

Home Office (1993) Digest 2: 'Information on the criminal justice system in England and Wales', London: HMSO.

hooks, bell (1992) 'Reconstructing black masculinity', in hooks, b. *Black Looks: Race and Representation*, Ontario, Canada: Between the Lines.

Hopcraft, A. (1968) *The Football Man*, Penguin: Harmondsworth.

Hopkins, A. and McGregor, H. (1991) *Working for Change: The Movement Against Domestic Violence*, Sydney: Allen & Unwin.

Hornby, N. (1992), *Fever Pitch*, London: Gower.

Hough, M. and Mayhew, P. (1983) *The British Crime Survey*, London: HMSO.

Hough, M. and Mayhew, P. (1985) *Taking Account of Crime: Key Findings from the 1984 British Crime Survey*, London: HMSO.

Hunt, J.G., and Hunt, L.L. (1977) 'Racial inequality and self-image: identity maintenance as identify diffusion', *Sociology and Social Research* 61: 539–59.

Hunt, J. (1990) 'The logic of sexism among police', *Women and criminal justice* 1(2): 3–30.

Inglis, S. (1983) *The Football Grounds of Great Britain*, London: Collins Willow.

Island, D. and Letellier, P. (1991) *Men Who Beat The Men Who Love Them*, London: Harrington Park Press.

Jarvie, G. and Walker, G. (eds) (1994) *Ninety Minute Patriots: Scottish Sport in the Making of a Nation*, Leicester University Press: Leicester.

Jefferson, T. (1992) 'Wheelin' and stealin'', *Achilles Heel* 13, summer.

Johnson, C. M. and Robinson, M. T. (1992) *Homicide Report*, Washington, DC: Government of the District of Columbia, Office of Criminal Justice Plans and Analysis, 717 Fourteenth St NW, Washington, DC 20005.

Jones, S. (1983) 'Community policing in Devon and Cornwall' in Bennett, T. (ed.) *The Future of Policing*, Cambridge: Institute of Criminology.

Jones, S. (1986) 'Women police: caught in the act', *Policing* 2: 129–40.

Jones, T., Maclean, B. and Young, J. (1986) *The Islington Crime Survey*, Aldershot: Gower.

Kalven, H. and Zeisel, H. (1966) *The American Jury*, Chicago: University of Chicago Press.

Kappeler, S. (1986) *The Pornography of Representation*, Oxford: Polity /Basil Blackwell.

Katz, J. (1988) *The Seductions of Crime: Moral and Sensual Attractions of Doing Evil*, New York: Basic Books.

Keating, F. (1993) 'One heck of a footballer', *The Spectator*, 6.3.1993.

Kelly, L. (1988) *Surviving Sexual Violence*, Oxford: Polity.

Kessler, S., Ashenden, D.J., Connell, R.W., and Dowsett, G.W. (1985) 'Gender relations in secondary schooling', *Sociology, of Education* 58 (1): 34–48.

Kidd, B. (1987) 'Sports and Masculinity.' in Kaufman, M. (ed.) *Beyond Patriarchy: Essays by Men on Pleasure, Power and Change*, Toronto: Oxford University Press.

Kim, J. (1981) 'The process of Asian–American identity development: A study of Japanese American women's perceptions of their struggle to achieve positive identities', unpublished doctoral dissertation, University of Massachusetts, Amherst, MA.

Kimmel, M.S. (1986) 'Introduction: toward men's studies', *American Behavioral Scientist* 29(5): 517–29.

King M.B. (1992) 'Male sexual assault in the community' in Mezey, G.C. and King, M.B. (eds) *Male Victims of Sexual Assault*, Oxford: Oxford University Press.

Klein, M.W. (1971) *Street Gangs and Street Workers*, Englewood Cliffs, NJ: Prentice-Hall.

Koss, M.P., Leonard, K.E, Beezley, D.A., and Oros, C.J. (1981) 'Personality and attitudinal characteristics of sexually aggressive men', paper presented at the American Psychological Association, Los Angeles.

Kozol, J. (1991) *Savage Inequities: Children in American schools*, New York: Crown Publishers.

Krisberg, B., Schwartz, I., Fishman, G., Eiskovits, Z., and Guttman, E. (1986) *The Incarceration of Minority Youth*, Minneapolis: H.H. Humphrey Institute of Public Affairs, University of Minnesota.

Lacan, J. (1953) 'The Function and Field of Speech and Language in Psychoanalysis' in Lacan, J. (1977) *Ecrits: A Selection*, London: Tavistock.

Laclau, E. (1980) 'Populist rupture and discourse', trans. Jim Grealy, *Screen Education* 34: 87–93.

LaGrange, R. and Ferraro, K. (1989) 'Assessing age and gender differences in perceived risk and fear of crime' *Criminology* 27(4): 697–719

Lanchester, J., (1989) 'The necessity of football' *London Review of Books*, 5.8.1989.

Lansky, M. (1984) 'Violence, shame and the family', *International Journal of Family Psychiatry* 5: 21–40.

Lansky, M. (1987) 'Shame and domestic violence', in Nathanson, D. (ed.) *The Many Faces of Shame*, New York: Guilford.

Larson, T.E. (1988) 'Employment and unemployment in young black males', in Gibbs, J.T. (ed.) *Young, Black and Male in America: An Endangered Species*, Westport, CT: Auburn House Publishing Company.

Larzelere, R.E., and Klein, D.M. (1987) 'Methodology' in: Sussman, M.B. and Steinmetz, S.K. (eds) *Handbook of marriage and the family*, New York: Plenum Press.

Lasch, C. (1977) *Haven in a Heartless World*, New York: Basic Books.

Lee, P. (1992) 'A strange kind of love: Manchester United, Sir Matt Busby and Europe' in Bull, D. (ed.) *We'll Support You Evermore*, Duckworth: London.

Lemelle, A. J. Jr. (1991) 'Betcha cain't reason with'em': bad black boys in America in Bowser, B.P. (ed.), *Black Male Adolescents: Parenting and Education in Community Context*, Lanham, MD: University Press of America.

Lempert, R.O. (1989) 'Humility is a virtue: On the publicization of policy-relevant research', *Law and Society Review* 23: 145–61.

Lerman, L.G. (1984) 'Mediation of wife abuse cases: the adverse impact of informal dispute resolution on women', *Harvard Women's Law Journal* 7: 57–113.

Lerman, L.G. (1992) 'The Decontextualization of domestic violence', *Journal of Criminal Law and Criminology* 83: 217–40.

Levi, M. (1981) *The Phantom Capitalists*, Aldershot: Gower.

Levi, M. (1987) *Regulating Fraud: White-Collar Crime and the Criminal Process*, London: Routledge.

Levi, M. (1991) 'Sentencing white-collar crime in the dark: the case of the Guinness Four', *Howard Journal of Criminal Justice*, 28 (4): 257–79.

Levi, M. (1994) 'Violent Crime', in Maguire, M., Morgan R. and Reiner, R. (eds) *The Oxford Handbook of Criminology*, Oxford: Oxford University Press.

Levi, M. (1993) *The Investigation, Prosecution, and Trial of Serious Fraud*, Royal Commission on Criminal Justice Research Study No.14, London: HMSO.

Levi, M. and Pithouse, A. (1992) 'Victims of fraud', in Downes, D. (ed.) *Unravelling Criminal Justice*, London: Macmillan.

Levi, M. and Pithouse, A. (forthcoming) *Victims of Fraud*, Milton Keynes: Open University Press.

Lewis, H.B. (1971) *Shame and Guilt in Neurosis*, New York: International Universities Press.

Liebow, E. (1967) *Talley's Corner*, Boston: Little Brown.

Lombroso, C. (1911) *Crime, Its Causes and Remedies*, Boston: Little Brown.

Luckenbill, D.F. (1977) 'Criminal homicide as a situated transaction', *Social Problems* 26: 176–86.

Lunneborg, P. (1989) *Women police officers' current career profile*, Springfield, Ill.: Charles Thomas.

MacDonald, D. and Sim, J. (1978) *Scottish Prisons and the Special Unit*, Glasgow: Scottish Council for Civil Liberties.

Macdonell, D. (1986) *Theories of Discourse: An Introduction*, Oxford: Blackwell.

McGrath, T. and Boyle, J. (1977) *The Hard Man*, Edinburgh: Canongate.

MacKinnon, C. (1983) 'Feminism, Marxism, method, and the state: an agenda for theory', *Signs: Journal of Women in Culture and Society* 8: 635–58.

MacKinnon, C. (1987) *Feminism Unmodified: Discourses on Life and Law*, Cambridge, Mass: Harvard University Press.

McMullen, R. (1990) *Male Rape*, London: GMP Publishers.

McRobbie, A. (1991) *Feminism and youth culture*, Boston: Unwin Hyman.

Madhubuti, H.R. (1990) *Black Men: Obsolete, Single, Dangerous?*, Chicago: Third World Press.

Maguire, M. and Corbett, C. (1987) *The Effects of Crime and the Work of Victim Support Schemes*, Aldershot: Gower

Majors, R. (1989) 'Cool pose: the proud signature of black survival' in Kimmel, M.S. and Messner, M. A. (eds) *Men's Lives*, New York: Macmillan.

Majors, R., and Billson, J.M. (1992) *Cool pose*, New York: Lexington Books.

Manning, P. (1980) *The Narc's Game*, Cambridge MA: MIT Press.

Marcuse, H. (1955) *Eros and Civilization*, Boston: Beacon Press.

Marcuse. H. (1964) *One Dimensional Man*, London: Routledge & Kegan Paul.

Mars, G. (1982) *Cheats at Work*, London: Unwin Hyman.

Martin, S. (1989) 'Women in policing: the 80s and beyond' in Kenney, D. (ed.), *Police and Policing Contemporary Issues*, New York: Praeger.

Marwick, C. (1992) 'Guns, drugs threaten to raise public health problem of violence to epidemic', *Journal of the American Medical Association*, 267, 2993.

Mason, T. (1980), *Association Football and English Society 1863–1915*, Brighton: Harvester.

Matthews, J.J. (1985) *Good and Mad Women: Historical Construction of Femininity in Twentieth Century Australia*, Sydney: George Allen & Unwin.

Matthews, R. and Young, J. (1992) *Issues in Realist Criminology*, London: Sage.

Mathiesen, T. (1990) *Prison on Trial*, London: Sage.

Matza, D. (1964) *Delinquency and Drift*, Englewood Cliffs, NJ: Prentice Hall.

Mauer, M. (1990) *Black Males in the Criminal Justice System*, Washington, DC: The Sentencing Project.

Maxfield, M. (1984) *Fear of Crime in England and Wales*, London: HMSO

Maxwell, G.M. and Morris, A. (1993) 'Family victims and culture: youth justice in NZ', Institute of Criminology, Victoria University of Wellington, Wellington.

Mayhew, P., Dowds, L. and Elliot, D. (1989) *The 1988 British Crime Survey*, London: HMSO.

Mayhew, P. and Maung, N.A. (1992) 'Surveying crime: findings from the 1992 British Crime Survey', Home Office Research and Statistics Department.

Meima, M. (1990) 'Sexual violence, criminal law and abolitionism' in Rolston, B. and Tomlinson, M. (eds) *Gender, Sexuality and Social Control*, Bristol, England: The European Group for the Study of Deviance and Social Control.

Messerschmidt, J.W. (1979) *School Stratification and Delinquent Behavior*, Stockholm: Gotab.

Messerschmidt, J.W. (1986) *Capitalism, Patriarchy and Crime: Towards a Socialist Feminist Criminology*, Totowa, N.J.: Rowan & Littlefield.

Messerschmidt, J.W. (1993) *Masculinities and Crime: Critique, and Reconceptualization of Theory*, Lanham, Maryland: Rowman and Littlefield.

Messner, M. (1989) 'Masculinities and athletic careers', *Gender and Society* 3 (1): 71–88.

Middleham, N. (1993) *Football Spectators and Policing*, Police Requirements Support Unit: HMSO.

Miedzian, M. (1991) *Boys Will Be Boys: Breaking the Link Between Masculinity and Violence*, New York: Doubleday.

Miliband, R. (1978) 'A state of desubordination', *British Journal of Sociology* 29: 4.

Miller, W.B. (1958) 'Lower class culture as a generating milieu of gang delinquency', *Journal of Social Issues*, 14(3).

Miller, W.B. (1980) 'Gangs, groups and serious youth crime' in Shichor, D. and Kelly, D. H. (eds) *Issues in Juvenile Delinquency*, Lexington, MA: Lexington Books.

Ministerial Review Team to the Minister of Social Welfare (1992) Review of the Children, Young Persons and their Families Act, 1989, Minister of Social Welfare, Wellington.

Mishkind, M., Rodin, J., Silberstein, L., and Striegel-Moore, R. (1986) 'The embodiment of masculinity: Cultural, psychological, and behavioral dimensions, *American Behavioral Scientist* 29(5): 545–62.

Monroe, S. (1988) *Brothers, Black and Poor: A True Story of Courage and Survival*, New York: Marrow.

Moorhouse, H.F. (1994) 'From 'zines like these', in Jarvie G. and Walker, G. (eds) *Ninety Minute Patriots: Scottish Sport in the Making of a Nation*, Leicester University Press: Leicester.

Morash, M. (1986) 'Gender, peer group experiences, and seriousness of delinquency', *Journal of Research in Crime and Delinquency* 23 (1): 43–67.

Morgan, D. (1987) 'Masculinity and violence' in Hanmer, J. and Maynard, M. (eds) *Women, Violence and Social Control*, Hampshire: MacMillan.

Morgan, D. (1992) *Discovering Men*, London: Routledge.

Morgan, J. and Zedner, L. (1992) *Child Victims: Crime, Impact and Criminal Justice*, Oxford: Oxford University Press.

Morgan, R. (1989) *The Demon Lover*, London: Methuen.

Morris, A. and Maxwell, G.M. (1991) 'Juvenile justice in New Zealand: A New paradigm', *Australian and New Zealand Journal of Criminology* 26: 72–90.

Morrison, T. (ed.) (1992) *Race-ing Justice, En-gendering Power: Essays on Anita Hill, Clarence Thomas, and the Construction of Social Reality*, New York: Pantheon Books.

Moss, J. (1991) 'Hurling oppression: overcoming anomie and self-hatred' in Bowser, B. P. (ed.), *Black Male Adolescents: Parenting and Education in Community Context*, Lanham, MD: University Press of America.

Muehlbauer, G. and Dodder, L. (1983) *The Losers: Gang Delinquency in an American Suburb*, New York: Praeger.

Mugford, J. and Mugford, S. (1992) 'Policing Domestic Violence' in Moir, P. and Eijkman, H. (eds), *Policing Australia: Old Issues, New Perspectives*, Melbourne: Macmillan.

Murdock, G. (1982) 'Mass communication and social violence: A critical review of recent research trends' in Marsh, P. and Campbell, A. (eds) *Aggression and Violence*, Oxford: Basil Blackwell.

Murray, W. (1984) *The Old Firm: Sectarianism, Sport and Society in Scotland*, John Donald, Edinburgh.

Nardi, P. (1992) 'Seamless souls', in Nardi, P. (ed.) *Men's friendships*, London: Sage.

National Research Council (1989) *A Common Destiny: Blacks and American Society*, Washington, DC: National Academy Press.

Nettler, G. (1974) 'Embezzlement without problems', *British Journal of Criminology* 14(2).

Newby, L. (1980) 'Rape victims in court: the Western Australian example' in Scutt, J.A. (ed.) *Rape Law Reform*, Canberra: Australian Institute of Criminology.

Newman, D. (1991) 'D Wing' in Selby, M. (ed.) *Riot: Reform in Our Time: A Report into Power Sharing*, conference held at HMP Grendon 20–21 August 1991, Springhill: Springhill Press.

Office of the Commissioner for Children (1991) 'A briefing paper: an appraisal of the first year of the Children, Young Persons and Their Families Act 1989', Office of the Commissioner for Children, Wellington, New Zealand.

Ogbu, J.U. (1978) *Minority Education and caste: The American System in Cross-cultural Perspective*, New York: Academic Press.

Oliver, W. (1989) 'Sexual conquest and patterns of black-on-black violence: A structural–cultural perspective', *Violence and Victims* 4(4): 257–73.

Parker, H. (1989) *Instead of the Dole*, London: Routledge.

Parker, T. (1990) *Life After Life*, London: Secker & Warburg.

Parsons, T. (1954) *Essays in Sociological Theory*, Glencoe: Free Press.

Patten, B. (1988) *Storm Damage*, London: Unwin Hyman.

Pearce, F. (1976) *Crimes of the Powerful*, London: Pluto.

Pearson, J. (1983) *Hooligan: A History of Respectable Fears*, London: Macmillan.

Perkins, U.E. (1975) *Home is a Dirty Street: The Social Oppression of Black Youth*, Chicago: Third World Press.

Phinney, J. (1989) 'Stages of ethnic identity in minority group adolescents', *Journal of Early Adolescence*, 9, 34–49.

Pileggi, N. (1987) *Wise Guy*, London: Corgi.

Pointing, J. and Maguire, M. (1988) *Victims of Crime: A New Deal?*, Milton Keynes: Open University Press.

Polk, K. and Ranson, D. (1991) 'Patterns of homicide in Victoria' in Chappell, D., Grabosky P. and Strang, H. (eds) *Australian Violence: Contemporary Perspectives*, Canberra: Australian Institute of Criminology.

Pollak, O. (1950) *The Criminality of Women*, Philadelphia: University of Pennsylvania Press.

Porter, J.R. and Washington, R.E. (1979) 'Black identity and self-esteem: A review of studies of Black self-concept, 1968–1978', *Annual Review of Sociology* 5, 53–74.

Powell, G.J. (1985) 'Self-concepts among Afro-American students in racially isolated minority schools: Some regional differences', *Journal of the American Academy of Child Psychiatry* 24: 142–9.

Poussaint, A. (1972) *Why Blacks Kill Blacks*, New York: Emerson Hall Publishers.

Ptacek, J. (1988) 'Why do men batter their wives?' in Yllo, K. and Bograd, M. (eds), *Feminist Perspectives on Wife Abuse*, Newbury Park CA: Sage.

Public Policy Research Centre (1988) Domestic Violence Attitude Survey, conducted for the Office of the Status of Women, Department of Prime Minister and Cabinet, Canberra.

Punch, M. and Naylor, T. (1973) 'The police: a social service', *New Society*, 17.5.1973.

Quicker, John C. (1983) *Homegirls: Characterizing Chicano Gangs*, San Pedro, CA: International University Press.

Rada, R.T. (ed.) (1978) *Clinical aspects of the rapist*, New York: Grune & Stratton.

Radford, J. and Russell, D.E.H. (1992) *Femicide*, Milton Keynes: Open University Press.

Rainwater, L. (1970) *Behind Ghetto Walls: Black Families in a Federal Slum*, Chicago: Aldine Publishing Company.

Real Rape Law Coalition (1991) 'Sexual assault: the law v. women's experience' in Law Reform Commission of Victoria, Rape: Reform of Law and Procedure, Appendices to Interim Report No. 42, Melbourne.

Reed, R. J. (1988) 'Education and achievement of young black males' in Gibbs, J.T. (ed.), *Young, Black, and Male in America: An Endangered Species*, Westport, CT: Auburn House Publishing Company.

Reiner, R. (1985) *The Politics of the Police*, Brighton: Harvester Wheatsheaf.

Reiner, R. (1992a) 'Police research in the UK: a critical review' in Tonry, M. and Morris, N. (eds) *Modern Policing*, Chicago: University of Chicago Press.

Reiner, R. (1992b) '*Fin de siècle* blues', Inaugural lecture, LSE.

Renzetti, C. and Curran, D. (1992) *Women, Men and Society*, London: Allyn & Bacon.

Retzinger, S.M. (1991) *Violent Emotions: Shame and Rage in Marital Quarrels*, Newbury Park: Sage.

Reuss-Ianni, E. (1983) *Two Cultures of Policing*, London: Transaction

Rice, M. (1990) 'Challenging orthodoxies in feminist theory: a black feminist critique', in Gelsthorpe, L. and Morris, A. (eds) *Feminist Perspectives in Criminology*, Milton Keynes: Open University Press.

Richards, B. (1990) 'Masculinity, identification and political culture' in Hearn, J. and Morgan, D. (eds) *Men, Masculinities and Social Theory*, London: Unwin Hyman.

Richards, J. (1990), 'The savage face of Britain', *Sunday Telegraph* 6.5.1990.

Rifkin, J. (1989) 'Mediation in the justice system: a paradox for women', *Women and Criminal Justice* 1: 41–54.

Rogers, C.N. and Terry, T. (1984) 'Clinical interventions with boy victims of sexual abuse' in Greer, J.G. and Stuart, I.R. (eds) *Victims of Sexual Aggression: Treatment of Children, Women and Men*, New York: Reinhold.

Roper, W. L. (1991) 'The prevention of minority youth violence must begin despite risks and imperfect understanding', *Public Health Reports*, 106(3): 229–31.

Rose, H. M. (1986) 'Can we substantially lower homicide risk in the nation's larger black communities?' in *Report of the secretary's task force on black and minority health*, vol. v, Washington, DC: US Department of Health and Human Services.

Rose, J. (1987) 'Feminity and its discontents.' In Feminist Review, (eds) *Sexuality: A Reader*, London: Virago.

Rosenberg, M., and Simmons, R. G. (1970) *Black and White Self-esteem: The Urban School Child*, (Rose Monograph Series), Washington, DC: American Sociological Association.

Rosenberg, M. and Sutton-Smith, B. (1972) *Sex and Identity*, New York: Holt, Rinehart, & Winston.

Rowlings, C. (1992) 'You don't look the type', in Bull, D. (ed.), *We'll Support You Evermore*, Duckworth, London.

Ruggiero, V. (1992) 'Realist criminology: A critique' in Young, J. and Matthews, R. (eds) *Rethinking Criminology: The Realist Debate*, London: Sage.

Russell, D.E.H. (1975) *The Politics of Rape*, New York: Stein & Day.

Russell, D.E.H. (1982) *Rape in marriage*, New York: Collier Books.

Russell, D.E.H. (1984) *Sexual Exploitation*, Beverly Hills: Sage.

Rutter, M. (1987) 'Psychosocial resilience and protective mechanisms', *American Journal of Orthopsychiatry*, 57(3): 316–31.

Ryder, R. (1991) 'The cult of machismo', *Criminal Justice* 9(1): 12–13.

Sampson, R. and Lauritsen, J. (1991) 'Violent victimisation and offending: individual, situational and community-level risk factors' unpublished paper, University of Missouri, St Louis.

Sanders, A. (1987) 'Constructing the Case for the Prosecution' *Journal of Law and Society*, 14: 229–43.

Sarat, A. (1993) 'Speaking of death: narratives of violence in capital trials', *Law and Society Review*, 27(1): 19–58.

Savage, M. and Witz, A. (eds) (1992) *Gender and Bureaucracy*, Oxford: Blackwell.

Scheff, T.J. (1987) 'The Shame-rage spiral: a case study of an interminable quarrel', in Lewis, H.B. (ed.) *The Role of Shame in Symptom Formation*, Hillside, N.J.: LEA.

Scheff, T.J. and Retzinger, S.M. (1991) *Emotions and Violence: Shame and Rage in Destructive Conflicts*, Lexington: Lexington Books.

Schulz, D. A. (1969) *Coming up Black: Patterns of Ghetto Socialization*, Englewood Cliffs, NJ: Prentice-Hall.

Schwendinger, H. and Schwendinger, J. (1985) *Adolescent Subcultures and Delinquency*, New York: Praeger.

Scraton, P. (1985) *The State of the Police*, London: Pluto.

Scraton, P. Sim, J. and Skidmore, P. (1991) *Prisons Under Protest*, Milton Keynes: Open University Press.

Scully, D. (1990) *Understanding Sexual Violence*, London: Harper Collins.

Scully, D. and Marolla, J. (1983) 'Incarcerated rapists: exploring a sociological model', final Report for Department of Health and Human Services, NIMH.

Scully, D. and Marolla, J. (1984) 'Convicted rapists' vocabulary of motive: excuses and justifications', *Social Problems* 31: 530–44.

Scully, D. and Marolla, J. (1985) 'Riding the bull at Gilley's: convicted rapists describe the rewards of rape', *Social Problems* 32: 251–63.

Scutt, J. (1983) *Even in the Best of Homes: Violence in the Family*, Melbourne: Penguin.

Scutt, J. (1988) 'The privatization of justice: power differentials, inequality, and the palliative of counselling and mediation', *Women's Studies Forum* 11: 503–20.

Segal, L. (1990) *Slow Motion*, London: Virago.

Seidler, V. (1989) *Rediscovering Masculinity: Reason, Language and Sexuality*, London: Routledge.

Seidler, V. (1991) *Recreating Sexual Politics*, London: Routledge.

Shapiro, S. (1990) 'Collaring the crime, not the criminal: liberating the concept of white-collar crime', *American Sociological Review* 55: 346–64.

Shapland, J., Willmore, J. and Duff, P. (1985) *Victims in the Criminal Justice System*, Aldershot: Gower.

Shepherd, J. (1990) 'Violent crime in Bristol: An accident and emergency department perspective', *British Journal of Criminology* 30(3): 289–305

Sherman, L.W. (1973) 'The sociology and the social reform of the American police: 1950–1973' in Neiderhoffer, A. and Blumberg, A. (eds) *The Ambivalent Force*, 2nd edn, Hinsdale, Ill.: Dryden.

Sherman, L.W. (1992) *Policing Domestic Violence: Experiments and Dilemmas*, New York: Free Press.

Sherman, L.W. (1993) 'Defiance, deterrence and irrelevance: a theory of he criminal sanction', *Journal of Research in Crime and Delinquency* 30.

Sherman, L.W. and Berk, R.A. (1984) 'The specific deterrence effects of arrest for domestic assault', *American Sociological Review* 49: 261–272.

Short, J.F., and Strodtbeck, F.L. (1965) *Gang Process and Gang Delinquency*, Chicago: University of Chicago Press.

Silverman, R.A. and Kennedy, L.W. (1987) 'Relational distance and homicide: The role of the stranger', *Journal of Criminal Law and Criminology* 78: 272–308.

Sim, J. (1987) 'Working for the clampdown: prisons and politics in England and Wales' in P. Scraton (ed.) *Law, Order and the Authoritarian State*, Milton Keynes: Open University Press.

Simon, R. (1977) *Women and Crime*, New York: Lexington Books.

Smart, B. (1985) *Michel Foucault*, London: Tavistock.

Smart, C. (1989) *Feminism and the Power of Law*, London: Routledge.

Smart, C. (1990a) 'Feminist approaches to criminology or postmodern woman meets atavistic man' in Gelsthorpe, L. and Morris, A. (eds) *Feminist Perspectives in Criminology*, Milton Keynes: Open University Press.

Smart, C. (1990b) 'Law's truth/women's experience' in Graycar, R. *Dissenting Opinions: Feminist Explorations in Law and Society*, Sydney: Allen & Unwin.

Smith, D.J. and Gray, J. (1985) *The Police and People in London: The PSI Report*, Aldershot: Gower.

Smith, J. (1989) 'There's Only One Yorkshire Ripper' in Smith, J. *Misogynies*, London: Faber.

Smith, K. (1989) *Inside Time*, London: Harrap.

Smith, L. (1989) *Concerns About Rape*, London: Her Majesty's Stationery Office.

Smith, M.D. (1990) 'Patriarchal ideology and wife beating: a test of a feminist hypothesis', *Violence and Victims*, 5: 257–73.

Smithyman, S.D. (1978) *The Undetected Rapist*, Ann Arbor, Mich.: UMI Dissertation Information Service.

Snider, L. (1990) 'The potential of the criminal justice system to promote feminist concerns', *Studies in Law Politics and Society* 10: 143–72.

Snider, L. (1992) 'Feminism, punishment and the potential of empowerment', submitted to *Canadian Journal of Law and Society*.

Solomos, J. (1988) *Black Youth, Racism and the State*, Cambridge, England: Cambridge University Press.

Soothill, K. and Walby, S. (1990) *Sex Crime in the News*, London: Routledge.

Spencer, M.B. (1982) 'Personal and group identity of Black children: An alternative synthesis', *Genetic Psychology Monographs* 106, 59–84.

Stafford, W. (1991) 'Pushed out of the dream: sorting-out Black males for limited economic mobility' in Bowser, B. P. (ed.) *Black Male Adolescents: Parenting and education in community context*, Lanham, MD: University Press of America.

Stanko, E.A. (1982) 'Would you believe this woman? Prosecutorial screening for 'credible' witnesses and a problem of justice' in Rafter, N.H. and Stanko, E.A. (eds) *Judge, Lawyer, Victim, Thief*, Boston: Northeastern University Press.

Stanko, E.A. (1985) *Intimate Intrusions*, London: Unwin Hyman.

Stanko, E.A. (1988) 'Hidden violence against women' in Pointing, J. and Maguire, M. *Victims of Crime: A New Deal?*, Milton Keynes: Open University Press.

Stanko, E.A. (1989) 'Missing the mark? Policing battering' in Hanmer, J., Radford, J. and E.A. Stanko, E.A. (eds) *Women, Policing, and Male Violence: International Perspectives*, London: Routledge & Kegan Paul.

Stanko, E.A. (1990) *Everyday Violence: How Women and Men Experience Sexual and Physical Danger*, London: Pandora.

Stanko, E.A. and Hobdell, K. (1992) 'Assault on men: Masculinity and male victimisation', *British Journal of Criminology*, 33(3): 400–15.

Staples, R. (1982) *Black Masculinity*, San Francisco: The Black Scholar Press.

Staples, R. (1989) 'Masculinity and race: the dual dilemma of black men' in Kimmel, M.S. and Messner, M.A. (eds) *Men's Lives*, New York: Macmillan.

Steinem, G. (1974) 'The myth of masculine mystique' in Pleck, J.H. Sawyer, & J. (eds) *Men and masculinity*, Englewood Cliffs, NJ: Prentice-Hall.

Stith, S.M. (1990) 'Police response to domestic violence: the influence of individual and familial factors', *Violence and Victims* 5: 37–49.

Stonequist, E.V. (1937) *The Marginal Man: A Study in Personality and Culture Conflict*, New York: Russell and Russell.

Straus, M.A. and Gelles, R.J. (1990) *Physical Violence in American Families*, New Brunswick, N.J: Transaction Publishers.

Straus, M.A., Gelles, R.J., and Steinmetz, S.K. (1980) *Behind closed doors: Violence in the American family*, Newbury Park, CA: Sage.

Stubbs, J. (1985) 'Domestic violence reforms in New South Wales: policy and practice', in Hatty, S.E. (ed.) National Conference on Domestic Violence, vol. 2, Canberra: Australian Institute of Criminology.

Sullivan, M. (1989) *Getting Paid: Youth Crime and Work in the Inner City*, Ithaca, NY: Cornell University Press.

Sumner, C., (1990) 'Foucault, gender and the censure of deviance' in Gelsthorpe, L. and Morris, A. (eds) *Feminist Perspectives in Criminology*, Milton Keynes: Open University Press.

Sutherland, E. (1983) [1937] *The Professional Thief*, Chicago: Chicago University Press.

Sutherland, E. and Cressey, D. (1978) *Principles of Criminology*, Philadelphia: Lippincott.

Sykes, G. (1971) *The Society of Captives*, New Jersey: Princeton University Press.

Sykes, G. and Matza, D. (1957) 'Techniques of neutralization: a theory of delinquency', *American Sociological Review* 22: 664–70.

Tavuchis, N. (1991) *Mea Culpa: A Sociology of Apology and Reconciliation*, Stanford: Stanford University Press.

Taylor, I. (1987) 'Putting the boot into a working class sport: British football after Bradford and Brussels', *Sociology of Sport Journal*, 5: 171–91.

Taylor, I. (1991) 'English football in the 1990's: taking Hillsborough seriously?', in Williams and Wagg (eds) *British Football and Social Change*, Leicester: Leicester University Press.

Taylor, R. (1985) '*The Death and Resurrection Show*', London: Blond.

Taylor, R. (1992a) 'Fans at the African Nation's Championships', Sir Norman Chester Centre for Football Research Working Paper, University of Leicester.

Taylor, R. (1992b) *Football and its Fans*, Leicester: Leicester University Press.

Taylor, R.L. (1989) 'Black youth role models and the social construction of identity' in Jones, R.L. (ed.) *Black Adolescents*, Berkeley, CA: Cobb and Henry Publishers.

Temkin, J. (1987) *Rape and the Legal Process*, London: Sweet and Maxwell.

Thrasher, F. (1927) *The Gang*, Chicago: University of Chicago Press.

Tolson, A. (1977) *The Limits of Masculinity*, New York: Harper & Row.

Tomlinson, A. (1991) 'North and South: the rivalry of the Football League and the Football Association', in Williams, J. and Wagg, S. (eds) *British Football and Social Change: Getting into Europe*, Leicester: Leicester University Press. 25–47.

Townsend, P. (1979) *Poverty in the United Kingdom*, Harmondsworth: Penguin.

US Bureau of the Census (1992) *Social and Economic Characteristics of the Population*, Washington, DC: Government Printing Office.

US Department of Justice (1992) *Uniform Crime Report: Crimes in the United States, 1991*, Washington, DC: Federal Bureau of Investigation.

Van Dijk, J., Mayhew, P. and Killias, M. (1990) *Experience of Crime Around the World*, The Hague: Klewer.

Vaughan, D. (1992) 'The macro-micro connection in white-collar crime theory' in Schlegel, K. and Weisburd, D. (eds) *White Collar Crime Reconsidered*, Boston, Mass: Northeastern University Press.

Veblen, T. (1967) *The Theory of the Leisure Class*, New York: Viking Press.

Von Hentig, H. (1948) *The Criminal and his Victim*, New Haven: Yale University Press.

Von Hoffman, N. (1993) *Capitalist Fools*, London: Chatto.

Vranitzky, Chancellor (1992) Opening address to the International Conference 'Test the West: Gender, Democracy and Violence', Vienna.

Wagg, S. (1984), *The Football World*, Brighton: Harvester.

Wagg, S. (1991) 'Playing the past: the Media and the England football team' in Williams, J. and Wagg, S. (eds), *British Fotball and Social Change*, Leicester: Leicester University Press.

Walklate, S. (1989) *Victimology: The Victim and the Criminal Justice Process*, London: Unwin Hyman.

Walklate, S. (1992) 'Appreciating the victim: conventional, realist or critical victimology?' in Matthews, R. and Young, J. (eds) *Issues in Realist Criminology*, London: Sage.

Wallace, A. (1986) *Homicide: The Social Reality*, Sydney: New South Wales Bureau of Crime Statistics and Research.

Walmsley, R. (1986) *Personal Violence*, Home Office Research Study No.89 London: Her Majesty's Stationery Office.

Ward Jouve, N. (1986), *The Streetcleaner*, London and New York: Marion Boyars.

Ward, C. (1989) *Steaming In*, London, Simon & Schuster.

Wardrup, K. (1982) 'The therapeutic community' in Carrell, C. and Laing, J. (eds) *The Special Unit Barlinnie Prison*, Glasgow: Third Eye Centre.

Warters, W.C. (1993) 'Collisions with feminism: perspectives of abusive men who've been challenged to change', unpublished manuscript, Department of Sociology, Syracuse University.

Watkins, B. and Bentovim, A. (1992) 'Male children and adolescents as victims: a review of current knowledge' in Mezey, G.C. and King, M.B. (eds) *Male Victims of Sexual Assault*, Oxford: Oxford University Press.

Weedon, C. (1987) *Feminist Practice and Poststructuralist Theory*, Oxford: Blackwell.

Weeks, J. (1981) *Sex, Politics and Society*, London: Longman.

Weisburd, D., Bode, N., Wheeler, S. and Wareing, E. (1991) *Crimes of the Middle Classes*, New Haven: Yale University Press.

Weissman, Eric. (1992) 'Kids who attack gays.' in Herek, G.M. and Berrill, K. T. (eds) *Hate Crimes*, Newbury Park, CA: Sage.

Wellman, B. (1992) 'Men in networks' in Nardi, P. (ed.) *Men's Friendships*, Newbury Park CA: Sage.

Wertham, F. (1955) *Seduction of the Innocent*, London: Museum Press.

West, C. and Zimmerman, D.H. (1987) 'Doing gender', *Gender and Society* 1 (2): 125–51.

Whannel, G. (1992), *Fields in Vision*, London: Routledge.

Wheeler, S. (1992) 'The problem of white-collar crime motivation', in Schlegel, K. and Weisburd, D. (eds), *White-Collar Crime Reconsidered*, Boston: Northeastern University.

Whimster, S. (1992) 'Yuppies: a key word of the 1980s', in Budd, L. and Whimster, S. (eds) *Global Finance and Urban Living*, London: Routledge.

Wiatrowski, M.D., Griswold, D.B. and Roberts, M.K. (1981) 'Social control and delinquency', *American Sociological Review* 46 (5): 525–41.

Williams, C.S. (1984) 'The classic rape: when do victims report?', *Social Problems* 31: 459–67.

Williams, J. (1987) 'Young people's images of attending football matches', Sir Norman Chester Centre for Football Research, University of Leicester.

Williams, J. (1991) 'Having an away day' in Williams and Wagg (eds), *British Football and Social Changes*, Boston, Mass: Northeastern University Press.

Williams, J. (1992) *Football Spectators and Italia '90*, Council of Europe, Strasbourg.

Williams, J. (1992) 'Lick my boots. . . . racism in English football', Sir Norman Chester Centre for Football Research, working paper, University of Leicester.

Williams, J. and Goldberg, A. (1990), *Spectator Behaviour, Media Coverage and Crowd Control at the 1988 European Football Championships*, Council of Europe, Strasbourg.

Williams, J. and Goldberg, A. (1991) 'England Fans and Italia '90', Sir Norman Chester Centre for Football Research, University of Leicester.

Williams, J. and Woodhouse, J. (1991) 'Can play, will play: Women and football in Britain', in Williams and Wagg (eds *British Football and Social Change*, Boston, Mass: Northeastern University Press.

Williams, J., Murphy, P. and Dunning, E. (1989) *Hooligans Abroad*, second edn, London: Routledge.

Williams, K.R. and Hawkins, R. (1989) 'The Meaning of Arrest for Wife Assault', *Criminology* 27: 163–81.

Willis, P. (1977) *Learning To Labour*, Farnborough: Saxon House

Willis, P. (1982) 'Women in Sport in Ideology', in Hargreaves, J. (ed.), *Sport, Culture and Ideology*, London: Routledge.

Willis, P. (1990) *Common Culture*, Milton Keynes: Open University Press.

Wilson, J.Q. and Herrnstein, R. (1985) *Crime and Human Nature* New York: Simon & Schuster.

Wilson, M. and Daly, M. (1992) 'Till death us do part' in Radford, J. and Russell, D. (eds) *Femicide*, Milton Keynes: Open University Press.

Wilson, P. (1978) *The Other Side of Rape*, St Lucia, Queensland: University of Queensland Press.

Wilson, W.J. (1987) *The Truly Disadvantaged*, Chicago: University of Chicago Press.

Wolfe, T. (1987) *Bonfire of the Vanities*, London: Paladin.

Wolfgang, M.E. (1958) *Patterns in Criminal Homicide*, New York: Wiley.

Wolfgang, M.E., and Ferracuti, F. (1967) *The Subculture of Violence: Towards an Integrated Theory of Criminology*, London: Tavistock.

Woodhouse, J. (1991) 'A national survey of female football fans', IT Working Paper No. 1, Sir Norman Chester Centre for Football Research, University of Leicester.

Wright, R. (1937) *Black Boy*, New York: Harper & Row.

Yllo, K.A. and Straus, M.A. (1990) 'Patriarchy and violence against wives: the impact of structural and normative factors', in Straus, M.A. and Gelles, R.J. (eds) *Physical Violence in American Families*, New Brunswick, N.J: Transaction Publishers.

Yllo, K.A. and Bograd, M. (eds) (1988) *Feminist Perspectives on Wife Abuse*, Newbury Park: Sage.

Young, J. (1986) 'The failure of criminology: the need for a radical realism' in Matthews, R. and Young, J. (eds) *Confronting Crime*, London: Sage.

Young, J. (1988) 'Risk of crime and fear of crime: a realist critique of survey-based assumptions' in Pointing, J. and Maguire, M. (eds) *Victims of Crime: A New Deal?*, Milton Keynes: Open University Press.

Young, J. and Matthews, R. (eds) (1992) *Rethinking Criminology: The Realist Debate*, London: Sage.

Young, M. (1991) *An Inside Job*, Oxford: Clarendon Press.

Zaretsky, E. (1976) *Capitalism, the Family, and Personal Life*, New York: Harper & Row.

Zeitz, D. (1981) *Women who Embezzle or Defraud: a Study of Women Convicted Felons*, New York: Praeger.

Zorza, J. (1992) 'The criminal law of misdemeanour domestic violence', *Journal of Criminal Law and Criminology* 83: 46–72.

Zuckerberg, R.M. (1989) 'From John Wayne to Tootsie: the masculine struggle with psychological integration' in J. Offerman-Zuckerberg (ed.) *Gender in Transition: A New Frontier*, New York: Plenum Medical Book Company.

Index